ARKANA

HOMAGE TO THE SUN

Kyriacos C. Markides, a native of Cyprus, is Professor of Sociology at the University of Maine. He is married to Emily J. Markides from Famagusta in Cyprus. They have two children, Constantine and Vasia. He has also written *The Magus of Strovolos: The Extraordinary World of a Spiritual Healer*, which began his account of the life of the mystic and psychic, Daskalos, and which is continued in *Homage to the Sun* and *Fire in the Heart*.

KYRIACOS C. MARKIDES

HOMAGE
TO THE SUN

THE WISDOM OF THE
MAGUS OF STROVOLOS

ARKANA

ARKANA

Published by the Penguin Group
Penguin Books Ltd, 27 Wrights Lane, London W8 5TZ, England
Penguin Books USA Inc., 375 Hudson Street, New York, New York 10014, USA
Penguin Books Australia Ltd, Ringwood, Victoria, Australia
Penguin Books Canada Ltd, 10 Alcorn Avenue, Toronto, Ontario, Canada M4V 3B2
Penguin Books (NZ) Ltd, 182–190 Wairau Road, Auckland 10, New Zealand

Penguin Books Ltd, Registered Offices: Harmondsworth, Middlesex, England

First published by Arkana 1987
5 7 9 10 8 6 4

Printed in England by Clays Ltd, St Ives plc

For Emily

Contents

Author's Note

The present work is in many ways a continuation of *The Magus of Strovolos* (Arkana, Routledge & Kegan Paul, 1985). It is also a study unto itself. The reader unfamiliar with the earlier work can proceed with the present study without the necessity of prior familiarity with *The Magus*. Those, however, who have read my earlier adventure into Daskalos' world will discover that the material in this study explores new and different aspects of his teachings not previously presented or developed. The glossary at the end may be a valuable guide to those not too familiar with Daskalos' terminology.

I have followed the same perspective and methodology as in my previous study. I employed a phenomenological approach, that is, I let Daskalos present his world and knowledge with hardly any theoretical intervention on my part. The technique I used to gather the material was through extensive taping of conversations and copious note-taking whenever taping was not possible. In cases where I was unable either to tape or take notes I simply reconstructed the events from memory as best I could and as closely to the way I experienced them.

I began my relationship with Daskalos in the summer of 1978. However, a substantial portion of the material for this second volume was gathered during the summer months of 1983, 1984 and 1985, as well as during a second sabbatical leave generously offered me by the University of Maine during the 1985–6 academic year. For that, and a summer grant provided by the same institution to complete my work, I remain forever grateful.

I have employed the same idiom as in *The Magus of Strovolos* in addressing male Greek names. Therefore, whenever I call on Daskalos directly I say Daskale. All names in the text are pseudonyms except historical names and those of my family. The name *Daskalos*, however, is not a pseudonym, it is the manner in which Daskalos' disciples address him. It is also a title with which people in the Greek world generally address schoolmasters and priests. It literally means 'teacher' or 'master.'

The list of people that I am deeply indebted to for the completion of this volume is considerably too long to mention them all here by name. But I do want to express my most profound appreciation to all those dear people who have become in one way or another a part of this book and a part of my life. The greatest debt goes, of course, to Daskalos, who allowed me to write about him and his teachings. My association with this master and with those close to him like Kostas, his successor, has been a most uplifting experience far outweighing any scholarly satisfactions that may have resulted from the actual writing of these volumes.

I am always greatly thankful to my colleagues in the Department of Sociology and Social Work of the University of Maine for their continuous support in my research activities. Special thanks to my fellow scholars and close friends Professors Steve Cohn, Stephen Marks and Michael Lewis for their personal involvement with and enthusiastic encouragement for my work with Daskalos and his circles. It has been a heartwarming experience that Michael's superb spiritual art has become an integral part of both *The Magus of Strovolos* and *Homage to the Sun*.

A salute to Marlene Gabriel, my literary agent, and Eileen Campbell, my editor at Routledge & Kegan Paul, for their exceptional professional expertise and for the personal and loving care they have shown in handling and promoting the material on Daskalos. Many thanks to Sue McLaughlin and Eva Meyn for typing the manuscript.

Finally, I want to extend my warmest affection to my relatives and friends in Cyprus who have always provided for my family and myself during our stay on the island a most congenial setting in which to live and work.

CHAPTER 1

The Healer

I have come to realize over the years that Spyros Sathi's reputation as a man of extraordinary psychic abilities was well founded. At first I was deeply skeptical of his alleged feats of miraculous healings, journeys out of the body, telepathy and similar forms of 'paranormal' phenomena. I had read about such matters reported by reliable observers but I could not personally be convinced.

I was trained within a positivistic tradition in sociology, a discipline at the pinnacle of modern secular, rational culture. By its very theoretical assumptions and methodologies such 'phenomena' as Spyros Sathi describes are discredited and debunked as nothing more than fairy-tales, fancy figments of weak and undisciplined minds, leftovers of a bygone and superstitious yesterday. I learned very early in my training that 'God is dead,' that religion is a neurotic projection of unconscious fears, an illusion destined to oblivion with the advent of science, psychoanalysis and 'enlightenment.'

Society, I learned, and later taught, gives birth to the gods it needs for the sake of its own maintenance. Therefore, when humans worship their deities, in reality they worship their society in disguise. As social scientists we were expected to consider axiomatic the notion that religion was nothing more than a reflection of society often serving as a diversion for the oppressed and ignorant masses. To be a part of the intellectual avant-garde, therefore, one had to be, if not a declared atheist, at least an agnostic and scoff at any claims remotely suggesting authentic power residing in mysticism, spirituality or religion.

Once God was pronounced dead, and buried under the weight of positivistic scientism, it was the turn of 'Man' (and 'Woman') to suffer a similar fate. Human nature, we were informed, does not exist. Humanity is either determined by 'conditioning' or by other social forces beyond one's conscious control. Freedom, along with God, was shown to be nothing

1

more than a figment of the imagination, another passing illusion. Leading beacons of contemporary culture sang with enthusiasm the epitaph of the mind. 'Man,' pronounced a celebrated French *philosophe*, 'is dead.' By the middle of the twentieth century *Homo sapiens* had become nothing more than a blank sheet of paper upon which society writes whatever it wishes.

Armed with this intellectual panoply and my own uncertain relationship to it I entered the world of Daskalos (Master), as Spyros Sathi was addressed by his followers and disciples. I never felt comfortable with scientific materialism. I accepted it as a tragic, perhaps unavoidable cost of modern intellectual life. Inside me there lurked a dormant, unmodern Dostoyevskian notion that 'if there is no God then anything goes.'

Because of my discontent I was perhaps more open to hear Daskalos' sacred version of reality with a minimum of theoretical interference on my part. I simply observed Daskalos during various healing sessions, listened to his talks and conversations and engaged him in dialogues using his own language and categories of understanding. I became a participant observer in the fullest sense of the term, including the practicing of meditation exercises he assigned for the development of alleged psychonoetic powers and systematic self-analysis for ego transcendence and transformation.

Daskalos accepted me as I was, a skeptic, a 'Doubting Thomas' as he was fond of calling me with mocking humor. He appreciated and sometimes even encouraged my skepticism. 'Accept nothing on faith. You must become a roving, blazing question mark, examining everything and always having as your compass self-mastery,' he once advised me.

My doubts about Daskalos' reputed abilities began to recede when I was personally able to observe him in action. At first I was impressed with the healing of a young Israeli woman who claimed to be possessed by demons. The psychiatrists and rabbis she visited in her home country were unable to help her and for a while she spent time in an asylum. The 'demons' continued to pester her to the point where she was unable to function, sleep, or be by herself. Daskalos, after diagnosing her problem as 'possession' not by demons but by two human spirits, Nazis to be specific ('husband and wife who died during the bombardment of Hamburg'), proceeded with exorcism based on formulas derived from the Cabbala. In the course of one meeting with Daskalos the patient was relieved of her problem. The voices were silenced and she was able to live a normal life again.

On another occasion Daskalos healed a middle-aged Cypriot woman suffering from a diseased spine. She was paralyzed and the doctors both in Cyprus and abroad advised her that she had to learn to live with her problem and that they could do nothing for her. In a matter of minutes, after touching and stroking her back, Daskalos got her out of the bed she had been lying in for the past six months. Her vertebrae had been realigned into their proper position and she was even able to exercise. What was so special about that cure was that the patient, not quite believing herself that she was cured so miraculously, visited her radiologist the same day. X-rays taken a week earlier had clearly shown a damaged spine. The new X-rays showed a perfectly healthy, normal spine. After that episode and many others that I was able to witness I had no doubt that Daskalos possessed unusual healing gifts that could not be explained by suggestion or other conventional medical or psychological theories.

Daskalos had other strange abilities that drew me slowly toward his world. One day as I was riding with him he began describing in detail the interior of our home in Maine. 'I like your house,' he remarked in passing, 'it has character.' He even suggested in jest that we ought to instal a telephone in our bedroom upstairs lest we roll down the steps whenever we rush to the kitchen when it rings. Daskalos had never visited us in Maine, at least not in his corporeal existence, nor did I ever describe to him either the inside of our home or the detail with the telephone. 'When you think of me with intensity I am with you,' he informed me. He 'visited' us, he said, several times in Maine with his 'psychonoetic body,' while in a state of *exomatosis*. That was how he learned of these details.

When we returned to Maine, Emily, my wife, had problems with her right knee. She had such severe pains that she could not bend it for any length of time, particularly when sitting in a car. One morning we received a letter from Iacovos, Daskalos' young apprentice. 'Emily should go to a doctor and have her knee checked,' he urged us. He claimed in that letter that he and Daskalos noticed that there was some problem with

3

Emily's right knee. Iacovos mentioned that he and Daskalos were doing their best to heal her but that she might also visit a doctor in any case. Emily's pains disappeared three days after we received Iacovos' letter.

A further opportunity to observe Daskalos' unusual qualities took place in the summer of 1984 during another of our extended stays in Cyprus. A good friend of mine, a psychologist, Professor Emeritus at an Ivy League university, visited us there to help organize an 'intercommunal workshop' in the hope of contributing to Greek-Turkish understanding on the island. It was his misfortune that prior to his arrival on the island, while taking a stroll on some Alpine mountain in Italy, he was seriously bitten on the leg by a dog, a German Shepherd. Being an elderly man, healing of his wound was slow and there was fear of infection. He was not, however, unduly alarmed. The physicians in Italy were reassuring. When he arrived on the island limping I suggested in passing that in addition to the doctors, perhaps he should allow Daskalos to take a look at his wound.

He vaguely knew of my research activities with Daskalos and more than once in his gentle and subtle ways expressed his fatherly concern about my academic reputation in dealing with 'such matters.' I reassured him that my approach in studying Daskalos' world was phenomenological and not propagandistic, not from the perspective of a true believer. He nodded with academic approval and after discussing my research with him in some greater detail he expressed an interest in meeting 'the healer,' as he referred to Daskalos.

It was in early August on a Wednesday afternoon that we visited Daskalos at Strovolos, a suburb of Nicosia. He welcomed us at the moment when he had just completed a session with the members of his 'inner circle.' They were still in the *Stoa*, a room in the back of Daskalos' house where they conducted their meetings and meditations. He introduced us to his disciples as they were taking off their white robes and stepping out of the Sanctum. After the others left we went into Daskalos' living-room for coffee and conversation.

With some hesitation in his voice my colleague opened the discussion. 'I am a psychologist,' he began, 'therefore we have a mutual interest in these matters.' After some talk about the state of psychological knowledge, Daskalos in no uncertain

4

terms expressed his repudiation of conventional psychology, claiming that it is still at its 'infancy stage of development.'

'The reason why psychologists and psychoanalysts have failed,' Daskalos said forcefully, 'is because they do not study themselves. One must go deep into oneself. Don't limit your research and observations to others, on patients, but in you,' Daskalos said with his finger pointed ominously at his visitor. Fortunately my friend's ego was quite secure and he took no offense at Daskalos' irreverent comments about his profession. In fact, judging from his reactions, I had the feeling he was not totally disagreeing with Daskalos' appraisal. A world-renowned social psychologist himself and a good listener with decades of experience in field research, he was more interested in hearing Daskalos' point of view than defending his own discipline or the intellectual tradition within which he built his career and reputation.

Daskalos went on to explain that the world within which he lives and works is very much a part of nature. People, therefore, wrongly call his 'science' metaphysics. There is no such thing, he insisted. 'Everything is physics. Just because we cannot see hydrogen it does not mean that there is no such thing. We employ,' he went on, 'a wider conception of reality which is beyond the senses yet it is quite tangible for purposes of research. That is why we call ourselves Researchers of the Truth. Most scientists today consider themselves materialists. But do they really know what matter is? Their understanding of matter is limited because they operate only on the gross material level. Now, we call it gross material because the other side within which we work is also material. The air is matter, invisible though. Ether was once discovered by conventional science and then it was foolishly dropped. But for us it is as real as electricity and we use it in therapy.'

I pointed out to my friend that what Daskalos was referring to, that is, the notion of etheric energy, is in many ways similar to Bergson's *élan vital*, to Reich's *orgone energy*, to Mesmer's *animal magnetism*, and to the Hindu concept of *prana*.

'I see,' my friend said thoughtfully and stroked his chin.

'Our difference from those who call themselves materialists is this: our laboratory is broader,' Daskalos said with a wide smile.

'So, you will say then,' my friend responded slowly, 'well,

after all we are dealing with the human brain and that is material too.'

'Now, just a minute,' Daskalos reacted. 'What you call brain is nothing more than the gross matter within the skull. There is another thing we call Mind.'

'Oh yes. Well, what is the difference according to you?' my friend asked.

'It is the difference between a generator and electricity. Electricity is everywhere,' Daskalos responded as he spread out his hands. 'Yet that instrument proves to us that electricity exists. But in itself it does not create electricity.'

Daskalos went on to explain that all of matter is Mind in various forms of 'vibrations.' Mind, he said, is not the Absolute, as he preferred to call what people understand as God, but the means by which the unmanifest Absolute manifests Itself. Mind is the 'supersubstance' with which the 'universes' are created. There is no 'dead matter.'

At the probing of my colleague, Daskalos elaborated that the gross material world within which conventional science operates is at the lowest level of vibrations of Mind. There are also the psychic worlds of the fourth dimension of existence where space as we know it does not exist, and the noetic world, the fifth dimension, where both space and time are transcended. Beyond that there are the higher noetic worlds, the worlds of the 'archetypes' and pure forms. One such archetype is the Idea of Man. Once an emanation from a 'Holy Monad' passes through this archetype, human existence begins. The eternal soul is dressed with a noetic body, a psychic body, and finally at conception and birth, a gross material body.

All three bodies that every living human being possesses are 'material' bodies at different levels of vibrations, Daskalos clarified. 'The tragedy with conventional science, including psychology,' he said, 'is that it recognizes only one, the gross material, and all scientific theories about human nature and the self are limited to the grossest level of existence.' Daskalos then claimed that his knowledge of these other dimensions is grounded on his own experience. He is in constant communication with these other worlds where he works with other 'invisible helpers' and masters.

Daskalos argued that when one dies one continues to live fully conscious within these other dimensions as a 'present personality' with one's psychonoetic body, the body of feelings, desires and thoughts, until the next incarnation when the ego will construct a new 'present personality' made up of a new noetic, psychic and gross material body. Through the inner self or the 'permanent personality' the essence of all the experiences of previous lives will be transferred to the new incarnation.

After further questioning from my colleague, Daskalos claimed that the aim of the cycles of incarnations is to acquire experiences and develop 'individuality within Oneness.' Through Karma, or the law of cause and effect, the ego will grow spiritually until the attainment of Theosis or the realization that one is an integral part of God or the Absolute. The human entity will then be liberated of the necessity of the cycles of existence and the descent into the 'worlds of separateness' and of gross matter. Daskalos emphasized that there is no 'sin' as such since there is no eternal punishment. There is only experience. All human souls will eventually be redeemed through the law of Karma, maturation and the assimilation of knowledge and wisdom. 'Today's murderer,' he once declared 'will become tomorrow's master of enlightenment.' Christ's parable of the Prodigal Son cryptically reveals to humanity its own destiny: return to the palace of the loving father after the trials and tribulations of earthly lives.

Daskalos went on further to elaborate on his cosmology, which according to him has as its source masters 'on the other side,' entities who live within Theosis, foremost of which is Yohannan, or John the Evangelist, who uses Daskalos' body to offer to humanity lessons on the nature of reality and existence.

My seventy-five-year-old friend listened with interest but without giving away any signs that he was either impressed or unimpressed with Daskalos' cosmological erudition. After a break of fifteen minutes when Daskalos attended to visitors seeking advice on some family problem, my friend proceeded to make further inquiries.

'I have a question about parapsychology,' he said and after clearing his throat a few times and receiving an encouraging nod from Daskalos he proceeded.

'This is not a challenge. I am just trying to explore your thinking.'

'Go ahead,' Daskalos said smiling as he folded his arms.

'Let us take a traditional experiment in extra-sensory

perception. There are these five cards,' my colleague said as he pointed to the imaginary cards lying on the coffee-table before us. 'One has a circle in it. The other has a square, and so on. And we know from many, many experiments that some people are able to say which card I have in my hand. And from your point of view and from every point of view we may not know how the transmission takes place.'

'But we do know,' Daskalos protested laughing.

'No, let me finish. According to parapsychologists there are some people that from a statistical point of view do better than chance. Whereas for ordinary people it is expected that they would be correct one out of five tries, or twenty per cent of the time, for these other people, they are correct seventy or eighty percent of the time. Now, that could not occur by chance,' my colleague said with excitement and with his forefinger pointing forward. 'This proves,' he went on, 'the reality of extrasensory perception. Now we agree on the facts. Some people can do it and some people cannot. Now we can accept it scientifically as something material in the sense that when I see you there are light waves coming from you to me and in that sense it is material.'

'Right,' Daskalos nodded.

'And we also know that radio waves can go through walls and so on.'

'That is material too,' Daskalos said smiling and with a hint of irony in his voice.

'So, this is all material. But my knowledge of the literature tells me that parapsychologists have not been able to train anybody on how to do it, on how to develop such abilities. Now from your point of view, based on your practice and experience, can you train someone to improve his or her parapsychological abilities?'

'First of all, my dear Professor, I find the experiments you mention silly. Parapsychology is also at its infancy stage. We are not interested in developing psychonoetic powers for their own sake, for the sake of creating phenomena. We want to develop such powers only for purposes of healing, to be of service to our fellow human beings. But yes, we do have a method, by teaching people how to handle Mind.'

'Yes, but what does that mean?' my friend asked.

'Look. As I said before, Mind as supersubstance is everywhere. Radio waves exist and if with appropriate materials we construct a receiving apparatus, a radio, we would be able to get any music or broadcast we wish by tuning into the appropriate channel. Our aim is to become a proper receiving apparatus of thought waves.'

'Yes, but how do you become a proper receptor?'

'Through certain meditation exercises of concentration we teach people how to handle this amorphous supersubstance of Mind and shape it into thought forms or mental images. The thought forms, or what we call elementals, have substance, they are made of Mind, and someone with clairvoyant abilities can see them.

'Normal human beings,' Daskalos continued, 'don't know how to handle Mind. The mind of most people is in its embryonic state. People cannot even concentrate for a single minute.'

'What about scientists?' I mentioned. 'Don't they know how to concentrate?'

'No. Not even scientists know how to truly concentrate. The kind of concentration that I am talking about is different. It is the ability to hold in one's mind an image over a period of time without any other thoughts interfering. This is not easy to do. Scientists concentrate but their concentration is the type that one thought succeeds another without absolute and fixed concentration on one single point or image. If scientists knew how to truly meditate and concentrate absolutely and undistractedly, their creativity would have increased tenfold. They would then experience what I would call *rush of understanding*, something which I cannot explain to you except to say that in a single moment you will be able to understand things that other people and scientists may require years of hard work to understand.'

'When you acquire these abilities without developing yourself as a spiritual being don't you become dangerous to yourself and others?' I asked.

'Of course. That is why we train people not only on how to develop their psychonoetic powers but also on how, through self-analysis, to overcome their egotism and cleanse their subconscious of destructive thoughts and desires.'

Daskalos went further to claim that ordinary people with a 'normal' state of consciousness live within a condition of semi-hypnosis, a mechanical state of existence. 'And I call normal state,' he said, 'a situation whereby one's attention is on outward things and one is oblivious to his inner reality.' This lack of awareness of or alienation from one's authentic self, according to Daskalos, makes people robots of external and, more often than not, destructive suggestions. 'People think they are living. In fact, they are not,' he claimed. 'They will truly live only when they discover themselves and instead of making use of their bodies, moving their hands and limbs and focusing on petty small matters, they will be able to truly use their divine inheritance of Mind and become masters of the world,' and Daskalos clenched his fist in a symbolic gesture of power.

'I have to be going soon,' my friend said after pondering Daskalos' statement, 'and I want to tell you something about the research of a friend of mine. It has to do with the chemistry of tears. He discovered that when you get artificial tears, such as when cutting onions, the chemical composition of tears is different from the chemical composition of tears resulting from sorrow. He discovered that there is real poison in tears of sorrow whereas there is no poison in the tears of onions. His theory is that in our society men are not supposed to cry when they are sad whereas women do. This poison he thinks has something to do with ulcers of the stomach. Therefore, the incidence of ulcers among men is greater than in women. Women express their emotions more easily and get the poison out of their system whereas men are supposed to be "men." This is still a theory at this point but I thought it would interest you.'

'I accept your colleague's findings. They make a lot of sense,' Daskalos replied and proceeded to offer his own comments on the subject. 'Tears are, let us say, a form of white bleeding. It is the equivalent of a hemorrhage of the blood. Now, suppose you cut your finger and blood is flowing. The chemical composition of your blood will be dependent upon your psychic state. If we examine the blood of a person under stress and anger and then under calm and peaceful conditions we will discover that there will be a marked chemical difference in the two types of blood. It is something similar to what your colleague has discovered about tears. And I have this to say, the synthesis and composition of all the body's liquids and bodily fluids, not just tears and blood but even urine and saliva, are analogous to the psychic state of the individual. Why? Because matter is governed by the etheric energy and this energy can be under either calm and peaceful vibrations or under violent vibrations. I know of a case in which a boy reputed to be "bad," in a rage bit another child and caused him blood poisoning. Under that rage his saliva turned into pure poison. When they checked his saliva after he calmed down, there was no poison. The chemistry of saliva is a reflection of one's psychological condition. It is true also with animals.'

'I suppose, Daskale, a similar principle applies in reference to *agiasma* (holy water),' I pointed out. 'As far as I know it has been argued by some researchers that the chemical composition of sanctified water is different than ordinary water.'

'Right. It is the effect of thought on matter,' Daskalos added. 'It is the impact of elementals that we as human beings create incessantly.'

'Can you please explain what you mean by "elementals"?' my friend asked.

'Every thought and every desire,' Daskalos replied, 'are psychonoetic energy charges that are projected into the environment. Once these "elementals" are thrusted outwards they have a shape and an existence of their own. Elementals, therefore, can affect others who vibrate on the same frequency as the person or persons who projected them. A Researcher of Truth must, through self-analysis and appropriate meditation exercises, project only benign elementals that can be of help to others.'

Daskalos went on to argue that one is always linked to and accountable for the elementals that one ceaselessly creates. Whatever kind of thoughts and desires, or elementals, therefore, we project outwards will eventually return to us either in this or future incarnations. It is the way the law of Karma works.

After further elaboration on the subject of elementals my colleague thanked Daskalos and we prepared ourselves to leave. But Daskalos had something else in mind.

'Now before you go, Professor,' he said playfully and with a smile, 'will you allow me to take a look at your leg? Kyriacos told me you were bitten by a dog.'

My friend was reluctant to untie his wound. He seemed rather anxious. But after a few seconds, at the encouragement of Emily and myself, he untied the gauze. Daskalos sat at his side and asked him to place his leg on Daskalos' lap. Then without touching the wound Daskalos concentrated and passed his hands several times over the affected area. While doing that he murmured to us in Greek that the wound was all right but he was worried about a blood clot. He had to 'dematerialize' it, he said, to prevent possible heart complications. Then he asked my friend to tie his wound again. 'For all practical purposes,' he declared, 'the wound is cured and there cannot be an infection.' He then placed his hand over my friend's head and for several minutes 'flooded' him with etheric energy.

'I feel okay but a bit dizzy,' my friend said after Daskalos ended the treatment. 'But of course,' he shrugged, 'I feel dizzy whenever I go to a doctor.' Later on he told me that while Daskalos held his hands over his head he felt a certain warmth passing through his body but was not certain whether that was simply his imagination or whether there was actual energy passed on from Daskalos' body to himself.

'I flooded you with my etheric,' Daskalos said confidently. 'This is what the Mesmerists call *magnetism*. You will feel it tonight while asleep. Your blood stream will work better. The blood clot is dissolved. You are all right. But I have to warn you,' Daskalos said gravely, 'you have an infection of the liver. You must avoid alcohol.'

My colleague did not seem to take seriously Daskalos' warning, particularly the prohibition against the consumption of any alcoholic beverages, and proceeded instead to ask further questions.

'Can you please tell me what you have just done? Because there is a material problem here. There is a hole on my leg. You say it is cured.'

'I will explain,' Daskalos said with determination. 'Assuming there is no infection, a wound will be cured by itself, within a certain specified period of time, within a few days. What is that thing that causes the curing? It is something within the body. Call it etheric, call it energy, call it magnetism, call it God, call it Holy Spirit, call it whatever you like. But it is that something which can heal the wound within twenty days, let us say. Is it not so? Now if I can inject two hundred times as much of that energy and vibrate it there the wound can be healed at an accelerated pace. This is pure mathematics,' Daskalos exclaimed with enthusiasm. 'This is what actually happens when a healer sometimes can cure a wound within minutes, assuming of course that Karma will permit it.

'When I look at a wound,' he went on, 'I can see inside it, I can see inside you. That means my *I-ness* can be inside you and whatever is in your body I can examine. When I closed my eyes I saw your leg cured. That means I have built a mental image of a cured leg and placed it there and injected it with etheric vitality. I have exercised my will-power that this leg of yours be cured. I constructed and placed there the mold, the mental image of a cured leg.'

'I am trying to assimilate what you have said so far,' my colleague said after a while. 'I am not skeptical except in one way. And that is in my life I have had somewhat similar experiences in meeting someone like you who claimed he had the truth. He was a philosopher, a psychologist and a doctor. William McDougal to be specific, an English professor. Of course Freud is another name that comes to mind. Now, what I find different about you, and we have been together only for a few hours, is that you have a complete view of reality. The Germans have a good word for this, *Weltanschauung*. You see the entire world. And you begin with prosaic things like the wound on my leg and then you talk about the beyond, God and so on. And it is all part of an organized system of thought. So I admire you or I admire the spirit that is within you, that you have this kind of *Weltanschauung*. The problem is that other people have had this too. How am I, a humble person working in God's vineyard, how am I to know?'

Daskalos smiled and for a few seconds pondered my friend's question. 'Well, my dear Professor, I cannot say that those others you mentioned are wrong. I cannot say that. But people present what they call truth with their name. Their personality and egotism are usually mixed up with their notions about the truth. This is wrong. I have never claimed that I have the truth. I can only say that we as human beings with our limitations can only have relative truth. We can never know the Truth. We can only know the conceivable, the understandable part of the Absolute, which is beyond human comprehension. That is why we must never come to conclusions but leave the borders open for correction. Therefore, we cannot be absolute about what we find and investigate, though these realities that I am talking about are more tangible to me than touching with my fingers this table in front of us,' Daskalos concluded and tapped the coffee-table as he leaned forward.

'I think I understand what you mean,' my friend responded slowly and with some hesitation in his voice, 'but in my intellectual tradition ... again, you see, I am respectful towards you ... we are trained to look for, putting it in one word, *verification*. Now, if I may use an analogy, suppose there are three chemists and each chemist has a different theory ...'

'But how could they since they have their laboratories?' Daskalos interrupted, laughing.

'No, you are moving ahead of me. Let's take the simplest illustration we have from chemistry, two parts of hydrogen and one part of oxygen. And this chemist,' my friend went on and with his finger pointed at some imaginary chemist standing at one corner of Daskalos' room, 'says, "when you get together two parts of hydrogen and one part of oxygen there will be a gas." This other chemist,' and he pointed at another corner, 'says, "nothing will happen. They have no affinity." This other chemist,' my friend continued and pointed at a third corner in the room, 'says, "if you put two parts of hydrogen and one part of oxygen there will be water." Then they try it out in their laboratories, in their material laboratories. This chemist,' my friend continued and pointed at the first corner, 'is wrong because there is no gas. This second chemist is also wrong because something does happen. And this chemist is right,' he said with emphasis, 'because there is water. His theory has been verified. So when I listen to you or to anyone or when I read anything in my tradition, my intellectual tradition, I think *verification* is important. And the problem of the beyond is not verifiable in most senses. But of course many things on this Earth of ours are extremely important yet they are not verifiable. I mean here I am in Cyprus. Why am I here? Because I think it is terrible that the Turks and the Greeks fight. And if I had a theory as to how I could bring them together this could perhaps verify the theory. It is the problem of *verification* in short that I wonder about at this point and that perhaps is my final question. And I mean it, very politely and humbly I ask you that,' my friend concluded and leaned back on his chair waiting for Daskalos' answer.

'I said it many times and I will say it again,' Daskalos replied, 'do not accept what I say simply because I say it. Give me your hand and we shall search together. This is what I do. I don't believe in anything and nobody should believe in anything because it is written or because it is said by this or that master unless one investigates it himself.' Daskalos then went on to state that he and his students are 'Researchers of the Truth,' not believers, and as such they advocate the freest possible inquiry into the nature of reality. 'In our circles,' he went on, 'we take seriously Christ's admonition "And the Truth shall make you free."'

'Daskale, the issue of verification is very important,' I pointed out, 'and a lot of transpersonal psychologists have extensively dealt with it. In conventional science we have a procedure in terms of getting certain results. And then in order to verify that what we are observing is real and not our fantasy, we have to confirm it with other scientists who are doing similar kinds of research.'

'Exactly,' Daskalos nodded.

'And you have to see it with your perceptions,' my friend rushed to emphasize.

'Now authentic masters, mystics, and gurus,' I went on, 'will tell somebody something like this: "Look, if you want to experience the world from this perspective, from our perspective, you have to go through a process of rigorous training just like you go through a long training with a professor of physics if you want to understand physics. And if you follow the steps I prescribe to you," the master will say, "you will get these results, these experiences." But somebody who does not have this specialized form of training cannot possibly experience these results. It is for this reason that people who come from different intellectual traditions have a hard time understanding one another, as it is to some extent our case today. So from the perspective of the practicing mystics, they have *consensual validation* of truth by virtue of long training and by following certain procedures that will lead them to experience similar kinds of results. But unlike conventional scientists the methods of the mystics are experiential and not experimental in the laboratory sense.'

'Very good,' Daskalos exclaimed, apparently pleased with my exposition. 'But Kyriaco, even those who do not follow such a rigorous training course can observe the effects of what masters do and draw analogous conclusions. Why do you suppose there are so many doctors in our circles? Because they have witnessed healings and they have seen this and that. Now, I have said it before, our approach is also scientific but our laboratory is broader. It is ourselves, including our gross material body. And whether you are a Cypriot, an American, an Englishman or a Japanese and follow the same procedures, and apply the same formulas, in this laboratory which we call ourselves, you will arrive at the same relative truths. And we are joyous when we realize on the basis of our own investigations that the formulas we apply or discover are identical with the formulas prescribed to us by great masters like Christ and the Buddha.'

My colleague left Cyprus toward the end of August. Three months later he informed me that sadly he suffered from hepatitis. I had completely forgotten about the details of our encounter with Daskalos. So when I wrote to him to express my sympathies I mentioned nothing of the fact that Daskalos did warn him of the impending problem. In his follow-up letter my friend wrote: 'In connection with my hepatitis I shall now confess that I deliberately withheld a question from you when I reported the dismal fact. I wanted to see whether you spontaneously might have the same impression I have, but apparently you have not. My memory may be playing me tricks, but I believe that the first comment of Daskalos to me was something to the effect that I was having trouble with my liver. Does that ring a bell for you? There is no reason why you would remember his comment and I may be imagining this. Now if he said that, then that was a noteworthy observation: the incubation period for this disease of the liver can be as long as three months, my physician has now told me, so that Daskalos may have been correct. I am certain I laughed inwardly at something he said because it seemed to be totally wrong.'

It so happened that I had recorded our encounter with Daskalos. After making a copy of the tape I sent it to him adjusting it to the spot where Daskalos made his remarks about my friend's liver. Just as Daskalos diagnosed, his hepatitis was not of a serious nature. So by the following summer when we met again in Cyprus to continue the peace efforts he had completely recovered from his illness. One of the things he wished to do while on the island was to visit 'the healer.'

After we sat down and had coffee, as it was the custom with Daskalos, my friend opened the conversation on the subject of his illness.

'I want to tell you the results of the experience I had with you last year. You meet so many people you probably don't remember but last year I was interested in meeting you as a human being and then Kyriacos here suggested that you might help me with my leg. It is all right now. Well, then you mentioned something to the effect that my liver was infected. At that time I ignored what you said. I had no jaundice and there were no symptoms.'

'But I saw it coming,' Daskalos said.

'You were right,' my friend said and pointed his finger at Daskalos. 'I mentioned to my physicians about what you told me and they were amazed and could not understand how you knew. From a medical point of view no instrument could have spotted the coming problem. But the virus must have been in my liver when you saw me because, as my physicians explained, there is an incubation period before the disease manifests itself.'

'Exactly,' Daskalos added.

'And you perceived the possibility of the hepatitis as the incubation period was going on.'

'I knew it would come,' Daskalos emphasized. 'It was not a possibility. It had to come.'

'Well, I have from a medical point of view recovered completely. They have taken blood tests again and again and the blood is normal, the doctors told me. When I had the hepatitis they said I shouldn't do this and that, I shouldn't drink alcohol and so on. And now I am allowed to do whatever I wish. So I feel as if I really recovered.'

'Yes, you have recovered completely. That is true,' Daskalos said thoughtfully. 'But you have the virus within you and although immune to the disease yourself you can give it to someone else.'

'Well, I am sorry, Sir. The physicians disagree with you on that,' my friend replied and moved within his armchair showing obvious discomfort at Daskalos' ominous statement.

'Let them disagree,' Daskalos replied with a mocking

17

intonation in his voice. 'I am telling you if your blood comes in contact with someone else's blood you could transfer the disease to that other person.'

'Look, I am not a medical person,' my friend protested, 'but what you are telling me now is what the doctors used to tell me when I did have the hepatitis. But now they say there is no problem. That is, I can no longer communicate the disease to anyone.'

'Did they say so?' Daskalos asked with irony in his voice, and then proceeded with a lowered voice. 'You have it dormant. Once you get it you are always a carrier. Have that in mind. If you go for blood transfusion and they examine your blood, they will discover it, not active but dormant. This thing you have inside you never dies once it enters your blood. You may be immune to it in the future, you may look perfectly all right, free from this illness but still you can pass on the disease to someone else through blood.'

'Are you saying, Daskale,' I tried to clarify, 'that he is contagious only to the extent of blood transfusions?'

'Only through blood,' Daskalos replied with certainty.

'Oh yes. The doctors did say that I should never give blood to anyone,' my friend remembered with a certain excitement in his voice.

'Exactly,' Daskalos replied. 'That is what I have been trying to tell you.'

'Oh yes, yes,' my friend said as he was obviously impressed with Daskalos' medical knowledge. Then after Daskalos re-established his credibility my friend asked for more clarifications of Daskalos' unusual ways of knowing. Daskalos smiled and proceeded to answer the question.

'How I do know is very difficult for me to explain. It takes many years of practice, concentration and meditations. Perhaps one lifetime is not sufficient to develop such abilities even though they are dormant within every human being. At the stage where I am now I can concentate on you and inside you, just like X-rays. In fact I believe quite often I can see better than X-rays and examine someone's state of health. From the colors and the luminosity that every part of the body, the lungs, the heart, the pancreas and so on, radiates, I can determine whether trouble may be coming. I saw the infection on your aura,' Daskalos claimed, and went on to say that before a disease appears on the gross material body it manifests itself first on the etheric-double which is identical in shape with the gross material body. The etheric double, he explained, is the energy field that keeps the gross material body alive. Without it no living organism can exist.

'Can you be more specific, Daskale, about this particular case?' Emily, who was with us that day, interjected. 'You diagnosed hepatitis, trouble of the liver, when you could have diagnosed many other different illnesses. Can you explain to us precisely what made you see trouble with the liver? Was it colors? What was it?'

'Yes, colors. Now when I was examining the Professor's injured leg last year and I concentrated within his body, I noticed inside the liver a little brown spot touching the bile. From experience I knew that there was trouble coming. I could even determine that it was Australian virus. You see, all these viruses have different shapes from one another. I can even see things that you cannot see with the microscope and make them as big as I want in order to examine them. From their shape I can then guess what kind they are. To my knowledge scientists don't know much about these viruses. Do they?'

'No, I guess not,' my friend said thoughtfully.

'When I concentrate in you,' Daskalos went on, 'what I see is in me. I become the mirror reflecting you. What is this mirror? Purified Mind. With our meditation and concentration exercises we are trying to develop these abilities that are dormant within us. Suppose, for example, you give me a picture of someone living in America. By touching it I come in contact with his aura. I become one with his aura. I could see what I concentrate on within myself, becoming myself the mirror that reflects anything I want to come in contact with. This is a new faculty, latent though within ourselves, that ultimately will be developed by the human race. What should we call it? I don't think we have a name for it. Do we?'

'How about extra-sensory perception?' Emily volunteered.

'Now, extra-sensory perception,' Daskalos repeated and made a negative grimace. 'The word "sensory" implies something belonging to the body. That is why I said we don't have a word for it. Because this is a faculty of the soul and not of the body. Unless you discover yourself as an ego-soul and not just a body you cannot develop these powers. These abilities are beyond the gross material body. As I said it is purified Mind as a mirror. You become one with it reflecting on it everything you concentrate at.'

CHAPTER 2

Madmen and mystics

A week later, after my friend returned to the States, I went to see Daskalos. It was late afternoon when I reached his home. Iacovos, his young apprentice, was also present. As we were chatting, a man in his middle twenties rushed into the house and began screaming hysterically about imaginary enemies that plotted his death. Among the plotters he included Ronald Reagan, several other world leaders and the American CIA.

Daskalos calmly and patiently listened until the unexpected visitor exhausted himself. Daskalos then advised him not to mention such matters publicly because he might be taken for a madman. 'Whenever you want to talk about this,' he advised the visitor, 'come to me.'

After promising that he would be careful, the young man quietly got into his brand new Volvo and drove off. Daskalos then asked Iacovos to go into the Sanctum at once, light a candle, and 'cover' him with white luminosity lest he get into an accident in the condition he was in.

'We are trying to rescue this lad from the asylum,' Daskalos explained to me. 'He is a bright mathematician and quite normal in every other respect. But occasionally he gets into fits of madness that may cost him his job.' Daskalos then at my probing proceeded to elaborate on the nature of madness.

'You will notice that in the case of some madmen, or what the psychiatrists call schizophrenics, there may be signs of malice which may in reality be a form of distorted affection. Such characters seem to be pathological liars because they cannot distinguish the difference between reality and fantasy. Here is a case that Iacovos knows about. A young man, at present in the care of his brother who himself suffered from a broken spine, became attached to me and began to visit me periodically. He was a karate expert. Why karate? Because aggressiveness was part of his make-up since childhood. His brother told me that when he was young he enjoyed throwing

21

other children onto the ground and beating them up. He probably brought these tendencies along with him from previous incarnations. Affection and hatred were muddled up in his mind. Such characters wish to humiliate the persons they love.

'I decided to pay some attention to this boy. He used to beat people up and then come to me and boast about it. One day, while serving in the army, he hit a brigadier general and had we not intervened on his behalf, goodness knows where he would have ended up.

'He asked me several times if he could come to my lessons but I refused to give him permission. He was not fit for the circles. Yet he went around boasting that he was my student and that I taught him all kinds of secrets. He later spread rumors that I did not want him as a disciple because I was afraid of him, afraid that he would learn my trade. He expressed affection towards me for which I did not care.

'What do you think he did once? While I was away from home he broke in, climbed up the steps to my bedroom, and created havoc. He took the Icon of the Holy Virgin from the wall and threw it on the floor. He scattered my books all over the room. He turned the bucket in which I urinate at night upside down. He took the carpet and rolled it over the bed. My room was unrecognizable. When I returned home I thought for a moment that perhaps Iacovos wanted to tease me. But after I talked to him I realized who the culprit was. Later I discovered that there were certain objects missing, including a golden pen, a gift from a friend. I found the cover right on the table next to my bed as if to tell me "I took it."

'Then,' Daskalos thundered angrily, 'he went around spreading rumors that I was a homosexual, that I wanted him as my lover but that he refused. I presume that had his case come to the attention of the police and the doctors, he would have ended up in the asylum. One day, as I was about to enter a bank, I saw him again. I stood still and looked at him. He froze. He tried to say something but could not utter a word. He could not move. I felt pity for him and let him go.

'He came to me one day and said, "I want you. I am sure you want me too." I said, "You are crazy, my boy. Go away."'

'He had a dream,' Iacovos, who appeared quite informed of the case, added.

'He had several dreams in which I appeared, having homosexual relations with people he knew. He lived in a world of fantasy and delusion.'

'But he believed in the reality of these dreams,' Iacovos emphasized.

'Of course he did,' Daskalos continued. 'He would not listen to what I said. I know he hates you and I would not be surprised if he attacked you one day.'

'What did Iacovos do to him?' I asked.

'He is jealous of him. If I do not help this lad, he will probably end up in the asylum. I help him in my own way.'

'How?'

'I send him appropriate elementals from a distance to bring him to his senses. One day after he had been beaten up he dragged himself to my house asking for help. He looked at Loizos, who happened to be with me, as if he were a criminal. "Have you changed your lover?" he asked. We helped him take off his shirt. His body was full of bruises and four or five vertebrae had moved. We put him on the floor and, with Loizos' help, I cured him. This happened about four or five o'clock in the afternoon. I emphasized that I did not want to see him again. I could work better on him from a distance. At one o'clock in the morning, however, I heard knocks on my door. I came down and opened the door. It was he again, asking for bread. "I am hungry. I haven't eaten since yesterday," he said. He had not been home since I had last seen him. I was ready to send him away but Father Yohannan intervened. When this lad knocked at the door my Master said to me, "Do not be angry. Do not be harsh with him." I had every desire to chase him out of the house once and for all.'

'Do you hear Father Yohannan as a voice?' I inquired.

'I feel him, he talks to me. Of course I hear his voice. Well, I had half a loaf of bread, three eggs, some bacon and sausages. I cooked for him. He ate it all, he was starving. He even helped himself to the refrigerator and took a Pepsi Cola. After he finished I said to him, "Listen, buddy, your actions do not make sense to me. I want to avoid getting into trouble because your presence here is not pleasant. Try to avoid bothering me in the future." Before he left, he grabbed my hand and started kissing it. And you know what he said? "I love you very much." "I prefer that you don't love me and leave me in peace," I replied. "I love you very much," he said again and left. I am sure he felt something for me but what he felt was, "I will destroy him so that nobody else will care for him." I have always had this problem. Several persons tried repeatedly to destroy my reputation in order to monopolize me for themselves. This kind of person may love and adore you, but when he sees others coming near you, he would do everything possible to poison your relationships. He will do his best to humiliate you, to trample upon you and then claim you as his own. I have had six cases like that of individuals that appear normal. If you fail to pay attention to them for awhile, they will do something, even something crazy, in order to attract attention. Should we call such people neurotics or schizophrenics? Since the Turkish invasion it is hard to find anybody who is sane around here.'

'We are crazy, too, to some extent,' Iacovos said, laughing.

'Of course we are,' Daskalos added. 'To a certain extent we are all sadists, masochists, and schizophrenics.'

'Maybe neurotic, Daskale,' I said, laughing, 'but schizophrenic . . . ?

'And what is the difference?' Daskalos replied with a mocking grimace showing total disrespect for psychiatric parlance.

'Well,' I said, trying to be serious, 'schizophrenics hear voices.'

'But we hear voices, too,' Daskalos quipped and burst into laughter.

I noticed that a considerable part of Daskalos' activities dealt with psychiatric problems and, from what I observed repeatedly, his success rate could provoke the envy of the best psychiatrists in America. The above two episodes offered an opportunity to discuss the nature of mental illness. The topic was of special interest to me. I had been teaching a course at the University of Maine on the sociology of mental illness, and, based on my studies, it was clear that the term itself is highly controversial and elusive. There is hardly any consensus among specialists as to the nature of insanity, particularly schizophrenia. An increasing number of 'anti-psychiatrists' claim forcefully that, contrary to conventional psychiatry, knowledge about the fundamental nature of insanity has not developed, not even one iota, since the Middle Ages, and that the psychiatric vocabulary is nothing more than a convenient label to stigmatize the underprivileged. Apparently Daskalos shared this perspective.

'Psychiatrists know nothing about what mental illness is,' he said with seriousness as Iacovos and I listened attentively. He then proceeded to elaborate upon the subject.

'In order to understand what mental illness is, we must explore the way habits are formed. When something gets imprinted in one's subconscious it tends to reach the surface of consciousness and presses for repetition. From our perspective we say that one projects an elemental which eventually returns to its source. It then absorbs energy from the etheric-double of the individual and becomes stronger. These habits and obsessions subconsciously become imprinted on the psychic and noetic body. When the vibrations of these elementals are very intense they can cause damage to the brain. These are sometimes the consequences of so-called mental illness and schizophrenia. Once the vibrations of the psychonoetic body quiet down, the brain also calms down and the otherwise insane individual behaves and thinks like any ordinary human being. One can observe, for example, that in mental hospitals, severely disturbed individuals have periods of lucidity and clarity of mind, until the turbulence in their subconscious starts again. Suppose that a person dies and we meet him in the psychic world. Will he still be insane? No. You may ask how could this be possible since the violent vibration is part of the self-conscious personality which includes the psychonoetic body. The personality as a whole vibrates violently but outside the prison-house of the material body and its brain no infirmity can be manifested. Violent vibrations in themselves do not lead to madness. Madness is the inability of the material brain and the solar plexus to express the inner condition of the psychonoetic body. Sometimes you will notice, for example, that before an individual gets into these fits of madness he may begin to feel pain in his stomach, bend down and start vomiting. The vibration that gets him off balance may start from the solar plexus.'

'Are you suggesting,' Iacovos asked, 'that all those who are insane have a biological brain damage?'

'No. Not necessarily. It is simply the inadequacy of the material brain to channel these intense vibrations.'

'This condition,' I added, 'could affect any ordinary human being.'

'Of course. How many times do people under the spell of an uncontrollable anger begin to stutter? Their material brain stops functioning and they are unable to reason. How many people under the influence of intense emotion destroy their bodies with a stroke or a heart attack?'

'Daskale, many schizophrenics report hearing voices which tease and torment them. What are these voices?' I asked.

'Schizophrenics get sounds from the psychic world.'

'In one study that I am familiar with,' I went on, 'the schizophrenics reported that they heard voices of two orders, the evil kind that appeared like little demons torturing them . . . '

'The elementals,' Daskalos interjected.

' . . . and more rarely,' I continued, 'they heard benign voices that were quite therapeutic in nature.'

'Yes, these are the angelic elementals. The schizophrenic enters the psychic realm unprepared and involuntarily. A mystic can enter the same regions through meditation.'

'Are you suggesting,' I said, laughing, 'that there is a common point that links the mystic with the madman?'

'Of course,' Daskalos said seriously. 'The mystic opens the doors of perception of vibrations that are interpreted as voices, but he is in full control over them. Furthermore, the mystic can differentiate clearly the gross material from the psychic dimensions. He does not mix them up and he can easily function in both worlds. The schizophrenic, on the other hand, opens the doors of perception as a result of violent situations but he is at a loss. He is confused and at the mercy of these voices. They are real. In what way you may ask? Hearing means receiving vibrations which are imprinted on the acoustic nerve and which then get transferred to the material brain. When these irritations occur we translate them as "hearing." It is the same with "seeing." The vibrations need not come from external sources to bring the irritation on the acoustic nerve. They can come directly from the psychic and the noetic worlds.'

'So what schizophrenics get are elementals from the psychic world created by others.'

'Precisely.'

'Is it not the schizophrenics themselves who create them?'

'Sometimes they create the voices themselves. A person will hear voices the moment he opens the gates of the centers of the material and the etheric brain. The voices that the mad person hears are real. The fact that you and others do not hear them does not mean that they are auditory hallucinations. If you coordinate yourself with such a person, you will hear the same voices. It is possible to shut the doors of perception so that the person no longer hears them. Psychologists sometimes use electro-shocks, which in reality implies closing the doors. The elemental is ejected and has difficulty in returning and imprinting vibrations.'

I mentioned to Daskalos that electro-shocks are discredited by modern humanistic psychologists and psychiatrists. He agreed that such methods may be cruel and may have negative side-effects on the body, but he insisted that the end result of such methods is to close the gates of perception.

'How do you help schizophrenics, Daskale, to overcome their problems?'

'One method that I use is to create contrary elementals which could bring about the balance. For example I had a case that Iacovos knows about. During the invasion this soldier, Petros was his name, was in the front lines and saw a lot of killing and bloodshed. He saw the head of his best friend blown up and the bellies of others torn apart, their guts spilled out. He went insane and was locked up in the asylum. He saw blood everywhere, killing, murder . . . '

'He saw what he experienced,' Iacovos added.

'Correct. But he was also getting images of similar experiences transmitted to him telepathically by others. When I took up his case I began the therapy with psychoanalysis, that is, I tried to examine and bring to the surface the events that tormented him and to create their opposites.'

'Can you give us a specific example?'

'After I saw in his subconscious the scenes of bloodshed, I explained that what he saw was not as tragic as he imagined. I talked to him about the law of Karma, and advised that he should eradicate the elementals that tormented him with appropriate thoughts and actions. I tried to show him that he should not indulge in dwelling on his past experiences and that he should focus his attention on the future.'

'So the kind of psychotherapy you practice is to bring

about a change in one's perception of life.'

'This is an important method but not the only one I use. For example, Petros was not very receptive to this approach. I therefore created opposite elementals with my mind, placed them inside him while he was asleep, and then I let him arrive at his own decisions, without his being conscious that his decisions were the result of an external intervention. I tried to cover the memory of what he saw that disturbed his balance. I believe that whatever is left of those memories is more like a dream to him which could not have the power of reality. It was the only thing that I managed to accomplish with Petros. Had I not done that I doubt that I could have saved him from the asylum. In his case it was necessary to bring about oblivion of the incidents that tormented him. In such cases, however, cure can never be total. You may heal the wound but the scar will remain. Sadness will always stay with Petros. He may appear merry and happy but this state will only be temporary. Is this not, after all, the case with three-quarters of the human race today?' Daskalos concluded.

'Perhaps much more,' I laughingly said. Then I asked Daskalos to explain to me what kinds of benign elementals he created and placed inside Petros.

'I replaced the elementals of hatred and hostility with those of love, peace and understanding,' Daskalos replied. 'But the meaning of these elementals cannot be understood unless appropriate circumstances are created. In the case of Petros I created, with thought, incidences opposite to those which tormented him, both in his daily life and in his dreams. Why do you suppose part of the training of a Researcher of Truth is to exercise with visual imagery? What do you think its purpose is? This is the reason, to create powerful and constructive elementals and then project them to combat the destructive ones.'

'Are you saying that you can construct a situation which will create for the patient the feeling of love?' I asked.

'I do not create the feeling of love. It is inside a person. I simply create conditions that may bring it to the surface so that this sentiment will not remain dormant inside him. Love is inside him, it is his nature. All I can do is to awaken it. Through visual imagery I create the benign elemental which then enters into his subconscious and leave it there to work.'

'Frankly, this is beyond me.'

'Let me explain. Say one is a drunkard. He comes home and beats up his wife. He starts all sorts of trouble. I will try to explain to him that what he does is wrong, that he should not do it again. He will react. At night he will see me in his dream advising him, "Had I been in your position I would not have behaved in that manner. What you did was irrational." You see, man is a bit of a monkey. He imitates both good and evil. Therefore, he may take what I suggest to him, he may make it part of himself without realizing that an external condition created it. This is how he could benefit. I would try to get him where I want him and then let him work out his own problem.'

Daskalos then said that sometimes, in order to calm down an insane person, he would take him out of his body and carry out the therapy on the psychic or astral plane. Then he would return the person back to his body. He said there are many ways of doing that but he did not care to elaborate.

'To help an individual,' Daskalos said after a few moments' pause, 'you have to adjust your methods and techniques to the nature of the case and the kind of person you are dealing with. You have to understand what makes the other person tick and then act accordingly. Take, for example, the case of Niciforos that you know about.'

Niciforos was a sixty-year-old businessman whose only son had been missing in action since the days of the Turkish invasion in 1974. Daskalos was particularly attentive to Niciforos and for a long time he would visit him daily. I thought, at first, that they were old friends and that Daskalos simply enjoyed his company. Niciforos seemed to be quite attached to him. I soon realized, however, that Daskalos' visits were not due to any desire for socializing but for therapy, even though he made it appear as if it were the former. Niciforos was an abusive character and his grief for his son aggravated his condition. The victim was his wife. Daskalos explained to me in all seriousness that this case was of particular interest to him because Niciforos' wife was Daskalos' mother in one of his incarnations in ancient Egypt. 'If for no other reason,' he confided in me, 'I owe it to her to help her husband.'

'In Niciforos' case I had to be very patient and get to his level in order to have any effect on him. Had someone heard me talk with him, he would be in for a shock.' Daskalos would often use the same vulgar language as that of Niciforos, a vocabulary replete with four-letter words. 'To help a madman sometimes you must behave and talk as if you were a madman yourself. In his case had I looked down upon him like some sort of Master passing judgment, I would have had no effect whatsoever.'

I asked Daskalos whether he was familiar with R.D. Laing's theory of schizophrenia, particularly as developed in his most controversial book, *The Politics of Experience.* Daskalos had never heard of Laing and began to laugh and shake his head when I mentioned that, for Laing, it is the schizophrenics who are in contact with Reality rather than those considered normal.

I proceeded to explain that Laing's method of curing the mad was to allow them to go through their schizophrenic trip, and come out of it supposedly wiser and more balanced. The psychiatrist, according to Laing, should simply provide a supportive environment for the patient's schizophrenic experience without trying to stop him or her through drugs or other methods.

'This is not always safe,' Daskalos said seriously. 'You may push the patient out of balance completely. He may go very deeply into madness and may not be able to return. It is sometimes pleasurable to remain there. It is also a way for the patient to evade his responsibilities.'

'I suppose from the mystical perspective, the patient's sacred discs may open up prematurely without the individual being in control.'

'Exactly.'

'I disagree,' said Iacovos, who often cherished playing the role of devil's advocate, even though Daskalos considered him one of his advanced students. 'You are talking as if the experience of illusions is the opening of the sacred discs.'

'But what are illusions?' Daskalos asked rhetorically.

'That mad mathematician,' Iacovos said, with an animated and impatient tone in his voice, 'claims that people accuse him of being a homosexual. On what grounds? Come, explain it to me. Does he really hear? He does not hear,' he concluded self-assuredly.

Daskalos insisted that it is a mistake to consider the crazy person's world as illusory. 'I know that many years ago, when he was a child, a homosexual tried to molest him. Even though he had never had a homosexual experience, he may have had certain latent tendencies. What he heard was his inner voice warning him, lest it happen. Do you understand me? These are not illusions.'

'It is an illusion,' Iacovos insisted, 'when you think that someone else is sending you such thoughts.'

'It was he who sent these thoughts to himself through the other,' Daskalos explained.

'But it is not the other who sent him these thoughts,' Iacovos added.

'How do you know?' Daskalos asked. 'It could be either way. Another person may have sent them to him or he may have used the other as subject, projected an elemental which hit on the aura of that person and then bounced back to himself.'

'Are you suggesting, Daskale,' I said with puzzlement, and unintentionally changing the subject, 'that everything is elementals?'

'Everything,' Daskalos retorted emphatically.

'Are these elementals products of the mind?'

'Precisely. As there is nothing without a cause, there is nothing without an elemental. Now where did this fellow fish this elemental of homosexuality? He himself may have picked it up and returned it to himself. He may have picked it up from the past or from the surrounding environment of elementals. It does not matter. There is nothing within the experiences of human beings without the existence of an analogous elemental.'

About a minute passed in silence as Daskalos munched on an apple that Iacovos had brought to him earlier. Then I broke the silence.

'Daskale, you mentioned that you were living consciously in the psychic realms very early in your life – from the moment you were born, as you once told me. You also pointed out that while growing up you had nobody in this world who shared your experiences and who could guide you. I frankly wonder how you managed to stay away from mental hospitals and how you remained sane.'

'I had masters on the other side who were my guides. They advised me what to do and what to say.' And as Daskalos munched on another apple he continued, 'I was not under the influence of wicked spirits who could have put me off balance.

31

My only mistake at the time was that I talked about my experiences. My mother was afraid and implored me to keep silent, otherwise people would think I was deranged.

'I remember, for example, the day I was born. When I grew up I described to my parents details of my birth. They were shocked. My father simply dismissed me and said, "You have been weird from the moment you were born anyway." His opinion of me never changed,' said Daskalos and burst into laughter. 'I remember that I was at the top of the ceiling and could hear and understand everything that was being said. I was both up there,' and Daskalos pointed at the ceiling, 'and inside my mother,' and he pointed at his navel.

'How could you remember the conversations in the delivery room? Did you know the language?'

'How could I? I was a Russian in my previous life. But I could communicate with their thoughts without the need of a language. I was in coordination with the vibrations of their thoughts. At the moment of my birth when I began to cry I was still at the top of the ceiling and also inside the newborn infant. When I noticed myself crying I sent signals to myself to calm down, and the infant stopped crying.'

Daskalos began laughing and tapped my knee with his right hand. 'To whom can I tell such stories and not be pronounced insane?

'One day while I was in the third grade I went to school unprepared. I failed to do my homework in arithmetic and had a premonition that my teacher would call on me to solve the problem on the blackboard. My fears were well founded. "Sir," I said to him, "I was not feeling well last night and did not do my homework." He insisted that I should go to the blackboard. I then felt the presence of one of my invisible helpers. It was Father Dominico. He was standing at my right side. "Come, my love, let us solve that problem together," he said to me softly. I went in front of the class, took a piece of chalk and started writing. Father Dominico held his hand over my own and simply guided it. The problem was solved in no time. The teacher was puzzled and wondered what reason did I have to tell him that I had not studied the night before. "Sir," I replied, "it was not I who solved that problem but one of my invisible helpers, Father Dominico," and I pointed with my hand to the space at my right. "Your who?" I repeated what I had said. My teacher was very angry. He thought I was trying to ridicule him in front of the class. He pulled me by the ear and took me to the principal. Fortunately he was a mystic himself who, after hearing my story, took me to one side and urged me not to talk to people about what I saw and heard because they were ignorant and could send me to a mental hospital. He urged me to come to his office whenever there were intermissions and gave me paper and pencil so that I could write down whatever I wanted. He would then study carefully everything I wrote. He was very good to me.'

Daskalos mentioned that throughout his life invisible helpers would assist him in solving problems. They even helped him once to give a solo piano performance at the Magic Palace, a theatre of old Nicosia. He was in high school at the time. When his turn came to perform, one of the invisible masters guided his fingers. It was such a virtuoso performance that he was given a standing ovation.

'It took me some time to realize that others did not share the same experiences that I had, that they were not like me. You see, contact with the other world does not necessarily lead you to paranoia or schizophrenia.'

'Has anybody ever called you crazy?'

'Many.'

'How did you react?'

'With total silence. I remember when I was a little boy, one day I abandoned the company of my friends and withdrew to a place near a creek surrounded with eucalyptus trees. There I played with nature spirits, those of flowers. They appeared to me like little boys and girls. A friend asked me what I had been doing there for such a long time. I replied I had been playing with "those," and pointed at the nature spirits. "Who?" My classmates could not understand. They thought I was out of my wits. One day they went to the principal and reported that I was playing and talking by myself.

'I was fortunate to have the guidance of masters like Father Dominico and Yohannan. They taught me not to feel hurt and embittered and not to counter-attack. Then they instructed me not to speak about my experiences to people who do not understand. Had I had evil predispositions and received no assistance from these invisible masters, I could have very easily attracted wicked spirits and elementals. Under such circumstances I would have gone mad.'

'Are you suggesting then that if one vibrates low one has greater chances of becoming psychopathic?'

'Yes. You attract evil. For example, what do you think kleptomania is? It is an elemental of "I take; I want to make it mine." A kleptomaniac is not master of himself. In order to get rid of this elemental a therapist must create opposite elementals. With words or with your thought you suggest to that person that it is not necessary to steal. "How would you like it," you ask him, "if someone stole from you?" When Jesus said that one should not desire objects belonging to others, he was in fact creating elementals opposite to those of theft.'

It was already late in the evening and Daskalos seemed tired and began yawning. We ended our discussion and agreed to meet the following day. In the meantime I sorted out what we had discussed so far. When we met again Kostas, his most advanced disciple and master unto himself, also joined us.

Daskalos resumed the discussion by expressing his disagreement with the psychiatric vocabulary in reference to mental illness. He said that psychiatrists are confused about what schizophrenia is because they study results without penetrating into causes.

'Once I asked a well-known English psychologist to identify for me the problem of those persons in the New Testament suffering from demonic possession. "Paranoid schizophrenia," he replied. "On what grounds?" I asked him.' Daskalos then proceeded to outline the various categories of insanity from his point of view.

'First there are those who suffer from a biological defect or injury to the brain. Second there are persons that we consider as suffering from evil elementals. We know how these elementals are created and how they move away from the person and later return to him. Jesus called them spirits mute and deaf. The overwhelming majority of schizophrenics suffer from these elementals, and more rarely from demons or departed humans.

'Incidentally, when the spirit of a departed human enters the body of a living person, it does not follow that this will necessarily lead to a mental breakdown.'

'How is that?'

'Suppose I die and then as spirit I enter Iacovos or Kostas or you. What do you think will happen? You would feel a pleasant loosening up while constantly thinking of me. You may ask, suppose the spirit of a departed criminal enters the body of a living individual. Would this not create a mental turbulence? Yes. He can enter only when the other person vibrates on the same frequency. Otherwise entrance is not permitted. For example, when I give my lessons, Yohannan often takes full possession of my body. I coordinate myself with this superintelligence during the lesson and I feel great joy. Could a demon enter me? Never. No one should be afraid of being possessed by a wicked spirit unless one vibrates on the same level. Like attracts like. Do you understand now? The spirit of a criminal can enter the body of a living criminal, but whatever the living criminal does would be analogous to what he would have been predisposed to do under the circumstances, regardless of being possessed or not. I know a case when the spirit of a departed criminal entered the body of another criminal and prevented him from committing a crime. The departed criminal was hanged and because of his experience he wanted to help the person who was about to commit a crime. Therefore this particular entrance was benign. But keep in mind that in the majority of cases of the so-called criminally insane, it is the result of elementals and not of possession by humans or demons.

'What should we do when faced with such cases? First we must determine whether there is damage in the material brain, in the nerves, in the brain cells. The very advanced Researcher of Truth can create with various colors conditions that can bring about complete recovery. Did we ever have such cases? Yes, many times. But we can never know whether we will succeed or not. Sometimes when a case appears hopeless you may have spectacular success and in other situations that appear simple you may not be able to accomplish anything. That young man you saw the other day was locked up in the asylum several times and he could have stayed there for good. In his case it was the elementals that he himself created that tormented him. At one time he stopped eating, except grapes, and he became extremely weak. Now he eats well and he has a well-paid job. There was no damage to his brain although there was partial paralysis of some nerve cells. Employing our own methods, by sending him therapeutic elementals, we were able to repair the damage.

'What psychiatrists consider psychosomatic cases are usually the accumulation of elementals within the personality of the individual that assume control of the material brain, the nervous system, the liver, the spleen and, in the case of sexual maniacs, the sexual organs. In these cases what can we do? Should the healer be a clairvoyant, he could see these elementals and force them out of the person. Is this permissible at all times?'

'I suppose,' I volunteered to answer, 'it would depend on the Karma of the person.'

'Correct. But we should keep in mind that sometimes to rid the person of all the elementals that trouble him could cause his physical death. Therefore we must be very careful. It may create chaos of expression and confusion to his present personality. We know from our lessons that the present personality is the sum total of all the elementals that one has created ever since one has passed through the Idea of Man. We must not therefore substruct a large portion of the elementals that compose one's present personality in order to have a phenomenal cure but one which can be fatal.'

'Have you ever encountered such a case?'

'Yes. But the Masters on the other side stopped me. I took up the case of a young man from Athens who very early in his life began to masturbate obsessively. Kokos, that was his name, was also predisposed to sodomy and while in school he was worked over by other boys. The elementals of masturbation and sodomy became an integral part of his personality. Later on he began drinking. These were different kinds of elementals. In addition, Kokos, being rich, was able to buy and use LSD. Then he became a gambler. His personality was in shambles. When his parents brought him to me I was at a loss. I was unsure as to what kinds of elementals I should leave intact and what to combat. Should I take, I wondered, the elementals of sodomy, of masturbation, of alcoholism, of gambling or of narcotics? It was a case which caused me tremendous anxiety. I decided to talk frankly both to his father and to his doctor who accompanied them to Cyprus. I asked why they kept it a secret from me that Kokos had these problems with sodomy. His father said, "I felt ashamed, Daskale, how could I tell you about such matters? You discovered them yourself." "If we free him from all his problems," I warned them, "we may harm him." His father implored me to go ahead and said that he would assume full responsibility. Reluctantly I dissolved the elementals of sodomy. I did the same with the elementals of alcohol, narcotics and gambling. So what did I leave him with? Nothing!' Daskalos said loudly as he criticized himself.

'When they took him back to Greece he had no desire for anything. They even had to wake him up in order to feed him. He had no appetite. He slept most of the time, peed and dirtied himself like an infant. So what good did I do to him? In six months they brought him to me again. "I warned you," I said. "What must we do now?" they asked. I told them that I was not sure. But I urged them to wake him up and prevent him from sleeping all day long. I advised them to get him back into society and allow him to express himself, assuming that he avoid drinking and narcotics. His father said, "We should marry him off." I protested. "What human being, mister, are you going to sacrifice in order to marry him?" Where do you think he ended up? To sodomy again. Fortunately he is no longer drinking or taking narcotics. Do you understand now? It is better this way.'

'You mean to say that you returned the elementals of sodomy back to him?' I asked.

'No. I let him recreate others. The sperm of these elementals was inside him. Had I taken the sperm he could have died. I left the sperm, it grew up again. I cleaned the weeds. The sperm grew up again. I told his father that from then on he had to tolerate him. Notice that in all other respects he was fine. I helped him develop a feeling for music and he taught himself how to play the piano. He is an intelligent lad. I helped him replace his interests. Instead of alcohol, narcotics, gambling and prostitution he now has music. His sodomy became civilized. Unlike before he became more discriminating. Now you may ask whether I could help him overcome that also. I cannot and I must not. This will have to wait for another incarnation.

'Here is another case. An old couple brought their son, Alecos, to me. He was a thirty-five-year-old high school teacher, quite intelligent and normal in every respect. But he had a weakness. He had a "lover." Who do you think his "lover" was? The glass of a kerosene lamp number four! Wherever he went he carried it along under his arm inside a velvet box. "Sit down, Aleco," I said, "let us see what is happening with you." He took his parents out of the house, locked them up inside the car, came back, closed the door and said to me, "Here is my lover, Daskale. Do you follow me?" Whenever he got sexually aroused, he placed inside his "lover" little sponges, soaked with olive oil and began masturbating. After he ejaculated he cleaned the lamp, kissed it and placed it back into the velvet box.

'His parents were going insane,' Daskalos continued with a grave look on his face, while the rest of us had a hard time controlling our laughter. 'They spied on him and watched him do it repeatedly. Alecos carried on this "affair" for six years. "If my lover dies," he said, "I will die in a week's time." I asked him, "How is the lamp going to die?" "When it breaks." "Aleco, what you are saying is crazy," I reacted.' Daskalos then explained that such an autosuggestion was very dangerous.

'He could have died,' Kostas retorted.

'He did die,' Daskalos said angrily. 'His idiotic father broke the lamp. Before they left my house I advised and implored him not to break it. He got annoyed. "Mister," he said, "we brought our son to you to have him cured. What sort of nonsense are you saying now? I will find a way to get it away from him." He broke it and left the pieces on the floor. "Now you can fuck the glass as much as you want," he told his son. Alecos died in a week's time.'

'Some powerful elemental he must have created,' Kostas murmured.

'Do you realize,' Daskalos continued, 'how monstrous such an elemental could be? It was the elemental which was linked to the lamp that killed him.'

'What could you have done, Daskale?' I inquired.

'They did not give me enough time to think. They did not give me any time.' Daskalos repeated with regret. 'They said he had had this problem for six years. I needed time to figure out what to do. The lad was in excellent health otherwise. He was lost because his crazy father broke the lamp.' When Daskalos finished his sentence, the phone rang. It was a call from Athens. Someone there was asking for Daskalos' help. He spent about fifteen minutes giving advice. When he finished he returned to his armchair and we continued. I noted that his method of curing mental patients was very different from that of classical psychoanalysis which concentrates on one's past experiences.

'Are you sure there can be a cure when you apply this method?' Daskalos asked. 'You may bring to the surface incidents that should be forgotten. Have you thought about this?'

'Sometimes,' Iacovos interjected, 'it may be necessary to dig into the past.'

'True. But you must be very careful. This method can strengthen destructive elementals deeply buried in the subconscious of the individual. When you conduct analysis, you place the patient, often unintentionally, in a state of semi-hypnosis. This is always the case whether you conduct conventional psychoanalysis or the kind that we employ. If you revive old memories while at the same time you explain to the patient how to handle these memories, then psychoanalysis could be beneficial. What you actually do is to bring destructive elementals to the surface, destroy them and replace them with life-serving ones. But if you just allow the patient to simply talk about his problems while you, as the therapist, listen or take notes and then suddenly wake the person up from his semi-hypnotic state, you can harm him. The monsters he awakened may devour him.

'Suppose, for example, someone in a state of drunkenness committed an act which has generated extreme feelings of guilt. You will notice, by the way, that such individuals quite often, in their desire to soothe their guilty feelings, may repeat the same act that caused their problem in the first place. It is a psychopathological state that can afflict even the greatest of scientists. As a therapist you must be on guard so that when the opportunity arises and the individual is engrossed with his guilt you may attack the elementals that torment him.'

'How?' I asked.

'You may tell him, for example, "Okay brother, whatever happened happened. You were drunk. You made a mistake, but you did not know what you were doing. It could have been worse. You did not mean it. You should not feel so guilty about it. It could have happened to any one of us." When he is receptive you may also tell him that perhaps it was Karma that caused him to act that way. Perhaps it was inevitable. You must engage him in a dialogue, otherwise the monsters could devour him. You should help him diminish the power of these elementals. After all this is what we therapists must do every night before we fall asleep. Through self-analysis we must try to weaken the negative elementals that take possession of us. A Researcher of Truth must constantly scrutinize and examine his thoughts and feelings. Is this not a form of psychoanalysis? It is a necessary work of fighting evil elementals. We have to do that systematically so that they do not get settled in our subconscious.'

'I do not believe, Daskale,' I responded, 'that psychoanalysts will quarrel with you about this practice. But they will not call them elementals.'

'They will call them "obsessive thoughts,"' Iacovos volunteered.

'It does not matter what you call them. To us what is important is their power, where it resides, what damage it does, and how to destroy it. By using the word "elementals," however, we transform them into something concrete which we can grasp and observe. In this way we give them form and power, as is, in fact, their nature. Elementals are different from one another both in form, energy and power. How is a psychoanalyst going to classify them and study them when they are labeled "obsessive thoughts"? One may have obsessive thoughts that urge him to drink, or to masturbate, or to boast, or to start fights, or to beat up his wife. We can put all these under the category of obsessive thoughts. But as elementals they are not alike. A clairvoyant notices that each one of these elementals has a different shape and therefore a different strategy is needed to handle each one of them. How is a modern psychoanalyst going to know what to do without being able to understand the true nature of the elemental that torments his patient? I believe that a therapist must also be a clairvoyant who, instead of working in the dark, has an understanding of laws and causes so that he can penetrate deeply into the subconscious of the person and eradicate what brings about the problem. That is why conventional therapists have few successes. I have this to add also. The conventional psychiatrist does not realize that what he considers obsessive thoughts in his patients could be gradually imprinted in his own subconscious. How many psychiatrists do you think have their wits intact today? I know so many of them that have more problems than their patients.'

'They are influenced by them,' Iacovos quipped.

'Had they known about the nature of elementals, they could

have protected themselves and with some self-analysis and appropriate meditation practices they could rid themselves of such elementals. I know psychiatrists who beat up their wives and then excuse themselves by saying, "It is because of my work, I lost my nerve," and then go on to swallow all sorts of sedatives.

'I believe the psychoanalyst needs special training so that he may know what Reality is. And Reality is in metaphysics. He must become a clairvoyant in order to understand the other person. Patients will tell him that they hear voices talking to them, that they listen to psalms, that they hear this and that. When the psychoanalyst himself is not clairaudient so that he may know what hearing means and in what way one checks what one hears, how is he going to help the person? We had a case like that with a good friend of yours. She used to hear voices . . . I am not sure whether she mentioned anything to you about this.'

I realized that Daskalos referred to the case of Aspasia, an old friend of the family. I learned of her tragedy before I met Daskalos. Her twenty-seven-year-old son died under extra-ordinary circumstances. He was an officer in the Cypriot Army and was at the front line during the Turkish invasion of the island in 1974. After the Turks stopped their advance and a cease-fire was established, he returned to Nicosia. He had the reputation of being good-natured but also a daredevil. While spending an evening with other officers at a local café, he tried to demonstrate his fearlessness of death. He pulled out his revolver and played Russian roulette. The fateful bullet killed him instantly in front of the horrified eyes of his friends.

His parents were inconsolable. He was their only child. Their grief was all the more intense because of the circumstances of his death. He survived a bloody invasion but not his own folly. The pain apparently was overwhelming for his father's heart which collapsed a month later. Aspasia remained all alone in the world and her extreme anguish literally crushed her. She reached the threshold of insanity. I was told that had it not been for Daskalos, Aspasia would probably have ended up in the asylum.

'Aspasia went to a psychiatrist who prescribed sedatives for her,' Daskalos continued. 'When she finally came to me I realized at once what had happened and asked her to stop

41

taking the drugs because they aggravated her situation. The elementals she created as a result of the shock she experienced from the loss of both son and husband led to the opening of her chakras at a time when she was least prepared. A human spirit who had lived with her in a previous life found the opportunity to get attached to her. Do you know how tiring it was for me to persuade this entity to leave Aspasia in peace? He was tormenting her. Whenever she went to bed he began talking endlessly to her and making demands.'

'How did you persuade this spirit to leave her?'

'First I brought him inside me. He himself was not aware of the change. He just felt that someone was communicating with him with intensity. He was unaware that he was disturbing Aspasia and assumed that it was his right to be attached to her because of their past association. I explained to him that he had to let her go because he was driving her insane. "If you have old rights," I said, "you have time to reactivate them in the future." This spirit was urging her to go sleep with any man. He created desires in her. He used to touch her at night and she would go wild. His ultimate goal was for her to bring him down to Earth. "This woman has no man to incarnate you with," I told him. "Therefore it is a closed case. Do you want to come down as a bastard? Stop. There is no chance for you here. Find another kindred spirit to get attached to and come down, assuming that it is granted from above."

'He said, "What if I don't stop?" I then used my last card and threatened him that I would force him out of her and that it would be very painful.'

'How would you do that?'

'By creating an elemental, attaching it around him and ejecting him into a psychic prison until he came to his senses. He will suffer in the meantime.'

'Is there a danger that this could be considered a form of black magic?'

'In this particular case it is not so. It is black magic only when you arrest an innocent person, put him in a psychic jail and torment him. It is not black magic when you grab a criminal who plans to kill someone and lock him up. Fortunately I managed to persuade him to leave her voluntarily. I then burned the elementals which opened her chakras and brought about the communication. You know, it took a lot of effort on my part to make him understand what was going on. Now Aspasia is fine.'

It was late in the evening when Iacovos, Kostas and myself bade farewell to Daskalos. We agreed to meet again in three days and continue our discussion on the nature of mental illness. It seemed as if Daskalos had an inexhaustible amount of cases that he was willing to share with us. In the meantime I contacted Aspasia and talked about her experience with Daskalos. She had no trace of her mental ordeal. In fact what impressed me about her was her calmness, earthy wisdom, and good humor. She was a forty-nine-year-old seamstress with only an elementary education. After her tragedy and her cure by Daskalos she became a devoted student of his and an avid reader, particularly of psychology. Her library was stacked with the works of Freud among others. When I visited her she was reading Eric Fromm's *To Have or to Be?*, a book which enchanted her, she said.

She explained to me that what drove her to Daskalos was her extreme anguish and her desire to communicate with her loved ones even though she was a skeptic at the time. When Daskalos realized what condition she was in, he tried to help her.

'I was in a desperate mental state. I walked the streets crying continuously. Daskalos sat down with me and tried to explain about Karma, about the psychic worlds, but I was reacting. I could not understand him.' He then brought her in contact with the 'boys,' as she referred to her dead son and husband. Daskalos put himself into a trance and communicated with them in her presence. As a result she became convinced that they were alive in some other world.

'I then began attending his lectures systematically. I had no idea at first about these matters. Gradually I got very involved, and was able to distinguish the gross material from the psychic world.'

'These lessons are theoretical. What evidence do you have that what Daskalos said about the psychic world was not convincing simply because you wished to be convinced in order to feel better?' I knew that Aspasia's psychological state was quite firm, therefore my question could not pose a threat to her mental balance and well-being.

'The exposure to Daskalos' teaching created in me a craving for knowledge. I began to read voraciously, and I diligently practiced the meditation exercises that Daskalos assigned. I was able to advance to the point where I began to have psychic experiences of my own, without causing any turbulence to my subconscious.'

Aspasia claimed that she could coordinate herself with the vibrations of her loved ones and be in touch with them any time she wished. It was her son, she said, that suggested to her the books she was reading. 'How could I,' she exclaimed, smiling, 'a poor seamstress with only an elementary education, know who Freud was?' Although she enjoyed her job as a seamstress, she wished she had more time for study.

'I learned through experience,' she said, 'that love is never lost. This realization totally transformed me. I became liberated.'

'What does liberation mean to you, Aspasia?'

'I am no longer enamoured with matter. But I do not reject it either, because it has a purpose. We are here to get experiences and must accept with patience and wisdom whatever happens to us. Everything is based on a Divine Plan. The boys came to this world, got whatever experiences they had to get, and then departed. Their time was up. They had to go. I accept the world as it is without being moralistic and without passing judgments. I know that we are here so that we can be of service to one another and learn how to love. Death is no longer a problem for me. It is simply a transformation, a temporary physical separation from people you love.

'I have suffered a lot,' she continued, smiling, 'but I have been rewarded with knowledge. I have never felt better in my entire life. Before, I lived in ignorance. Now I know.'

Aspasia said to me how lucky I was since I entered the path of knowledge through my studies without having to experience a personal tragedy. 'In my case I had to be jolted into knowledge,' she added with a smile.

According to Daskalos, Aspasia had become so advanced as a healer that he planned to assign her a circle of students of her own. In her spare time she was already acting like a good social worker, practicing the healing arts taught to her by Daskalos. On several occasions she assisted him. She mentioned to me that she was present when Daskalos handled the case of a twenty-two-year-old girl from Larnaca who, since birth, had had a crooked spine, and one leg was an inch shorter than the other. Daskalos, Aspasia claimed, made her spine completely straight and the legs became even. But because of the girl's chronic problem, she could not believe, at first, that she was cured. Daskalos had to convince her. Then she began to walk straight.

I have met with Aspasia on many occasions. We became good friends. In fact during the early stages of my research, before I established a close rapport with Iacovos and Kostas, it was through her that I contacted Daskalos.

CHAPTER 3

Three bodies

When I arrived at Daskalos' there were some visitors who apparently faced a serious family crisis. After he introduced me I discreetly sat next to Kostas who happened to be present. A middle-aged man who seemed to be the head of the family looked deeply distressed and on the brink of tears. His wife and daughter were in a similar emotional predicament.

'You advised us,' the man said, 'not to interfere with him and instead show him love and understanding. Now he has almost ruined me financially and I don't know what to do. There is a struggle inside me whether to forgive him or not. I often wonder whether forgiveness is not a form of weakness.'

'You assume you have been unjustly treated,' Daskalos stated.

'I *was* unjustly treated,' said the visitor with emotion. 'It is proven.'

'In what way?' Daskalos asked.

'The police arrested him and it is up to me whether I testify against him or not,' said the man, a pharmacist and a member of Daskalos' circles. Kostas explained to me in a low voice that several months back the pharmacist noticed that large sums of money as well as inventory were missing from his shop. He resorted to Daskalos to discover the culprit. Daskalos told him, correctly, that the thief was none other than his own stepson, who assumed that what he stole was rightfully his. Daskalos advised them not to confront him but to show patience and affection on the assumption that this would bring him to his senses. The stepson, however, continued to deplete the pharmacy of cash and products. He finally burglarized a neighbor's shop and the matter got into the hands of the police. The legal entanglements were such that it was up to the stepfather whether the young man was to remain in jail or not.

'I ask myself,' the man said bitterly, 'shall I testify against him or not? Should he not suffer some punishment in order to reform? What about the law? Is he or is he not a wound on society?'

'He is a wound,' Daskalos added, 'but the wound is on himself.'

'But shall I become his accomplice or should he be punished?'

'It depends on the punishment. It could destroy him. I cannot tell you what you must do. But I can tell you what I would do in your case. If you wage a war against him because he has hurt you, you will create a bigger evil than the one he has already inflicted on himself. As you know, whatever act we commit encloses within itself the analogous punishment or reward. There is no human being without a conscience. If I were you I would talk to him in private, embrace and kiss him and reaffirm my love for him. Then I would give him a couple of slaps in the face and tell him, "You fool, come to your senses before it is too late. You are destroying yourself." I will have put fire in his heart to awaken his conscience. I would not testify to the police. This would ruin him. Show him love for the evil he has inflicted. This is the greatest punishment that can bring him to the right path.'

'But Daskale,' a man who accompanied the family protested, 'he stole from them hundreds of pounds.'

'It does not matter whether he stole a handful of dirt or a sack full of dirt,' Daskalos snapped and then turned to the pharmacist.

'Let me ask you something. Do you love your stepson?'

'I loved him.'

'Do you love him?' Daskalos asked loudly.

'I loved him,' the man repeated, close to tears. 'I adopted him when he was very young and raised him as my own. What has he done to me now? He has deliberately tried to destroy me.'

'Forgive him if you want to find peace,' Daskalos urged him softly.

'I wish I was dead,' the man said and burst into tears. Several minutes passed in silence while father, mother and daughter wiped their eyes.

'I will let things follow their course,' the pharmacist said with determination as he calmed down and dried his eyes. 'I will not testify against him.' He then thanked Daskalos for his time and left with his family and friends.

'Unless he forgives him,' Daskalos murmured to Kostas as the others left the house, 'he will not find rest. It is he who is going to suffer.'

'The other day,' Daskalos said as he sank back into his chair, 'a couple I know complained about their son. They loved him, they said, and made great sacrifices for his medical education until he decided to marry a girl they disapproved of. From their "doctor," their "pride," their "love" he was transformed overnight into the ungrateful and contemptible son. So great was the father's anger and bitterness against his son that he even wished his death. "I hope they bring him dead in front of me on a stretcher," he said to me. "Shut up. Are you mad?" I screamed and felt like slapping him in the face. "But I loved him," he said. "Nonsense," I shouted. "You have never loved him. It is only yourself you loved and turned your son into a mirror to see and take pride in your own reflection."

'I hope now that he has become a grandfather I will be able to reconcile them. Love, to me, means giving,' Daskalos continued, 'not receiving. One who loves gives of oneself. That is how I understand love. Someone might ask, "And where is love in this world of ours?" It will evolve gradually. Now we are in a period of confusion,' Daskalos concluded and drank the glass of water Kostas had fetched him a few minutes earlier.

'Kyriaco,' Daskalos said to me as he put his glass on the table, 'will you come with us to Larnaca?'

'What are you going to do there?' I asked.

'We have a meeting of the Larnaca circle.'

It was late afternoon when we started for the coastal town. The sky was covered with heavy dark clouds and before we reached the outskirts of Nicosia there was a torrent of rain followed by lightning and thunder. Daskalos, oblivious to the cataclysm outside, continued an animated discussion we had started earlier on the local political situation with its chronic crises. Although Daskalos never tired of impressing upon us that 'topo-chronic' (space-time) realities are of no ultimate value, he himself was not a mystic detached from earthly concerns. It was perhaps because of this habit of 'coming down' to the concerns, and sometimes even petty concerns, of ordinary people that made him so accessible to his fellows. I once informed him, only half in jest, that I was more impressed with his knowledge and understanding of the metaphysical world than his expertise on local and international politics. Daskalos, unmindful of my irreverence, laughed heartily at my insinuation.

I often had the uncanny feeling that Daskalos would deliberately present himself as an ordinary mortal with common weaknesses in order to debunk the myth of the perfect master. More than once he expressed his objections to the personality cult characteristic of other mystical traditions, particularly those offering and promising instant and effortless enlightenment.

Beyond the outskirts of Nicosia, well on the way to Larnaca, the rain had stopped, the clouds were breaking and a rainbow decorated the horizon in the distance like a majestic celestial ornament. It was early November and the Cypriot countryside was coming to life after a long dry summer. I had not experienced fall in Cyprus for many a year and the exposure filled me with nostalgia rekindling in me memories of a world long gone.

We passed by several Greek villages crowded with refugees from the north. The road to Larnaca ran parallel to the 'Green Line,' the division between the occupied north and the south which remained under the control of the Greek Cypriots. Protest banners in English, an apparent attempt to impress foreign visitors, welcomed the motorist at the entrance of every village: 'We want to return home,' 'Justice for Cyprus,' 'Refugees in our own country.' At the village of Lympia there was a most unlikely sight. High on the hilltop overlooking the village there was a small church dedicated to the prophet Elias. Right next to the bell tower a Turkish flag flew defiantly. Below there was a sandbag embankment and Turkish soldiers kept watch over the Greek village below. Between the village and the Turkish stronghold there was a United Nations observation outpost and further down an encampment of Greek Cypriot national guardsmen. The entire scenario was a constant and depressing reminder of the fragility of peace prevailing on the island. It became an almost masochistic habit of many refugees living next to the 'Green Line' to climb nearby hills on Sundays and with binoculars gaze at their now inaccessible villages located north of the dividing line.

By six o'clock we were at Theano's, an old *archontiko* facing the waterfront with its promenade and series of palm trees. Theano, a lively and lovable woman in her sixties, was a member of Daskalos' inner circle. After the hugs and kisses we sat in her antiquarian living-room full of relics of her late husband-poet and disciple of Daskalos. On the wall over an ancient piano there were three paintings by Daskalos, a cactus, a cyclamen and one portraying two dark exploding volcanoes.

Theano as usual brought forward glasses of lemonade, cups of coffee and pieces of various cakes she had baked for the occasion.

Daskalos' disciples arrived one by one, sat around with the rest of us and helped themselves to the pastries while listening to Daskalos' yarns and humorous anecdotes. By seven-thirty as many as thirty people were present, ranging in age from twenty-two to seventy.

We moved to a larger room to begin the lesson. Kostas lit a white candle, burned in a small container some church incense and stood on Daskalos' right side. On his left there stood Iacovos. Daskalos closed his eyes, slightly bent his head and turned his palms upward. We stood with our heads slightly lowered as Daskalos murmured the familiar short prayers starting with 'Our Father who art in Heaven.'

'Tonight,' Daskalos began, after everybody sat down, 'we will summarize and review some of the material that we have covered so far in regard to the nature of the etheric-double and the three bodies of man. You will have a chance to ask whatever questions you may have about these topics.'

Every human being, Daskalos taught, lives simultaneously in three planes of existence, the gross material, the psychic and the noetic. All three are material universes but at different levels of 'vibrations.' The gross material, namely the three-dimensional world, is at the lowest level. It is the world where we experience space and time, a 'topo-chronic' condition, as Daskalos was fond of saying. The psychic, or what is often called the fourth-dimensional world, is also material but at a higher level of vibrations. Space is neutralized and the individual can move over vast distances momentarily. The laws that govern the psychic dimension are different from the laws that govern the third dimension, the world of gross matter. The noetic, or fifth dimension, is also material, but governed by a different set of laws. In this fifth dimension both space and time are transcended. The vibrations are of a more rarefied order and the individual can move and act much more freely than within the other two dimensions. The individual, as self-consciousness, can travel instantly, not only over vast areas of the Earth, but also across time.

Every individual has a corresponding body for each of these three worlds. In the world of the three dimensions we live with the gross material body. In the world of the fourth dimension we live with the psychic body, the body of emotions and sentiments. In the fifth dimension we live with the noetic body, the body which makes possible the expression of concrete as well as abstract thoughts. The noetic body is divided into the higher and lower body. All the three bodies make up the present self-conscious personality.

Daskalos further argued that there is nothing within the gross material universe which does not have a psychic and noetic counterpart. The Earth too, he said, is a living being. No object or atom is in reality 'dead.' However, the psychic and noetic counterparts in the mineral, plant and animal kingdoms do not form a psychic and noetic body which can function independently from the gross material. Animals do not have self-consciousness. Only man is an eternal entity.

'Human consciousness,' Daskalos stressed, 'came neither through the animals nor minerals as some fools have argued. Yes, the body of man is related to animals, plants and minerals since we must eat in order to sustain the material body. But animals and plants have nothing to do with the inner self, the permanent personality. Man descended through the Idea of Man as a complete eternal entity, creating shadows to express itself. One of its shadows is the present personality.'

Daskalos quickly clarified that the psychic body is not identical with the psyche of a person or the soul. The latter is eternal and beyond all manifestations. The psychic body eventually dies just like the gross material body and the noetic body. With every incarnation the self-conscious soul manifests itself with a new noetic, psychic and gross material body. The three bodies are the garments that the self-conscious soul wears to express itself from one incarnation to another.

The three bodies that make up the present personality can exist independently of one another. The gross material body,

51

however, always has within it the other two. Similarly, the psychic body always has within it the noetic body. The latter, however, can exist by itself and can be a vehicle for the full expression of a self-conscious soul.

A personality can abandon the gross material body and, through the psychic body, the body expressing feelings and sentiments, can live fully conscious within the psychic worlds. It is similarly possible that one can live fully conscious only with the noetic body after abandoning first the gross material and then the psychic body. At death the individual withdraws with his psychonoetic body and lives in the psychic worlds in a similar manner as he did within the gross material world. Daskalos maintained that most people often do not, upon death, realize the transition.

'An advanced mystic,' he went on, 'who has reached the point at which his present self-conscious personality is in attunement with his self-conscious soul is a master of all three bodies. Such a mystic, who may live in the noetic spheres, having only a noetic body, can create at will a psychic body and materialize within the psychic worlds. He can further materialize at will a gross material body and become visible to personalities that live on the gross material plane. Therefore such a mystic, after abandoning both the gross material body and the psychic body, can be in constant contact with the other two worlds. For example, such a mystic can materialize in front of people, talk to them, shake hands with them and be of assistance. He can materialize himself on a battlefield and help a wounded soldier or stop a hemorrhage. Bear in mind that for an advanced mystic it is not necessary to abandon the gross material body permanently in order to accomplish such a feat. Whether he lives in a gross material body, in a psychic, or in a noetic body, he masters all three and can at will express himself within the three worlds by using the analogous bodies.

'Daskale,' someone asked, 'what is the difference between the higher and lower noetic body?'

'The lower noetic body has form and shape. You can travel with your lower noetic body and have exactly the same physiognomy that you now have within gross matter. Even though the lower noetic body is in a different dimension, having different properties, its image is identical with the psychic and gross material bodies. The higher noetic body on the other hand is shapeless. It exists within the higher noetic world. The higher noetic body concerns laws and causes. The higher noetic body is the set of those vibrations that maintains the cohesion of forms and images at the lower levels. It is the abstract, which is the real. What is considered to be concrete is only phenomenally real.'

'Therefore, when we exist only with our higher noetic body we are closer to reality than when we exist with the other bodies,' someone observed.

'Correct. We have three mirrors that distort us, gross matter, psychic matter and noetic matter. We take our shadows as ourselves. We smile at the mirrors and take as ourselves our reflections. But our true self is something else. When we discover our self, we will no longer be concerned about breaking the mirrors.

'The three bodies,' Daskalos continued, 'that make up the present self-conscious personality are linked together through their corresponding etheric-doubles. Each body is surrounded and penetrated by a life-giving ether that keeps it alive. We call it etheric-double because it is identical with the gross material body and is one with it, but consisting of a different texture. The relationship of the body to its etheric-double is equivalent to the relationship between a battery and the electricity within it. It is the etheric-double that keeps the body alive. The moment the etheric-double is detached from the body the latter begins to disintegrate. This applies to all the three bodies with their corresponding etheric-doubles. It is through these etheric-doubles that the three bodies are linked together and influence one another.

'For the human body to maintain itself in life it requires not only food, oxygen and water, but also life-giving ether. It is through the centers of the etheric-double that this life-giving ether is absorbed and channeled into the human body. The Indians call it *prana* and one source is the Sun. This ether, or *prana*, is widespread in the atmosphere during the day when the Sun is up and it is low when the Sun sets. It is for this reason that at night the condition of patients worsens. The body absorbs a smaller amount of ether after sunset. Through deep breathing one can absorb this kind of vitality, however, at any time.

'In addition there is a higher form of ether that comes through space. Nightfall is no obstacle to it nor is any material object or celestial body. We can harness this energy through the appropriate meditation exercises, store it in our etheric-double and use it at will for healing purposes.'

Daskalos went on to say that the ether which is necessary for the maintenance of life has four basic properties or functions: kinetic, sensate, imprinting and creative. Every atom and every cell of the etheric-double is imbued with all four properties working simultaneously.

'The creative property of ether is the most important and it is under the direct control of the Holy Spirit and Christ Logos. A very advanced mystic who becomes master of this property can literally dematerialize and materialize cells and carry out therapies such as the removal of a cancerous tumor or the elongation of a short leg. The creative function of etheric vitality makes possible the construction and maintenance of the body. It can do that in conjunction with the other functions. For example life cannot exist without the kinetic property. It cannot exist without movement, without blood-flow, heartbeat, pulsation of the lungs, movement of the limbs, metabolism and so on. You will learn how to master the kinetic property of ether through various exercises that I will teach you. By mastering this function you can also become masters of your own autonomic nervous system.

'The sensate property of ether,' Daskalos continued, 'is that part of the ether that makes possible the existence of sense experience, feelings and sentiments. Ether flows within the nervous system like electricity within a cable. It is in this manner that irritations are transferred from the surface of the skin to the center of the brain.

'The imprinting property of ether enables us to construct images, that is, it makes possible thought itself as well as phenomena such as telepathy, telekinesis and exomatosis. Is it then possible, I can ask, for a personality to detach the etheric-double from the gross material body and use it as a separate body? Never. It is an integral part of the gross material body. Once the etheric-double is detached from the gross material body we have the phenomenon of death and the body will begin to disintegrate. When one dies he will continue to live in the psychic worlds through his psychonoetic body. The etheric-double of the gross material body is now useless and will be dissolved.' Daskalos stopped for a few seconds apparently awaiting questions from his attentive audience.

'Daskale,' I asked, after noting that no one else was ready for a question, 'does the etheric-double of the gross material body grow old in a similar manner as the material body?'

'No. There is no young and old etheric energy. The etheric-double, as a model within which the material body grows, undergoes changes itself but it is not an aging process. For example, the etheric-double of a fetus is not identical with the etheric-double of a grown man. Similarly the etheric-double of a young woman is not the same as that of an old one. But I will repeat, the changes that the etheric-double undergoes are not equivalent to the process of aging. For example, we will not notice any wrinkles on the etheric-double of an aged person, even though his gross material body may be covered with them. What we will notice, however, are changes in terms of the shape of, and the work that, the etheric-double performs *vis-à-vis* the body. The work and shape of the etheric-double of an infant are different from that of a grown person. The etheric-double is the continuously changing model within which the gross material body is built and which in turn obeys the laws of the completion of the cycle of existence.

'I have this to add: the etheric-double of the gross material body is relatively similar in all human beings whereas the etheric-double of the psychic and noetic bodies is very dissimilar. Each person is unique in terms of character and personality. And it is the noetic and psychic bodies that constitute the personality of an individual. The composition of noetic and psychic matter varies radically from individual to individual.'

Daskalos then mentioned what I had heard him repeat time and again. The present personality is the sum total of all the experiences the self-conscious entity has accumulated and all the elementals it has created from the very moment of its descent into matter and the beginning of the incarnational cycles.

To make his theoretical formulations on the existence of ether more concrete, Daskalos proceeded to perform a rather unusual demonstration. Theano left the room and at the request of Daskalos brought a three-inch needle from a room next door. Daskalos then stood up and pulled up his shirt sleeve from his left arm.

'It is possible,' he said, 'to anaesthetize part of the body by removing the sensate property of ether with our thought without using any drugs. We can even operate on the body without any pain being transferred to the brain.' In a state of deep concentration he slowly passed his right hand over his left arm several times. When he finished he picked the needle up with his right hand and passed it in front of his open mouth as he forcefully exhaled a few times, 'to sterilize it.' He then asked Iacovos to pinch with his fingers a portion of Daskalos' flesh from the latter's bare arm. With a quick movement of his right hand, Daskalos pierced the protruding flesh as if he were sewing a piece of leather, the tip of the needle coming out the other side. I noticed no pain expressed on Daskalos' face. He left the needle in his arm for about a minute so that everyone could inspect it. He then pulled it out and softly and quickly rubbed his arm. There were no blood marks and no trace of the operation was left on his arm. He then asked for volunteers. Iacovos went first, succeeded by several others from the audience. Daskalos followed the same procedure with the same results. Nobody expressed pain and no marks were left on their arms. I gathered my courage and asked Daskalos to do it on my own arm. If for no other reason, I felt that I owed it to my research role as a participant observer to try it out. Naturally I had seen enough of Daskalos' strange gifts to have at least a minimum of trust that nothing serious could possibly happen to me. Like the others I experienced no pain whatsoever and no marks remained.

'Unless you remove the sensate property of ether you will feel pain and blood will flow. Who would like to try?' Daskalos inquired after a few moments' pause. Nobody volunteered. I inspected the needle and touched my skin with it. I could not imagine trying it on myself without prior preparation through Daskalos' 'magic.'

Daskalos assured his disciples that they could one day easily accomplish such feats assuming that they regularly practiced the meditation exercises he assigned so that they became masters of the various properties of ether. Once they acquired such mastery they could then accomplish healing phenomena that presently appeared 'miraculous.'

Daskalos then asked Kostas to carry on another experiment as a way of demonstrating experientially the principles of the etheric-double and its properties. Daskalos has taught that a

Researcher of Truth that has become a master of his etheric vitality would be capable of 'projections,' that is, through concentration he could pass on energy to another person who could feel it, regardless of how far away one is from the other. Through this method healing can take place at a distance.

Kostas stood in front of the first person next to him. 'Close your eyes,' he asked the thirty-year-old woman, 'and try to guess what I am doing to you. Make sure you don't open your eyes, okay?'

'Okay,' she replied as she straightened up, closed her eyes and placed her hands on her lap. Kostas bent forward and began slowly passing his right hand a few inches away from the woman's right arm. He appeared in a state of deep concentration as his palm vibrated slightly from the intensity of his effort. Kostas was careful not to touch in any way the woman's arm or any part of her clothing.

'What am I doing to you?' Kostas asked after he passed his hand up and down her arm a few times. The woman answered correctly, that she felt a current of warm energy moving up and down her right arm.

'Next,' Kostas commanded as the woman opened her eyes and moved to another chair. Everyone including myself, participated in this experiment. Kostas would sometimes pass his palm over the left and sometimes over the right arm of the other. It was done in a random manner. Therefore there was no way that one could predict on which arm Kostas was concentrating his attention.

I watched the experiment carefully, as everyone else did, and kept count of the successful replies. All of us who gave the correct answer described the experience in identical terms, a warm sensation moving up and down our arm. From a statistical point of view, the experiment was quite impressive. Twenty-six of the thirty-two persons present gave the correct reply with the first try. I knew that assuming there was no 'cheating,' and I had no reason to suspect any, the high correlation of correct answers was extremely significant and unlikely to be the result of pure chance. Kostas was a powerful healer enjoying great respect among the spiritual underground of Daskalos' circles.

The validity of Daskalos' teachings on the etheric energy and its therapeutic properties was confirmed for me one day as I was glancing through the science section of *The New York Times* (26 March 1985). It was discovered by scientific researchers in nursing that under carefully controlled experimental conditions the traditional healing method of 'laying on of hands' resulted in bodily effects on the patients that 'go beyond the well-known placebo response, in which patients improve because they believe the therapy is beneficial. In this and other studies, therapeutic touch was found to have health benefits even without direct contact between the healer's hands and the patient's body and even if the patient had no knowledge of what the technique was supposed to achieve.' The key to this healing, according to the researchers, was the ability of the healer to 'concentrate' on the patient. The researchers, however, could not offer an explanation as to *why* it works.

Once Kostas completed the experiment Daskalos asked him to continue and instruct us on an exercise for the mastery of the sensate, kinetic and imprinting properties of etheric vitality.

Kostas commanded us to sit as comfortably as possible, close our eyes, loosen every muscle within our body and begin to breathe deeply and with ease.

'You will now begin to exercise the sensate property of etheric vitality by feeling the soles of both your feet. Only the soles,' Kostas said slowly in a mesmerizing tone and repeated his instructions. 'You feel only the soles of your feet. No other part of your material body attracts your attention. You are at the soles of your two feet. You feel a soft vibration at the soles of your feet, only of your feet.' After a few moments' pause he continued his instructions, in the same slow and semi-hypnotic tone.

'Now the kinetic property. Proceed slowly upwards toward the ankles of your feet. With the sensate property of ether you feel now the part of your body from the soles to the ankles.' After about half a minute Kostas continued.

'The kinetic property again. Proceed gradually from your ankles to your knees. Now you feel your legs from the soles to the knees. No other part of your body should attract your attention. You are employing the sensate property of ether from the soles to the knees. The kinetic property again. Move slowly upwards through the thighs and reach up to the points where your legs join with the pelvis. Through the sensate property of ether feel your two legs from the soles to the pelvis. Remember, no other part of your body attracts your attention.

'Now,' he continued, 'utilize the imprinting property of your etheric vitality. You visualize your two legs covered by an all-white irradiance. Only white light covers your two legs from the soles to the pelvis. With your thought make a strong wish that only health should reign within your legs.

'Through the kinetic property of your etheric vitality,' Kostas said after about half a minute as we kept our eyes closed, 'proceed upwards through the pelvis, the abdominal region and arrive at the chest. Exercise the sensate property of ether up to the chest. Just remember, do not lay off the sensate property from the previous parts of your body that you have just covered. You feel your body from the soles of your feet up to your chest. Concentrate over that region.

'Now use the imprinting property,' Kostas went on after a minute. 'Observe inside and around your abdominal region a white-blue light in the form of a nebula. It is a white-blue irradiance inside and around your abdomen. With your thoughts, wish that full health should reign within your gross material existence.

'The kinetic property again,' Kostas said after a minute of silence. 'Move upwards and proceed within your chest. Through the sensate property of ether feel the entire region of your chest and through the use of the imprinting property visualize a white-rose irradiance in the form of a nebula to cover the entire region of your chest, inside and outside. With your thought,' Kostas continued after half a minute or so, 'will that complete health should reign within your psychic body. Make a strong wish that complete health must reign within the world of your sentiments. Peace and tranquility may prevail within your present self-conscious personality.

'The kinetic property of ether again,' Kostas continued after a minute. 'Move upwards through your shoulders and begin gradually to descend through your arms. Reach down to the palms and fingers of your two hands. Through the sensate property of etheric vitality feel now your two hands from your shoulders down to your palms and fingers. Now,' Kostas proceeded slowly, 'through the imprinting property visualize your two hands covered with a white irradiance. Do the same with your two legs. Your arms and legs are now covered with a vibrating all-white luminosity. Wish that complete health may prevail within your two hands. Wish that these two hands become agents for healing the pains of your fellow human beings.

'Kinetic property again upwards,' Kostas went on after a minute. 'Come up all the way to your thyroid. Through the imprinting property of ether visualize the thyroid region covered within an egg-shaped white-orange irradiance. A nebula of white-orange light covers the region of your thyroid. Again wish that complete health reigns within your gross material existence.

'The kinetic property of ether again,' he said after half a minute. 'Begin to slowly enter upwards inside the head. Through the sensate property feel your head. Imprinting property now. Visualize a golden nebula, a white-golden irradiance covers the inside and outside of your head. Wish that complete health must reign within your noetic body. Wish for right use of the divine gift of thought, wish for right thinking.

'You are now,' Kostas continued after a few seconds of silence, 'inside every particle and every cell of your material existence. White-golden light covers your head, white-rose light covers your chest, white-blue light dominates your abdominal region, your legs and hands are covered with white light. Now visualize that you are surrounded by an egg-shaped vibrating white luminosity. You are at the center of this luminosity. Pay attention, it is not something solid, it is an all-white light and you are inside it. Wish that this egg-shaped luminosity protects your present personality from external threats, from whatever is trying to hurt you. Will that this luminosity neutralizes and dissolves anything that lurks against your present personality. It must neutralize it and not send it back from where it came from. Be careful about that. Wish that complete health may reign within your present self-conscious personality.

'That will be all,' Kostas concluded as we came out of our meditative state, opened our eyes and stretched. I looked at my watch. It took about half an hour to complete the exercise. Daskalos, after thanking Kostas, instructed that for the following month we should practice daily with this exercise. 'It is training,' he said, 'for mastering three of the four properties of etheric energy. It will also keep our three bodies in good health.'

After most of Daskalos' students had left, Theano and another member of the Larnaca circle set up a feast in honor of Daskalos. All the out-of-towners, which included Iacovos, Kostas, another member of the inner circle from Nicosia and myself, were invited. It was a ritual that after the monthly Larnaca meetings there followed a dinner which inadvertently turned out to be a more informal continuation of Daskalos' lessons, and was always accompanied with good humor and lightheartedness.

We had barely finished eating when we heard a car stop outside and quick footsteps coming up to the door. It was Lisa, one of Daskalos' students of the Nicosia circle. She looked very upset. Lisa was also a family friend and confidante of Daskalos'. Through him I got to know her fairly well. We drank innumerable cups of coffee together and endlessly chatted on every possible subject, from the problems of her teenage daughter to the attainment of Theosis. Lisa had a striking resemblance to Leonardo da Vinci's *Mona Lisa* and we would often jokingly refer to her as 'La Gioconda.' 'Mona Lisa?' Daskalos exclaimed one day laughing and joking. 'She is more like "DeMona Lisa"' – Daskalos who was particularly fond of Lisa was alluding to her dynamism and piercing intelligence.

'Daskale,' she said, breathing heavily, 'my son has beaten up his sister and unless certain things get straightened out, I don't know what's going to happen.' She nervously grabbed from her purse pictures of her son and daughter, and explained what took place. Her son, an officer in the Cypriot army, lost his military insignia and apparently his sister was responsible for giving them away to a cousin. So they were lost. In his rage he hit her. He was afraid of a court martial and of the humiliation that would follow. Lisa was very upset because of the discord in her house. She gave the pictures to Iacovos and Kostas first, and then to Daskalos. They went into another room and whispered among themselves. The whole episode appeared to us rather absurd as it was felt by some of us that the fact of her son losing his insignia should not have created so much turmoil. Driving all the way from Nicosia was thought totally unnecessary and out of proportion with the case at hand. Lisa's argument was that the army could have called him for duty that very night. Her son was in the military police, and he would have no insignia to wear. The discipline in the Greek

Cypriot National Guard was severe enough to generate anxiety in her family.

In about an hour, while Daskalos and the rest of us tried to reassure Lisa and calm her down, the telephone rang. It was her husband, a physician, also a disciple of Daskalos. He informed us that the insignia had been found and that everything was fine. Lisa sighed with relief. As she was about to leave for Nicosia I asked her privately whether she thought Daskalos was responsible for finding her son's insignia. She threw her hands upwards. 'Only God knows,' she exclaimed. Lisa had no doubts of Daskalos' power. She had, in her own way, studied Daskalos over the years. On other occasions she conveyed to me stories of extraordinary feats Daskalos had performed in her presence.

In addition to Daskalos' reputation as a healer, clairvoyant and spiritual master, he was known for his ability to locate lost objects. A woman had once told me that Daskalos helped her locate the grave of her son who had been missing in action since the days of the Turkish invasion.

It was a little after eleven o'clock when we left for Nicosia. Kostas drove to Limassol and Daskalos, Iacovos, myself and the other brother from Nicosia drove back to the capital in the latter's Volvo. By that time there was little traffic. We were all silent throughout the trip listening to Mozart playing on the state radio. The combination of a full moon, the Cypress trees on both sides of the road and the music made the trip a relaxing and memorable experience, somehow a befitting scenario to complete the spiritually intense evening.

CHAPTER 4

Sacred discs

Daskalos looked sad that morning when Emily and I visited him. Theophanis, his close friend and disciple for over forty years, was present listening to Daskalos' lamentations.

'There is so much confusion all´around,' Daskalos said after we inquired about what was going on. He went on to inform us that a student who was very close to him, as close as any daughter could be, was getting divorced. What made it even more painful was that her husband was a member of his circles and himself very close to Daskalos. In spite of his mediation efforts Daskalos was unable to help reconcile their differences. Karma would not permit it.

On top of these problems Daskalos had received a message that the local priest in the previous Sunday's sermon had given an impassioned diatribe against Daskalos. He had urged his flock to avoid Daskalos because he was an 'instrument of the devil.' It was a problem that Daskalos faced continuously. Only Daskalos' diplomatic skills and good relationships with some of the higher clergy saved him from excommunication.

'At first I thought of suing the old fool but then I changed my mind,' Daskalos said with exasperation. 'Instead I wrote him a letter informing him that he did not know what he was saying. I even told him that some of his superiors in the church were members of my circles.'

'There is no reason for you to get upset,' Theophanis, who rarely spoke, said reassuringly as he tapped Daskalos on the left shoulder.

'But how can I not get upset when people spread such vile rumors about me?'

'Daskale,' I added, 'Theophanis is right. On the basis of what you yourself teach you should not be bothered by the way some ignorant people define you. Aren't you above all that?'

'My dear Kyriaco,' Daskalos replied with a sense of protest in his voice, 'what bothers me is not the way I am being defined

63

by others. I do not need people to provide me with my self-identity. When people like him spread such nonsense, persons who would have come to me for help may stay away.'

We reassured Daskalos that the teachings that come through him cannot be suppressed with such petty methods. Daskalos calmed down and in a few minutes he was again his ebullient self, ready for endless conversations and humorous anecdotes.

In the absence of any visitors seeking his help that morning Daskalos at my instigation proceeded to describe to us in detail the strenuous relationship he had with the local church. During my early encounters with Daskalos I learned that the bishops, many years back, encouraged by several theologians from Greece, tried to excommunicate him, accusing him of being an apostle of Lucifer. The late Archbishop Makarios, who was on good terms with Daskalos, was on an extended absence from the island. It was the bishops' chance to undo 'the Magus.'

Memories of that episode were no longer painful for Daskalos. In fact, reminiscing about those events brought forward hilarity and laughter. And Daskalos was a man that, regardless of the nature of his situation, never lost an opportunity for laughter and comic relief. It was an attribute of his character that added immensely to his attractiveness as a charismatic personality and an effective healer.

'The Patriarch of Alexandria found out about the bishops' machinations and sent me a reassuring letter,' Daskalos began after I helped Emily to prepare four cups of coffee. '"They have no right to excommunicate you," he wrote. "Their actions could harm the Church of Cyprus."

'It was clear to me,' Daskalos went on as he sipped from his cup, 'that the Patriarch had ulterior motives, to use me in order to take control of the Cypriot Church, something that the patriarchate was unable to do for centuries.'

In the early part of the fifth century the Patriarch of Antioch, by resorting to clever and weighty theological arguments concerning the apostolic foundation of the Church of Antioch, demanded the recognition of its supremacy over Cyprus. The Cypriot bishops and clergymen vigorously resisted the patriarch's attempt to take over the Cypriot Church. Their efforts, however, were bound to fail as the Patriarch was a friend of

Zeno, the then Emperor of Byzantium. A well-timed 'miracle,' however, saved the Cypriot Church. Anthemios, the Archbishop of Cyprus at the time, had a vision in which the location of a lost copy of Matthew's gospel was revealed. He discovered in his vision that Mark, the evangelist, placed it on the chest of Saint Barnabas, the founder of the Cypriot Church, when the latter was buried in Cyprus during the first century AD.

A Cypriot delegation visited Constantinople and presented Matthew's gospel as a gift to the Emperor. The Antiochian claims collapsed now that Cyprus could demonstrate that its Church also had an apostolic foundation. The grateful Emperor accorded the Cypriot Church total autonomy and certain unprecedented privileges reserved only for Byzantine emperors. The Archbishop of Cyprus was to carry an imperial sceptre of silver and gold, with an orb and a jewelled cross at the summit. In addition he was to wear an imperial purple cape and sign his name in red ink. The Archbishop of Cyprus, fifteen centuries later, continues to enjoy these privileges, with serious and far-reaching repercussions for the social and political life of the island.

'I showed the letter to Gennadios, the Bishop of Paphos,' Daskalos went on. 'He gasped with fear. "Let us kneel down and pray to God, my son, so that we may be forgiven," he said. "Kneel down and ask forgiveness yourself," I told him. "I am not afraid of God. I love God."'

'Did that letter save you from excommunication?' I asked.

'Not really. As soon as Archbishop Makarios learned what his bishops were engineering in his absence, he gave orders to cancel the proceedings.'

Daskalos then mentioned to us that the Archbishop in fact was receiving taped talks from Daskalos and through meditation exercises he was beginning to develop his psychonoetic powers. Daskalos went on to say that unfortunately the Archbishop abused those powers. For example, in order to impress the other bishops at a banquet he allegedly made the plates 'dance by themselves.' I was intrigued by what Daskalos said about Makarios, who served as the first President of the Republic of Cyprus. I knew that just before the bishops tried to defrock him (they were later defrocked themselves by Makarios after a protracted crisis within the Church) one of them, Anthimos, had written a short pamphlet accusing his superior of magic practices and recounted the incident of the dancing plates. Makarios, the bishop hypothesized, learned these evil tricks from a yogi when he was on a state visit to India. I was able to confirm the Archbishop's interest in esoteric teachings after a casual conversation I had with a foreign correspondent who interviewed Makarios a month before his fatal heart attack in 1977. This journalist claimed that Makarios had no interest in discussing politics. Instead, his primary concern with spiritual questions reminded the journalist of the teachings of the Rosicrucians, a spiritual cult with some similarities to Daskalos' teachings.

'Without his intervention the circles may have closed down long ago,' Daskalos claimed. The majority of the clergy fought Daskalos and for a long time they tried to undermine his authority as a healer and a psychic. In fact one archimandrite offered a lad a certain sum of money to spread rumors in the coffee-houses that Daskalos was a homosexual. One day Daskalos was in a coffee-house with several of his students when this young man entered and boasted about his alleged carnal adventures with the 'Magus of Strovolos.' Daskalos' students asked him to identify Daskalos in the room. Having never met him, the young man failed the test. The students then grabbed him by the collar of his shirt and forced him to reveal who had sent him around to spread such vile rumors.

'My students then paid a visit to this archimandrite. Without any shame or hesitation he said that in fact it was he who had sent the lad around to spread the rumors. He told them, "I will fight your master with whatever means necessary." He then had the audacity to come to my house and repeat the same words to my face. "Had we lived during the Middle Ages I would have roasted you like a lamb," he threatened me. Then he went on to say, "We monks are like charcoal. When lighted we burn, when extinguished we stain." "I shall wear special shoes with iron soles to protect myself," I replied.'

'You mean you intended to harm him?'

'Of course not. I simply wanted to frighten him a little so that he would leave me in peace.'

Daskalos then proceeded to elaborate further on his relationship with Archbishop Makarios. After the tragic events of 1974 he sent Makarios a taped message pointing the finger at him as shouldering the heaviest responsibility for the disaster.

'"Had you shown less egotism and more understanding towards your political opponents," I said on the tape, "there would have been neither a coup against you nor an invasion of our island." Theophanis was reluctant to deliver the tape. He thought it was too critical and insulting. I insisted that he should deliver it at once.

'Theophanis,' Daskalos continued, 'presented the tape to Makarios and offered his apology. "You need not say a word," replied the Archbishop as he listened to the tape; "it is my conscience that speaks now."

'As soon as he died, Makarios visited me. I was in the living-room with my son-in-law and Theophanis when I felt him inside the Sanctum. I rushed to the Stoa with the other two. Makarios was on his knees praying in front of the altar. He came with his etheric body as he had not ascended as yet to the psychic planes. He turned and looked at me for a couple of seconds. "Spyro," he said, "will you dress me with the white robe? Our black robes can hide a lot of dirt. On your white robe a single fly will show."

'I immediately proceeded with the ceremony. I asked my son-in-law to assume the role of the Archbishop and put on the white robe. At that very moment the Archbishop's spirit took possession of my son-in-law. It was as if I had Makarios in front of me. Even his facial features became distorted and strikingly resembled those of the Archbishop.' Daskalos paused for a few moments and then he repeated that in spite of his limitations as a present personality, Makarios was a great soul. Daskalos emphasized this point several times because he knew how critical I was of the deceased Archbishop's political career.

'Is that why you have his picture hanging on the wall in your living-room?' I said smiling, with a dose of irony in my voice.

'He himself asked me to do that so that I won't forget him,' Daskalos replied, laughing.

'Suppose,' I said, 'he had been unwilling or unable to rescue you from excommunication. Would you then have accepted the help offered you by the Patriarch of Alexandria?'

'Under no circumstances would I jeopardize the autonomy of the Cypriot Church. How could I? I was once one of its central pillars.'

'I don't get that,' I exclaimed. 'In what way were you a central pillar of the Cypriot Church?' Daskalos went on to say matter-of-factly that in one of his incarnations he was a Cypriot clergyman by the name of Spyridon.

'You mean Saint Spyridon?' I uttered in amazement, not knowing whether to take Daskalos seriously or not. I soon realized that he was not joking. He was dead serious about his identification with the island saint highly revered within Orthodox Christendom.

'You think he was a saint?' Daskalos responded with a mischievous look on his face. 'Believe me he was no such thing. He committed an act of black magic for which he paid dearly. My incarnation as Spyridon was in fact a spiritual fall.'

'In what way?' Emily, who shared my incredulity, inquired.

'At the ecumenical council in Nicaea in 325 AD,' Daskalos went o.ι to explain, 'the Church fathers convened to resolve a theological conflict that plagued the Church during its early formation. The dispute was between those who argued that Christ was a man that attained godliness versus the others who insisted on His divinity. Arius, the leader of the dissenters, was an urbane, well-educated and articulate theologian who preached that Jesus should be considered as a great master like the Buddha. He had a strong following and his chances were excellent to win his argument and establish a new doctrine for the Church. Most of the clergymen in Cyprus were followers of Arius. As Spyridon I opposed this doctrine and insisted on the divine supremacy of Christ, that Christ was the embodiment of the Logos, the incarnation of God. For me it was blasphemy to argue otherwise.

'The governor of Paphos [south-west city in Cyprus] and most of the higher clergymen of the island were followers of Arius. They passed a decree prohibiting my departure from Cyprus so that I might not be able to attend the meeting at Nicaea. No boat was allowed to have me on board.

'I was illiterate but had powers. I spread my gown on the ground, sat on it, floated in the air until I reached a boat at the harbor. I told the crewmen, "Here I am, not in a boat. Take me on board."'

'You did what?' I asked.

'Levitation, Kyriaco, levitation. What's so surprising about that?' Daskalos replied and spread his hands, feigning impatience in order to impress upon me that by now such stories, which appear incredulous to the uninitiated, must be of no shock to me.

'The boatmen were terrified when they saw me in that condition and had no choice but to take me aboard. That is how I managed to escape from Cyprus and attend that most crucial gathering of Nicaea. Before my departure I sold my golden crown, put on a white robe and on my head I placed a woven basket. I also held a wooden stick which I carved and decorated myself.

'The other church leaders who attended the Nicaea meeting were accompanied by their entourages and wore royal garments, holding silver sticks on top of which two serpents were engraved. I had no need for silver serpents myself. I was master of the living ones. Arius, who came from an aristocratic background, referred to me as the "stinking peasant." He was right. Unlike himself I was uneducated and smelled of sheepskin because, in addition to being a clergyman, I was also a shepherd.

'I knew I had no chance to win the debate. Arius had great oratorical skills but he was wrong on the theological doctrine. I had to convince those attending of the falsity of his arguments, not with words, but by demonstrating my powers. In front of the others I grabbed a brick, squeezed it and turned it into fire, water and earth. Arius responded, "Only a mason is interested in bricks." I then made a terrible curse. "If God is listening to me now and if indeed you are fighting the Truth, let your bowels flow down from you." Immediately Arius bent down from extreme pain in his belly and dropped dead. Some holy man I was all right,' Daskalos exclaimed and laughed. 'I would never do such a thing now,' he added reassuringly.

'Upon my return to Cyprus the governor and the other followers of Arius, including all the bishops, ordered my arrest. Many fanatical supporters of mine were present while they dragged me to prison. "They don't deserve the heads they carry on their shoulders," I muttered to myself, referring to the governor and the bishops. It was as if I had invited the fanatics to do just that. What I had muttered to myself they took literally and slew the governor and all the bishops. I then proceeded to appoint new bishops and life moved on. But I did pay heavily for what I did to Arius.'

'I wonder what?' I mused.

'I lost my daughter Erene who has reincarnated in this life as my older daughter. Whenever we violate the law of Karma,' Daskalos said slowly, 'we must pay.

'As Spyridon,' Daskalos added, 'I conducted church services at the village of Tremedousia. Because the chanters could not always be relied on to be in church on time for the services, as they had their fields to tend, I created angels who sang along with me. I insisted that the liturgy begin on time. The chants of the angels were often heard by others. These phenomena can be observed today with seances, the hearing of voices and the like.' Daskalos then proceeded to recite the wording, in Byzantine Greek, of Spyridon's hymn, sung in church to this day in homage to the Cypriot saint.

'If Spyridon was no saint as you claim,' I said half jokingly, 'then people are really deceiving themselves when they light candles and pray for his help. They are actually praying to someone who does not exist now as Spyridon and who once committed an act of sorcery.'

'It does not matter whether Spyridon was a real saint or not. Believers pray to the elemental of Spyridon that they themselves have created with their thoughts and sentiments. They will get the benign effects. Spyridon as self-consciousness exists no more. He is now Daskalos. But the shadow of Spyridon will always remain within Universal Memory and can be activated and imbued with therapeutic qualities by the worshippers themselves.'

'Was the incarnation of Spyridon your only bond with the Orthodox Church?' I asked after a short pause.

'No, there were more.'

'I am very curious to know about them.'

Daskalos seemed to be reluctant at first to pursue the subject but with further probing on my part he finally revealed that in one of his incarnations he was none other than Origen himself, the early Christian mystic and Neoplatonist philosopher. The church fathers fought Origen as a heretic for his teachings which included the doctrine of reincarnation and the eventual salvation of all human beings.

'As Origen I was an intellectual and fought for the preservation of Orthodox Christianity. By orthodoxy, of course, I do not mean the temporal dogmas of the priests. I mean the essence of Christianity which is virtually identical with the essence of all the great religions. Do you see now why I am so attached to Orthodox Christianity?'

'That I may be able to understand. What I do not understand is why, as Origen, you cut your genitals,' I replied trying hard to remain serious.

Daskalos laughed and shook his head when I brought up this issue. Origen, according to historians, cut his genitals for unknown reasons. A plausible explanation that has been suggested is that Origen committed the unspeakable act because of his extreme asceticism, to avoid the temptations of the flesh. A historian colleague of mine, a specialist in early Christianity, said in a conversation I had with him, that it was a puzzle to him how an advanced thinker like Origen could commit such a ridiculous act.

'No doubt,' Daskalos said, 'what Origen did was preposterous. But the reasons why he did it were different from those proposed by the historians. In order to discredit his teachings, the religious hierarchy of the time spread rumors that he was a seducer of women. He therefore cut his genitals to protect the teachings. You may say that Origen as a personality had some problems but what he taught was true.'

Daskalos had no doubt in his mind that he was once incarnated as Origen. It would have been easy for me to dismiss him as a madman suffering from delusions of grandeur had I not been exposed to him for such a long time. From his point of view it was perfectly natural to have memories of past lives. When one reaches a certain state of superconscious self-awareness one can remember in great detail episodes of the various 'roles' one has played in the 'theater of planet Earth.' Daskalos never talked of his previous lives openly. He was fully aware that this type of discussion 'scandalizes' people. He talked of his past lives only in private and only in the presence of his closest associates.

It was close to noontime when we left Daskalos' house. He reminded me that a meeting of the Nicosia circle was to take place in the late afternoon and that it was assumed that I would be present. I told Daskalos that I was aware of the scheduled meeting and that I would, of course, be present.

The discussion about Saint Spyridon and Daskalos' alleged

memories of past lives has always puzzled me and in a strange turn of events it became interwoven with my own experience. The episode took place months later in Orono, at the University of Maine, while I was working on the story of the Cypriot saint.

I was in my office engrossed in the field material. I was having difficulties with the translation of the Byzantine hymn dedicated to Spyridon, as recited to me by Daskalos. I gave up and decided to write a letter to a friend of mine at the Cyprus Social Research Center in the hope that he would locate for me an official church translation. In the meantime I took a break from my writing and walked to the library to read the newspapers. I picked up the topmost issue on the shelf of the *Hellenic Chronicle*, a Greek–American weekly which routinely reported summary news on Cyprus. I was particularly eager to find out whether there was any progress on the long, and so far fruitless intercommunal talks for the resolution of the Cyprus conflict. Habitually I would take a look only at the first page and the editorial. I ignored most of the other pages as they pertained to local issues. That day, however, I casually flipped the pages and suddenly my eyes stopped at a full-page article on Saint Spyridon. I felt my heart pumping fast. Cold sweat dripped down my spine. I felt dizzy for a moment and noticed my hand trembling slightly. I sat down in an armchair to read the article. The author, a Greek theologian, eulogized Spyridon as an 'ecumenical beacon.' Most of the article was about the Nicaea synod of 325 AD and the description was almost identical to the manner that Daskalos described it to me.

Saint Spyridon's influence at the Synod was profound from the very fact that he was . . . illiterate. However, when he confronted the heretic Arius, who was well versed in church law and one wielding much influence throughout the area, the faith of Spyridon was so overwhelming that the heretical teachings of Arius and his followers were shown for what they in fact were: diabolical machinations. . . . Saint Spyridon had taken a brick in his hand and immediately asked the assembled delegates a question relating to the component factors of a brick. They replied: Earth, Water, and Fire. At that moment, it was written, Saint Spyridon squeezed the brick; immediately, water trickled to the floor,

fire emanated from his hand, and earth remained in the palm
of his hand. This miracle was his reply to those who doubted
the substance . . . of the Blessed Trinity.

The article ended with the official church translation of
Spyridon's hymn as chanted in church on his name day and as
recited to me in Greek by Daskalos.

> Thou, our father, divinely inspired Spyridon,
> didst show thyself at the first synod a
> champion and wonder-worker; wherefore
> thou didst speak to one dead on the tomb
> and didst change a serpent to gold, and in
> the recitation of thy holy prayers, thou O Holy
> One, hadst angels to assist thee. Glory to Him
> Who glorified thee; glory to Him Who crowned
> thee; glory to Him Who through thee works
> healing for all of us.

The experience overwhelmed me. For an instant I felt as if
some invisible force beyond my rational comprehension guided
me to the exact spot to get the information I needed.

It was not the first time that such a strange coincidence had
taken place in my life since I started my association with
Daskalos. When I started focusing my attention on them I
began to re-evaluate the notion of 'coincidence' itself. In all
honesty I could not afford not to raise questions in my mind
whether perchance Daskalos and some of his close associates
indeed lived consciously, as they themselves claimed, within a
realm of reality that no matter how exotic and radically
different from ours it seems, is nevertheless as real if not more
so. Coincidences, said Jung, do not exist. And on that note he
developed his controversial thesis on 'synchronicity,' a motif
elaborated further by contemporaries like Arthur Koestler and
several celebrated 'quantum' physicists. It has been a theme put
forward by the great sages of humankind, that nothing in the
Universe is accidental.

That afternoon at the scheduled meeting, Daskalos asked,
after he completed the short prayers, whether there were any
questions from his audience. I was about to ask the first
question when an Armenian, a fifty-year-old businessman who

spoke Greek fluently, asked Daskalos to elaborate on the nature and functions of the 'sacred discs.'

Daskalos taught that the human body with its etheric-double has several energy centers that manifest themselves like revolving discs. It is through these centers or 'chakras,' as the Hindu mystics call them, that the body absorbs etheric vitality from the cosmos. To 'open up' one's chakras is the aim of all mystics and a precondition for the development of one's clairvoyant and other psychonoetic powers.

'Two of the most important centers of the etheric-double,' Daskalos began without delay, 'are right next to one another at the center of the brain between the two lobes and the cerebellum. The sacred disc which is linked to its corresponding center in the brain lies over the head about half a foot and revolves in a clockwise direction. This is the normal movement of all the discs. Sometimes, however, depending on one's mental and emotional state, this disc may revolve in the opposite direction. This happens when the individual is fickle in his thinking and way of life. Such an individual lacks the capacity to reason and is under the spell of violent psychic vibrations such as anger, intolerance, hatred and the like. You will notice that when one is overwhelmed with such emotions, his capacity to reason is virtually non-existent. Under such states the sacred disc over the head moves counter-clockwise. When the person calms down and begins to reason again the disc re-acquires its normal revolution. There are individuals whose chakras always revolve counter-clockwise. These are persons who have no goodness in their hearts and whose behavior is continually hateful, aggressive and evil.

'From the very moment one is born all the sacred discs begin to move. The way they move will be analogous to the maturity of the center that the disc is linked to. In infants these discs look like small coins. Their movement is very slow and accelerates with the growth of the person.'

'Daskale,' I interjected, 'do all the discs have the same speed right from birth?'

'No. The center of the etheric-double which begins to move first with speed is that of the solar plexus. Actually that disc begins to move normally while the fetus grows in the womb. How do you think that embryo gets fed? Is it not through the umbilical cord which becomes later the navel? It is right at that spot that we notice the disc of the solar plexus.

'Actually in a fetus we observe two sacred discs springing from the same center. One which has the size of a two-shilling coin is inside the abdomen of the fetus at the spot of the solar plexus. There is another disc on the outside, right at the place where the umbilical cord touches the navel. When the infant is born and the umbilical cord is cut that disc withdraws inside the abdomen and is absorbed by the other disc which is inside. A clairvoyant can see all these. The moment the external disc recedes inside the disc of the solar plexus the infant begins its separate existence. However, it takes some time before the external disc becomes completely absorbed by that of the solar plexus. Therefore, an infant, for a certain period of time, is telepathically connected with its mother. Physicians have noticed, for example, that quite often when an infant experiences pain the mother may begin to have pains also. After that the infant calms down. The pain is transferred telepathically to the mother.

'The disc at the heart begins to revolve simultaneously with the movement of the disc at the solar plexus. It begins revolving while the infant is still in the womb. The two discs, that of the solar plexus and of the heart, are responsible for offering us the phenomenon of life. After birth the sacred disc at the heart is also responsible for energizing the movement of the lungs.

'The sacred discs of the heart and the solar plexus are completely independent of the present self-conscious person-ality. They are under the direct and omniscient supervision of the Holy Spirit which sets these two discs into motion, making possible the functioning of the material body.

'The two discs at the head are responsible for the development of the personality and offer us the potential of self-consciousness. The sacred disc that exists at the base of the nose right between the eyes looks like a revolving flower with many petals. On the other hand, the disc over the head looks like an all-white lotus having myriads of petals. This disc is a relatively large one right from birth. The first disc to begin moving and functioning is that which lies between your eyes. It begins to move when the infant learns to focus and is able to see. The more the infant learns to do that, the more intensely and harmoniously the disc revolves.'

'Is it possible, Daskale,' I asked, 'for the sacred disc in front of the eyes not to move in a normal fashion?'

'Of course. When a person tries to focus his attention on something and is incapable of doing so the disc moves sometimes in one direction and sometimes in the opposite direction.'

'When does the disc over the head begin to move normally?' I probed further.

'It begins to move very slowly right at birth and it gradually develops as the child learns how to concentrate and reason. The discs of the head move in accordance with the development of the personality unlike the discs of the heart and of the solar plexus that are holyspiritual in nature. The latter, that is, are under the control of the Holy Spirit, without the self-conscious personality playing any direct role in their movement.

'Now, it is possible that a person may spend a lifetime with the disc over his head never moving in a normal and harmonious manner. This may happen when the person is overfocused on and overdetermined by earthly material existence. I have noticed that for a lot of people that disc hardly moves. I said "hardly" because in reality that disc always moves at least a little for all persons regardless of their mental and spiritual development. However, for these earthly people the disc remains atrophied. It maintains the size which it had when the person came into the world.

'The development of this sacred disc will depend on the person's self-consciousness, the way the person thinks, the way he handles noetic substance. It starts to grow and move harmoniously when the person makes proper use of the power of thought.

'When the individual learns how to consciously leave his body, the disc moves very fast in a normal clockwise direction, and the petals of the lotus open up completely and all the colors become apparent.

'The disc over the head can develop through appropriate meditation exercises of concentration. But it can also develop without the individual consciously trying to develop it. Sometimes this may be a more preferable way. There have been people who through virtue, reason, powers of observation and through self-discipline managed to develop the disc over their heads without ever learning of its existence, and never consciously trying to open it and develop it. On the other hand there are Researchers of Truth who learn about these centers on the etheric-double by reading books from the Orient. Through practice they may begin to move that sacred disc rapidly and open it up. But unless they also develop their characters, they will not accomplish much. In fact they may prematurely open their sacred discs, which could be damaging to their present personalities. The safest method of developing this disc is through self-analysis, reason, and the right way of living. When a Researcher of Truth combines self-analysis with meditation practices, the results will be significant.

'Notice that the two discs of the head, the centers of which are next to each other, are interdependent and influence each other. The centers from which they originate touch each other. In fact for all practical purposes they spring from the same center within the brain. Let me give you an example. Seeing is made possible through the disc in front of the eyes. And when I say "seeing" I do not only imply that which we acquire through ordinary sight but through clairvoyance. Now, is it possible to "see" anything without thinking about it? No. Therefore, the two discs are linked together through a common center in the brain.

'The disc in front of the eyes is like a mirror. For an ordinary person this mirror is covered with etheric mist that will not allow the proper reflection of images. This is how life begins for ordinary people. For most people this mirror never clears up. They never learn how to focus their attention, how to concentrate. Therefore the way to advance the proper functioning of this disc is through the development of the power to concentrate, to hold in one's mind a noetic image and maintain it for a period of time without distraction. Through concentration exercises the surface of this disc will clear up allowing the proper reflection of images. Whether a person will make good use of this center will depend on how advanced he is as a present self-conscious personality. When the mirror develops and clears up it will not only reflect images coming from the outside but it will begin to reflect images that spring from the center of the disc, from within. It is at this point that space, which is an obstacle to ordinary eyesight, is transcended and clairvoyance begins. In a state of clairvoyance ordinary sight is temporarily closed off and concentration from within begins. Then the clairvoyant, like a television camera, begins to receive images from places anywhere on the planet or from any condition of the psychic realms. At this stage the individual is in a position to have an understanding of what Reality is. When eyesight and clairvoyance are transformed into knowledge and understanding we observe the harmonious movement and the opening of the disc over the head. And when the mystic advances further he enters into a state of ecstasy at which point the disc in front of the eyes plays hardly any role. It is the disc on top of the head which takes over completely. In ecstasy a person becomes one with the Divine, with the higher spheres. One experiences a form of clairvoyance. Some mystics who, in such a state, perceive the Divine and Eternal Light assume that the disc in front of the eyes must be playing some role. That is not the case. Another clairvoyant who can see a person in a state of ecstasy notices that the sacred disc over the head moves fast and beautifully while the movement of the disc in front of the eyes slows down.'

'How does that happen?' someone asked.

'The entire energy from the center moves upward and this occurs when the Sacred Fire is awakened and, through the spine, rushes upward. After reaching the center in the brain it proceeds towards the lotus over the head, absorbing at the same time the surplus energy from the disc in front of the eyes. The extra energy results from the intense concentration that precedes the ecstatic rapture. The state of ecstasy lasts only briefly and only while the present self-conscious personality in coordination and oneness with the permanent personality is focused on the higher spheres. There are more functions of these centers within the head that we will examine later.'

I asked Daskalos to explain to me the meaning of the 'Sacred Fire' as it was the first time I heard him mention it. 'It is,' he said, 'what the Indians call Kundalini.

'We sometimes call it the Sacred Serpent because it looks like a serpent. Its tail touches the sacred center of the sacrum right at the base of the spine. Like a serpent the Sacred Fire revolves upward around the spine in a sevenfold spiral and its luminosity energizes the genitals and, to an extent, via the bone marrow, all the organs of the body.'

Daskalos said that the Sacred Serpent has the color of dark red which symbolizes fire and heat. At the center of the sacrum, he said, there is a great charge of energy controlled by the Holy

Spirit and other entities – Laws. In the Orthodox Religion the Sacred Fire is symbolized by the rotating fiery sword of Archangel Michael, the master of fire.

Daskalos said that once the individual becomes master of the Kundalini, once he 'moves' the Serpent, he will be able to accomplish feats that appear miraculous or extraordinary from the perspective of ordinary consciousness. The myth of Hercules strangling the serpents, he said, is a cryptic symbol of this great truth.

Daskalos ended the meeting by urging his students to practice systematically their meditation exercises. 'For the next month,' he said, 'I want you to practice the following. Sit in front of a table covered with a white tablecloth. Close your eyes and place your right elbow on the table. Feel your right arm from the shoulder to the palm and fingers. Rest it on the table from the elbow to your palm facing upward. Feel effortlessly your arm and visualize an all-white arm interpenetrating the material arm. Slowly raise your material arm and rest the palm on your shoulder. Slowly again lower your hand and place it on the table, the palm facing upward. Feel continuously your arm and visualize the all-white arm inside the material arm. Repeat this movement five times. Then leave the material arm on the table and with your thought remove, slowly-slowly, the all-white arm and bring the etheric palm to rest on your shoulder. Then, slowly, again lower the etheric arm and place it inside the material one. Repeat this for five times. While you do so your concentration must be on the etheric arm which you should feel as if it were a material arm. Practice this exercise ten minutes each day.

'Do not forget,' Daskalos went on, 'to carry on your self-analysis for five minutes just before sleeping. This is important for your spiritual growth. Bring to your memory one of the day's episodes. Relive it with every detail and study your feelings, thoughts and behavior. Avoid turning into lawyers and apologists for your present personality. Avoid also masochistically judging your actions. We should examine these episodes with detachment, impartiality and objectivity. Study the events around the episode you are reviewing and critically examine your behavior as well as that of others, and draw your own conclusions. This practice will help you understand the power of your ego. Unless we cleanse ourselves from all traces of egotism, we cannot become masters and we must not develop our psychonoetic powers. May the love of the Most Beloved One be with you and in your homes and with the whole world.'

CHAPTER 5

Thorisis and Rasadat

I went to Strovolos in the early afternoon. Theophanis and Iacovos were there drinking coffee and conversing with Daskalos. Little Marios played outside with snails he had gathered from his grandfather's yard.

A few minutes after I joined them a young woman knocked at the door asking for Daskalos' help. Her brother-in-law had a tumor in the brain and the doctors were pessimistic about the prospect for a recovery. Her mother vigorously opposed the idea of bringing her brother-in-law to Daskalos. She was a staunchly religious woman and deeply suspicious of the 'Magus of Strovolos.' The young woman had heard of Daskalos' reputation on healing from a friend but her mother insisted that 'Satan wears the clothes of an angel.' Her mother preferred instead to light candles in front of the Icon of Saint Nectarios, her patron saint.

'Do not bother to change your mother's opinion of me,' Daskalos said somewhat sadly, 'her mind is already made up. I know who put these ideas into her head.' Daskalos then mentioned that the director of the Saint Nectarios foundation, a theologian-priest, spread rumors against him. 'And yet whenever he sees me, he is so friendly. "Oh my dear Spyro, how are you . . . " Sometimes it is not pleasant to read people's thoughts.'

Daskalos took the picture of the patient in his hand and closed his eyes for a minute. 'I am afraid,' he said, 'his case is hopeless. It is questionable whether he will live for another six months. We shall do, however, whatever we can, beyond that it is up to God. Does your mother love her son-in-law?'

'Yes, very much so,' said the young woman.

'Good. This will help. In his case it is better to work from a distance without anybody knowing about it.'

Daskalos gave the picture to Iacovos and Theophanis who

supported Daskalos' diagnosis. He then called Marios to come into the house.

'Come, my love,' he told the little boy, 'tell us what you see in this picture.'

Marios took the picture in his hand, looked at it with seriousness, turned it around as if to explore it from all angles but said nothing.

'Tell us,' Daskalos said in earnest, 'what do you see?' Instead of a reply Marios sighed and placed the picture on the table.

'That is his answer,' Daskalos said slowly.

'My love,' Daskalos said to his grandson, 'will you work with me and try to help this fellow?' The child nodded and without a word ran outside to play with his snails.

On several occasions Daskalos had mentioned to me that his grandson had been a Polish bishop and a great mystic in a previous life and that when he grows up he, along with the others, will carry on the work of the circles. In fact I had heard rumors that Marios, with the help of his grandfather, allegedly removed a tumor from the neck of a woman from Athens. When she returned to Greece she went to her doctors and told them that a boy in Cyprus cured her. The stunned physicians began to call Daskalos for more information. 'What an irony of nature,' Daskalos said to me once as he pointed at his grandson. 'Here is a great master who has to wait until his body develops before he can fully express himself.'

'I hope you don't need this picture,' Daskalos said to the woman, 'because I will have to burn it eventually.'

'Why do you have to burn it?' I asked.

'I have to pass it over fire so that the cancerous cells may be burned,' Daskalos replied and asked me to take the picture and place it in the Sanctum right in front of Christ's icon.

When I returned from the Sanctum the visitor was already gone. Daskalos commented that cancer has reached epidemic proportions both in Cyprus and elsewhere.

'I have noticed,' he added, 'that a lot of children are getting it now.'

'The more we pollute the environment,' I volunteered to add, 'the more people will get cancer.'

'That is not how to explain it,' Daskalos replied, apparently not very impressed with my sociological insight.

'But, Daskale,' I persisted, 'we know, for example, that in the New Jersey area in America, the cancer rate is one of the highest in the country. It is also one of the most polluted parts of the country. Why can't we say that a basic cause of cancer is the pollution of the environment?'

'This is not the way to explain it,' Daskalos repeated with emphasis. 'Those who get cancer do so for karmic reasons. Look, the twentieth century has been a bloody century. We have had two world wars. Many of those who participated in those atrocities are beginning to get reincarnated in order to pay their debts. It is not accidental that someone finds himself in a polluted place and gets cancer, just as it is not accidental that a group of people board a plane and collectively meet their death in an air crash. Do you follow me?

'Theophani, I had a strange dream last night,' Daskalos said abruptly and turned towards his friend who as usual listened quietly.

'A huge green snake tried to swallow my right arm. My entire arm almost disappeared inside its belly when I said to the snake, "You silly creature, don't you know that if I twist my arm all of your teeth will fall out? Come, let go of my arm." The more I implored the snake, the more its teeth gnawed into my flesh. Suddenly, with a twist of my arm, all of its teeth fell to the ground, along with the snake.

'Iacovos was next to me,' Daskalos continued, pointing at his mischievously smiling young disciple, 'and urged me to grab an ax and snatch the head off the snake. It was bound to grow back its teeth, he said, and repeat its actions. "I can't do it," I told him, "I can't kill the poor snake." The snake grew its teeth back and began to swallow my arm once again. "You have not learned your lesson, have you?" I said to the snake. The more I implored, the more it persisted. "Didn't I tell you?" Iacovos said. "You should kill the damn thing." I refused. Instead I again twisted my arm and the snake's teeth fell out on the ground. Iacovos then distracted my attention by pointing towards the other direction. As I focused there he grabbed an ax and split the snake's head in two. When I looked dismayed, he said, "Don't worry, your Leonidas will grow his head back." "What Leonidas?" I answered back. "There is your Leonidas," Iacovos said and pointed at the snake. "Take it and look at his head. It is Leonidas." I took the snake's head and looked but saw no Leonidas. "You don't want to see," Iacovos replied.'

'Your dream is so clear it does not need any interpretation,' Theophanis remarked.

Leonidas, a nephew, had created problems for Daskalos and brought about havoc in the family of his younger daughter. He was the leader of a militant semi-underground organization. Daskalos was concerned that the 'madman' could become the cause for bloodshed on the island.

'He once accused me of "diverting the attention of the masses from the real issues." The idiot,' Daskalos said and shook his head. Leonidas was allegedly his son in a previous incarnation. 'He was as crazy then as he is now.

'Iacovos has been urging me to strike back because Leonidas continues to bother us. I refuse to use psychonoetic powers for such purposes. I cannot betray the seven promises of the Researcher of Truth that Yohannan gave me when I was seven years old. I did not accept them then in order to betray them sixty-four years later because of problems I now face. My dear Iacovo, let us not forget the fifth promise, "To love and serve my fellow human beings sincerely from the depths of my soul and heart, no matter what their behavior may be towards me."'

'Daskale,' I asked, 'was the dream a form of exomatosis?'

'Naturally.'

'But was Iacovos actually there?'

'Of course he was,' he answered and Iacovos nodded in agreement. He repeated that he and Iacovos are so attuned psychically that what one experiences the other also shares. Their 'auras' merge as it were.

'Sometimes when in exomatosis,' Theophanis volunteered, 'you perceive things symbolically and sometimes you experience them directly. In my case I usually perceive things symbolically.' With these comments Theophanis stood up and got ready to drive back to Paphos, a three-hour journey. It was already late afternoon. I was pleased to hear that Daskalos was free for the evening so that we could continue our discussion.

'Daskale,' I said after we finished a dinner of roast chicken that we bought from a nearby take-out restaurant, 'I am always puzzled by the ease with which you claim you remember past lives. I am eager to learn more about such experiences.' As a field researcher I was very fortunate because Daskalos would hardly ever refuse to answer my questions.

'The common denominator in all my incarnations,' he began while Iacovos and I listened attentively, 'was to be of service to my fellow human beings and to balance reason with emotion. In all my incarnations, whether it was as musician, as painter, as writer, or as psychic, I struggled to reveal to my fellow human beings what is beautiful about God.'

'Daskale,' I interrupted, 'how can you be certain that you were the persons you claim you were? How can you be certain that what you consider as memories of past lives are not in fact well-meaning illusions, fantasies or hallucinations?'

'I will tell you,' Daskalos said confidently. 'It is very easy to be misguided. I have met many people who claimed they had glimpses of past lives. In my own way I could see through their illusions. Their fascination and attachment to a person of the past attuned them with the elemental of that person and convinced them that they were that person.

'In order to be certain of the reality of a past incarnation you must be able to relive the entire life from birth to death with the greatest ease. You must become fully aware of all major events. Every time you focus on that incarnation you must be able to consistently perceive the same results. When I close my eyes I can see the details of an absolutely conscious life. I can see myself in a previous incarnation with all my faults, and all my virtues and weaknesses.'

'Do you imply that others who get only glimpses of a past life simply imagine things?' I asked.

'Not necessarily. In such cases you cannot have the absolute certainty as when you can relive the past life in full detail. I know many cases when students of mine re-experienced fragments of their past that were genuine. I had a student whose memory of a past life came back to him at the moment when he was about to be initiated and become a white-robed brother. He fell on the ground and began sobbing. I took him in my arms and tried to calm him down. It was a devastating realization for him.'

'Why so?'

'Because of what happened to him and to me in that incarnation.'

'Can you tell us more about it?' I pressed Daskalos.

'Many centuries back,' he went on, 'I was a Tibetan lama

and he was one of my disciples. He demanded of me to give all the wealth of the lamasary to the poor. I was against it. The lamasary had little wealth to begin with and I could not see in what way the precious stone at the forehead of the Buddha could rescue the poor from their poverty. He was well meaning but stubborn. He came in contact with what he thought were revolutionaries and led them into the temple to get the jewels. In reality they were common criminals. When I tried to stop them they stabbed me to death. He rushed to stop them but it was too late. When he realized what he had done he committed suicide by throwing himself into the precipice. When the memory of that episode came to him it was too devastating. I tried hard to soothe his pain. "Look," I said, "don't you see? I am not dead!"'

'How old were you,' I asked thoughtfully after a few seconds' pause, 'when you became conscious of past incarnations?'

'I knew who I was from the day I was born,' Daskalos replied in all sincerity.

'I find it very hard to accept that a two- or four-year-old can have consciousness of past incarnations,' I added somewhat irritated.

'And I tell you that I had such knowledge not only in this but also in previous incarnations.'

'But was it not necessary to gradually bring back these memories?' I asked.

'No, no. At the point where I am now I don't need to gradually recall the memories. I have them.'

'What about him?' I asked and pointed at Iacovos who seemed to find my debate with Daskalos rather amusing.

'Iacovos,' he replied, 'has yet to bridge the memory gap because he is still too attached to his present incarnation. But he can enter into his own reincarnations and get glimpses of who he was. I know that as of late he has been able to remember fragments of one of his incarnations in ancient Egypt.'

'That's true,' Iacovos added in all seriousness.

'Do you yourself, Daskale,' I asked, 'have to concentrate before memories of past lives can come to you?'

'There is no need for concentration at the stage where I find myself now.'

'You mean to say you know all your incarnations?' I snapped

86

with an element of impatience in my voice.

'I remember only those that I am interested in. I have had many other incarnations but they don't interest me.'

'When you came into this world,' I pointed out as I tried to sort out in my mind the nature of his experience, 'you had a feeling that you were a certain person in some incarnation and another person in another incarnation. As you grew up in this life, and with experience, the memories of those past incarnations came back to you.'

'Not exactly,' Daskalos responded, somewhat disappointed that I could not grasp what he was telling me. 'I know who I was,' he said slowly and emphatically. 'It is not a question of remembering.'

'How could a two-year-old child,' I repeated and raised my voice in protest, 'be conscious of who Spyridon was or Origen or the others that you told me you were?'

'If he had been these people he could be conscious. I know because I was. At the age of two I could not express myself. But inwardly I knew who I was. And I waited for this body to grow so that I would be able to express myself as I do now. Of course the material body is a limitation to express who we truly are. It is not easy to explain. Believe me there was no time that I was not fully conscious of who I was.

'In some of my incarnations,' Daskalos reminisced, 'they praised me. I know that I was not as good and holy as they now eulogize me. They ignored my faults, even my petty crimes that I committed as I wore my saintly robes,' he said in a self-mocking tone.

'I suppose you imply your acts as Spyridon,' I commented.

'Yes.'

'Most of the so-called saints,' Iacovos chuckled, 'were sorcerers who often committed acts of black magic.'

Daskalos went on to say that his knowledge of several languages was the result of previous incarnations. He claimed he had never had training in the Russian language, yet he knew Russian because in his last incarnation he was a Russian writer. In the same way Daskalos knew Armenian and some Italian.

'Now I ask you,' Daskalos said and clapped my knee for emphasis, 'how could I know these languages without any formal training? I brought this knowledge with me. When you go to bed at night and you wake up in the morning do you remember that you are Kyriacos or do you know you are Kyriacos? It is the same thing with me. I do not remember who I was, I know who I was.'

'Have you had any evidence other than your own subjective awareness that you were the persons you say you were?' I asked.

'A great deal.'

'What, for example?'

'I know places and streets that have never been mentioned in any books.'

'How do you know these streets are not imaginary?'

'They cannot be imaginary. I know how to differentiate fantasy from what I call "seeing in the Akashic Records" and reliving the way I had lived them and undergoing the same experiences. If anyone can fully remember the life of a past personality, then he is that person. I mean reliving the past life in every detail, with all its weaknesses, with all the actions that made you ashamed or made you proud. Do you understand what I mean? I do not only remember past events in previous lives but also the sentiments I experienced through these events.'

'Have you ever met anyone else who has this kind of awareness of previous lives?' I asked, fully conscious of the incredulity of our conversation.

'You mean to the extent that I have it?'

'Yes.'

'No. I have never met anyone. I have only met people who remember fragments of previous lives.'

'Does that mean that you are the only human being on Earth who has such an ability?'

'I can't say that. Do I know all the people of this Earth?' Daskalos said with humor in his voice.

I reminded Daskalos of a promise he gave me sometime in the past to recount in some detail his experiences in one of his incarnations in ancient Egypt. It was one of his most intense incarnations, Daskalos said, when he and Iacovos were hierophants at the temple of Aton. I thought our conversation to this point provided the appropriate ambiance to reminisce about the land of the Pharaohs.

'If Iacovos does not object I'll tell you about it,' he said and we both looked at the young disciple.

'I don't mind,' he said softly. Daskalos then breathed deeply, leaned back in his armchair and began his narration in a low voice.

'During the time of Ikhnaton there was a great conflict between the followers of Amon-Ra and of Aton. The followers of Amon-Ra believed in the material sun. They carried out human sacrifices and worshiped a dog-like deity as well as sharks, crocodiles and the like. Aton's followers, on the other hand, opposed these practices. They believed in a psychonoetic sun, in one deity, and denounced human sacrifices.

'One of the early worshipers of Aton was a cousin of the Pharaoh. He had two sons. The older was called Rasadat. The two brothers strikingly resembled each other. Rasadat was eventually brought to the temple by his father to become a hierophant of Aton.

'Rasadat's father had a cousin named Chapsitou. Her husband was a Greek by the name of Ares who served in the Pharaoh's army. His wife gave birth to Thorisis, myself. When Ares returned from a war against the followers of Seton, the Sudanese of today, he brought along with him and adopted a dark-complexioned child he had found among the captives. He is as treacherous today as he was during that incarnation. When he grew up he started a relentless war against Thorisis who decided to leave his father's house and go to his uncle, the father of Rasadat. The first to enter Aton's temple was Thorisis. Rasadat, a year younger, followed. A great friendship developed between the two.'

While Daskalos continued his tale, Iacovos had his eyes closed, sitting in a meditative position. It appeared as if he were reliving the experiences of Rasadat in ancient Egypt, induced by the mesmerizing narrative of Daskalos.

'When Thorisis was eighteen years old there was a contest to select a successor to the master hierophant. The contestants were expected to answer successfully three questions posed to them by the master hierophant. Whoever was able to answer the questions in the most satisfactory manner would be the one chosen to succeed the master hierophant. The latter would then pass around the waist of the white-robed initiate a golden girdle.

'There were three candidates, Rasadat, Thorisis and a twenty-four-year-old neophyte. Both Rasadat and Thorisis were clairvoyants and could read the thoughts of others. Therefore, before the hierophant posed the questions they both knew the answers.

'The first to be tested was Thorisis. He answered all three questions correctly. He was then followed by the twenty-four-year-old candidate. When Thorisis came out into the corridor of the temple, Rasadat was there waiting for his turn. He grabbed Thorisis by the waist and demonstrated to him that he knew both the questions as well as the answers. After the second candidate completed and failed the test Rasadat was called in. He gave the correct answer to the first and third questions but left the second unanswered. It appeared that Thorisis had won. The hierophant then called all three of them back into the temple. He said that Rasadat failed the test because he did not answer the second question satisfactorily. Thorisis reacted. "I don't accept that," he said. "When we were outside in the corridor Rasadat told me what the three questions were and gave the correct answers, exactly the same way as I answered them. He could have given the correct answer. Why did he not do that?" "I think I know why," said the master hierophant. "When I was examining the other candidate I was with both of you in the corridor and heard your conversation." Thorisis continued to protest and announced that he could not accept the girdle. Right at that moment Rasadat kissed the hands of the master hierophant, to get permission, and grabbed the golden girdle. "Here", he said to him, "put it around him or I will do it myself." "You do it," replied the hierophant. Rasadat then put the golden girdle around Thorisis and said, "Go on your path. I shall follow you." Thorisis then embraced Rasadat, kissed him and said, "We are again one, we shall always be one." "I know it," Rasadat replied, "I would also like to feel it."

'Rasadat,' Daskalos said somewhat sadly, 'did not feel it,' and looked at Iacovos who had kept his eyes closed in meditation.

Daskalos mentioned to me repeatedly that Iacovos and he were twin souls but to this day Iacovos is more cerebral and intellectual, whereas Daskalos has always been more emotional and sentimental. In fact this is a characterization that one could apply in describing both of them in their current lives.

'I am curious,' I asked, 'to learn what the three questions were.'

'The first was on the nature of one's being and one's relationship to Aton. We had to prove the reality of Aton and that behind the material sun there was the psychonoetic sun. Part of the test was aimed to transfer fire through our thought from one place to another.

'The second question was on the nature of love. "Love," I answered, "is what creates matter and maintains the unity and harmony of the Universe. To the lower world it is attraction. It is fire that causes pain and that causes wood to sputter when it burns. It is fire that creates smoke and fills the eyes with tears. But it is also light that shines. It is a sun that warms and enlivens."

'The third question was about the difference between love and life. We had to demonstrate that there is no life without love and that love is life itself.

'It was not sufficient to answer these questions with words. It was necessary to create the appropriate noetic images and vibrations of the meanings of these words so that the hierophant himself would be able to experience them. You had to prove that you possessed psychonoetic powers. Religious functionaries had power during those days. Now, whether it be Christianity, Buddhism, Islam or whatever, religious functionaries express nothing more than the shortsightedness of men. The great truths have been covered with very base and earthy meanings and religion turned into a form of business.

'I remember,' Daskalos continued, 'that our temple was on a small islet of the Nile. Around it there were eight more temples very near each other. We moved from islet to islet either by boat or by walking when the waters were no higher than our knees. The homes of the hierophant students were built on these islets. Rasadat and Thorisis were always together living in the same house. I remember how Rasadat enjoyed lying on the white marble floor of the yard with his feet in the water. Whenever Thorisis would come near him he would splash him with water. They played like little children, in spite of the fact that they were mature hierophants.

'In the meantime,' Daskalos continued his reminiscences as he changed his narrative to the first person, 'my father discovered my whereabouts and visited me at the temple. He was Greek and believed in the gods of the Greeks and

91

Egyptians. I told him, "Father, I will go and visit my mother but I will return to the temple. I belong to Aton now."

'When the followers of Set started a war against Kami [Egypt], the adopted son of my father who was by then a grown man, joined the invaders, his compatriots. One day they burned the house of Ares. They then marched against our temples.

'Incidentally, our job as hierophants was not only to pray and conduct religious activities. We cultivated our farms and we gave the surplus produce to the people. One day when I was on a trip to the northern villages to distribute food, the invaders attacked and burned the houses around the temple. When I realized what had happened I rushed back and searched for Rasadat. I reached the house and found his sandals stained with blood and saw his body floating on the Nile. I fell on the ground. I remained there crying continuously, unable to act or think. I then saw Rasadat's father in a boat coming towards me. When he arrived I pointed at Rasadat's body. "I know," he said. "I see him. Come, get into the boat. The enemies are still around burning houses." "I am not going anywhere," I said. "I will swim and get Rasadat's body." "Don't be a fool," he implored me. "They will kill you too. He is my son. Do you think I feel less pain? I want you to come to your senses. Lie down inside the boat. We will have to go through the bulrushes so that they won't notice us." I remember as we were moving slowly through the bulrushes a water snake passed by and as I was lying in the boat I put my hand into the water to grab it. Rasadat's father signaled me to leave it. "This is no time for such things," he whispered. It may interest you to know that Rasadat's father was Theophanis. That is why the two are so close in this incarnation.

'When we reached another temple down the river,' Daskalos went on, 'we were out of danger. I fell asleep on the marbles. When I woke up I saw Rasadat's body next to me. It was full of wounds from the stabbings. The Nile brought it to the temple where the priests picked it up and prepared to embalm it. Rasadat's father urged me not to look at him any longer because my love was becoming savage, he said.

'The hierophant of the temple promised to be in touch with me. He was going to see the Pharaoh who blamed the followers of Aton for the war. "I can see the future, my son," he told me, "you must know that the evil will get worse."

'I was brought in front of the Pharaoh and ordered to convert, renounce Aton and become a follower of Amon-Ra. I refused. Finally I gave in, on the surface, that is. In reality I never betrayed Aton. I was ordered to remain in the temple and worship Amon-Ra. I was psychologically crushed after the loss of Rasadat and the destruction of our temples. Resistance seemed futile at the time.

'One day, I remember, some people came to the temple and plunged themselves into the sacred lake to be devoured by the crocodiles, so that they could go to their "paradise." A woman was getting ready to throw her baby into the lake and then jump in herself. She wanted to go to her dead husband. I rushed forward and succeeded in snatching the child from her hands. But I was unable to save her. She was eaten up by the crocodiles. I took custody of the baby and named it Rames. Later on, with other secret followers of Aton, we killed all the crocodiles.

'The Pharaoh was very angry at me. Consequently he sent me away to his colonies, to Cyprus. He changed my name from Thorisis to Korraton which in ancient Egyptian meant "he who has been deceived by Aton." I said fine, since you burden me with this name let it be so. It will remind me of Aton the only God.'

Daskalos then elaborated on his duties in Cyprus which were primarily commercial. His task was to ship to Egypt Cypriot products such as copper and wheat. Cyprus was a major producer of copper in ancient times and its name was in fact derived from this metal. Daskalos said that because of his familiarity with ancient Cyprus he was able, in his present life, to assist a European archaeologist to unearth Alasia, a town which was discovered near the ancient city of Salamis.

'When I returned to Egypt the followers of Amon-Ra plotted against me. They demanded that since I had a princely status I should go through an initiation ceremony which eventually was to cost my life. Inside the temple there was a huge golden disc which symbolized the sun. It was hanging from the ceiling. Underneath the disc there was a stone ladder and Korraton had to stand on the third step right under the huge idol. When the ceremony began the priests of Amon-Ra, through the power of thought, severed the chain and the disc fell on me. Immediately they accused me of sacrilege. The chief hierophant, after declaring that god Ra was sentencing me to death, opened up my stomach with a knife. They proclaimed me ungodly took me outside of the temple, disemboweled me and filled my belly with tar. They covered all of my body with tar and put me in a standing position inside a grave. It was like a small hut which they also plastered with tar. Then they put out a decree that whoever came to Korraton's grave to mourn would be put to death on the spot.'

'Why did they do that to you, Daskale?' I asked. 'I mean why did they cover you with tar?'

'It was a form of black magic. They wanted to keep me entrapped within the etheric world so that I would not be able to reincarnate. Well, at night, Rames, now a grown man, visited my grave and wept. One night as he had his hands spread out on the door of my grave crying, they nailed him with a spear.'

Daskalos said that Rames was Father Dominico, a Catholic priest and great master who lived in the psychonoetic world. He had been one of Daskalos' invisible guides since childhood. The same entity that incarnated as Rames was also the entity who lived as Father Dominico in his last incarnation on Earth.

'With these acts of black magic they kept me imprisoned in the other world for two hundred years. You see, the functionaries of ancient religions did have these kinds of powers. When I managed to escape the prison they put me in, I incarnated among the Aztecs. Rasadat followed me there. Again I became a hierophant and in our religion at that time we practiced human sacrifices. One by one I managed to incarnate within the Aztec nation almost all of my former enemies of Amon-Ra. As soon as they reached their eighth birthday I would sacrifice them to the god of war. I would open their chests with a stone knife and with my bare hand I would pull out the heart while it was still pulsating and then roast it over burning coals.'

'How could you act in such a macabre manner, Daskale?' I protested.

'They were horrible acts for which I am paying to this day. Why do you think I am suffering from my heart? In all my subsequent incarnations since that time I have had heart problems. I was carried away with a vengeance. It was a spiritual fall. It was before the coming of the Most Beloved One who taught us how to love even our enemies.'

Daskalos claimed that he incarnated several times as an Aztec and remembered the period of the Spanish conquests. In one of his incarnations he was the cousin of Montezuma, king of the Aztecs during the conquests. Iacovos was Daskalos' nephew and the son of Theophanis, then brother of Montezuma. Daskalos went on to express his abhorrence of 'barbarous' Cortez, the Spanish conquistador, and of the greediness of the Spaniards for gold. He spoke with such pathos that I felt as if he were reliving the injustices inflicted upon the Aztecs by the conquistadors.

'One day when Theophanis, who was in charge of the aqueducts, was away, the Spaniards arrested Iacovos. To save him I tried to make a deal with the general in charge. "If you give him back to me," I said, "I will pay you his weight in gold." He gave me his word. "In the name of our God Jesus Christ," he said, "I promise we shall let him free." We were so naive that we assumed the Spaniards were operating with the same values as we were. You see, after Christ's Ascension He appeared among the Aztecs and they saw him as the White God. Since then a legend had spread that the White God was to return. The Aztecs refused to kill any white man lest they kill the White God. The Spaniards wiped them out and they stuck to this myth, the fools.

'When I led the Spaniards into the temple with the gold it never crossed my mind that they had no intention of keeping their oath. When they saw the treasures they went wild. The general in charge took out his sword and killed both Iacovos and myself.'

Daskalos went on to say that the 'general' was none other than Mr Prasinos, one of Daskalos' disciples and a member of the inner circle. When Daskalos introduced him to me I tried to keep a straight face. Somehow the image of Mr Prasinos, a fifty-year-old, bespectacled, frail, short and smiling bookkeeper, as a ferocious Spanish conquistador was deeply amusing.

'It was Karma,' Daskalos claimed, 'that brought him to the inner circle. Only God knows how much he must have gone through to erase the negative elementals he created as a Spanish conqueror. Now he is a brother in love. But let me tell you,' Daskalos confided, 'there is still a certain amount of distance between us. Even though he is a brother and we love him, the scars are not completely gone from that episode. It takes many aeons before all the scars of such encounters can be totally erased.'

'Of all the incarnations you know, Daskale,' I asked, 'which one do you cherish most? Which one do you consider your best?'

'As Thorisis,' Daskalos replied without hesitation.

'How can you call an incarnation a good one when you met such a violent death?' I asked.

'It does not matter how you go,' Daskalos replied with a raised voice and his eyes beamed with heroic intensity. 'What matters is how you live, not how you die.'

For a few seconds I felt dizzy as if someone had given me a jolt in the stomach. Daskalos' statement moved me deeply and I felt my eyes watering. His words kept spinning in my mind as if at that moment Daskalos implanted a mantra inside my head whose echo kept repeating itself: 'What matters is how you live, not how you die.' During those few moments my whole life flashed in front of me forcing me to re-examine the value of my entire existence. My years in America, my perennial yearning for and ambivalence towards my native culture, my agony over the fate of Cyprus, all paraded within my awareness like a movie screen. I am not certain how long it took me to come out of that state. But I am certain Daskalos noticed the profound impact his statement had on me.

During his incarnation as Thorisis, he went on to say, he had had the most emotionally close and uplifting relationship with Rasadat, a soul destined to reunite with him in Theosis.

'Sometimes I forget myself and call Iacovos Rasadat. He once took my head with two hands and shouted at me to forget Rasadat. "I am Iacovos, not Rasadat," he said.

'I have met repeatedly with Rasadat since then, in over twenty incarnations, but in none of them was the psychic connection as close as at that time.'

'I was under the impression that the more you encounter someone from one incarnation to the next, the closer you come to that person,' I commented.

'This is not necessarily so. It is possible that you may come closer to that person spiritually but move a little away from him emotionally and sentimentally. The desire for creating this distance has not been mine. He wants it so, even to this day,' Daskalos said with emphasis and pointed at Iacovos, who had come out of his meditative state and was listening without saying a word.

It was already late at night and we decided to disperse. I was to meet with Daskalos the following morning. I had more questions that I wanted to ask.

'Iacovo,' I asked, as I was about to drop him off outside his home, 'can you please explain to me why you have been killed so many times?' When I said that, I was fully conscious of the bizarre nature of my question, yet it was a fully legitimate question from within Daskalos' world view.

'I'll tell you of an aphorism by an Indian master,' he replied with a smile.

> '"Whoever seeks me finds me
> Whoever finds me knows me
> Whoever knows me loves me
> Whoever I love I kill."

'Do you understand now?'

'No, I do not understand,' I said in protest and drove off as I tried to digest his chilling answer.

CHAPTER 6

Exomatosis

It was early evening when I reached Daskalos' home. The front door was open. I knocked but there was no reply. There was light in the living-room and I heard someone speaking. I assumed Daskalos was taping a lesson for his overseas circles. 'The tape recorder,' he once marveled, 'is such a magnificent invention. It has made our work so much easier.'

I knocked again, still no answer. I was getting ready to sit in the hallway and wait when Iacovos made his appearance. We exchanged greetings and he asked me to join him inside. I suggested that they continue with the taping.

'I am not taping anything,' he replied, 'I am listening to the radio. Papaioannou is speaking in the house of representatives.' It was Thursday, the day the Cypriot parliament held its weekly meetings. We both sat down as the radio continued broadcasting the speech.

'Who is your favorite politician?' Iacovos suddenly asked.

'I don't have one. They have caused such a mess,' I responded wryly, suggesting by the intonation of my voice that I had no desire to discuss politics. But Iacovos, like Daskalos, seemed to have a penchant for political gossip.

'I like Papaioannou,' Iacovos continued, and gave me a side look trying to see my reaction. 'He seems to be down to earth and doesn't talk nonsense like the others.' How amusing, I thought, a Christian mystic enamored by the oratorical virtuosity of the chief communist of the island.

'Lyssarides,' Iacovos went on, 'is such an extremist. What kind of a socialist is he, anyway?' Iacovos seemed to be engrossed in the issue being debated and was in the mood of carrying on the conversation along political lines.

'Is Daskalos home?' I inquired, trying to shift the discussion to a direction more relevant to matters pertaining to the beyond. Just as I finished my sentence Daskalos walked into the room.

'Good evening, good evening,' he said as he rubbed his hands with an air of exuberance. 'Is everything okay?' he asked in English.

'Everything is fine,' I said in kind, 'but I don't seem to be able to get rid of this head cold,' and pointed at my head.

'Come and sit on this chair,' Daskalos commanded. 'Perhaps we can get rid of this head cold of yours.'

I did as he told me. Daskalos came from behind and placed his hands over my head. I felt as if a light electrical current rushed from the top of my head down to my navel. It was a strange sensation that went on for as long as Daskalos held his hands over my head, about seven minutes.

'Now you are filled with etheric vitality and your cold will be gone,' Daskalos announced as he walked to the kitchen to fetch me a cup of the warm chocolate milk he had previously prepared for his grandson. 'Drink this and it will make you completely well,' he reassured me.

To my surprise Daskalos' 'magic' worked. My head cleared up and the heaviness was gone. I was getting ready to have a long discussion.

'Come, I have something to tell you,' Daskalos waved at me as he walked out of the living-room and into the hallway. He closed the door behind him after letting me through. That is odd, I thought. What could Daskalos tell me that Iacovos, one of his close adepts, should not hear?

'Please,' he whispered, 'do not mention to Iacovos what I told you about him the other day, unless he himself volunteers to do so. He does not like to be talked about. Every person has his oddities and we must respect that.' Daskalos referred to some experiences Iacovos had had before and some healings he had performed.

I promised Daskalos that I would mention nothing of the conversation we had had about Iacovos' experiences unless he himself volunteered it. Daskalos was content. 'Iacovos,' Daskalos said in a low voice, 'has a great potential to become a master. But he is still too young. That worries me a lot. In fact Yohannan once cautioned me not to expect too much from Iacovos. He needs to grow up and mature first.'

When we re-entered the living-room Iacovos was sitting silently, apparently unperturbed that Daskalos had spoken to me in private.

'There is very little that I can add to what Iacovos can teach you,' Daskalos said with a raised voice as Iacovos smiled shyly. Daskalos then excused himself and walked upstairs. His granddaughter was impatiently waiting for him to get some help in math. To spend the evening productively I began asking Iacovos questions about his association with Daskalos. The young adept seemed to have expected my 'interrogation' and was prepared to cooperate. Whenever I was with Iacovos, Daskalos or Kostas I never lost any chance to ask questions. They accepted my inquisitiveness and often joked about it. Their attitude made my work ever more enjoyable.

'Iacovo,' I asked as I comfortably sank into an armchair, 'I am curious to learn how you first met Daskalos.' My question animated him. Without second thoughts he began to talk in a slow, confident voice. The aura of authority was clear. He was no longer the young refugee from the occupied village of Ayios Georgios, but an experienced apprentice. Yet he spoke without pretense.

'Very early in my life, in elementary school, I was interested in philosophical and religious questions. They used to call me "the wise one." I wondered how the world was made. How it would have been without human beings. I tried to perceive the void. In spite of the atheism of my parents I accepted the existence of a Supreme Being. My faith was not a reaction against my parents. No. I simply felt the presence of the Absolute. I also had the feeling that one day I was destined to meet someone I already knew who was going to change my life.

'When I was twelve years old, as I told you before, my father got a tumor on his neck. He felt extreme pain but the doctors could do nothing. An uncle of mine mentioned a certain "fakir" at Strovolos who might be able to cure him. I overheard the conversation and urged my father to go to him. During that year Daskalos was visiting our area once a month. He was giving lessons to a group of people at the Five Mile Beach near our village right at the spot where the Turks first landed.

'Daskalos removed the tumor from my father's neck by just placing his hand on it. From that day on, I attended Daskalos' lessons regularly.'

'How did you feel when you first met him?'

'We started talking as if we had known each other for years. I felt I knew him from before, but the full memories came back gradually. We laughed and laughed for hours that night. Intuitively I knew who he was.'

'Are you saying that at the age of twelve you believed in reincarnation and you felt that you knew Daskalos from a previous life?' I asked.

'I had never heard the word reincarnation but I knew I had lived before. In particular I felt that I had had war experiences from a previous life and I feared that I would die young. In reality this happened in an earlier life. I very vividly remember Ancient Egypt. I remember the Pyramids, the Nile, the temples. It was a very intense life. They must have attacked us at the temple. It was not only in this life that I was taken captive. When the Turks put us on the boats for Turkey people were screaming with despair in their faces. Similar scenes from other captivities came to my mind. I relived them all. When we were taken prisoners we all felt lost. The conditions were such that we expected to be executed at any moment as had happened to many others during the early phase of the invasion. As I told you before on the way to Turkey I felt the Logos coming to me in the form of white light. I then became very peaceful in spite of what was happening around me.'

'Did you have any other contact with Daskalos before the invasion?'

'Yes. I used to go and listen to his lectures at the Five Mile Beach. The first time I went there I felt great familiarity with what he was saying. From the very first day, when we began the meditation exercises, he took me to the side and said that he expected a lot from me because I was doing the exercises better than anyone else. I became extremely interested. Had I not had in my subconscious previous experiences and therefore the inclination for such matters, I would not have continued. I would have started with enthusiasm and then given up, as happens with so many others.

'From the moment of my imprisonment in Turkey I tried very hard to make psychic contact with Daskalos until I finally succeeded.'

'How did you do that?' I asked.

'I focused my attention and I felt him near me. After that I felt him next to me constantly. My morale soared. I used to get information about what was happening in Cyprus.'

'You mean you heard a voice giving you such information?'

'No. As I was sitting absent-mindedly thoughts would come into my mind. I knew, for example, how and where my parents were, information that I confirmed after my release. I also knew that negotiations were under way about our release and told the other prisoners when that would happen.'

When Iacovos was released he went to Daskalos, who cured him of ailments resulting from his five-month ordeal. Daskalos then invited him to join the inner circle. From then on Iacovos became one of Daskalos' close apprentices.

'Iacovo,' we heard Daskalos calling from upstairs, 'we need some help. Would you please come up here for a few minutes?' Apparently Daskalos was having some problems with his granddaughter's math exercises and needed assistance from Iacovos. In about ten minutes the three of them walked downstairs. Daskalos complained that teachers had gone mad. They were overworking their pupils, leaving them no time for anything other than homework. He then left us to continue our discussion while he walked his granddaughter home. As soon as he stepped out of the house something very strange happened. The door of the living-room began shaking violently as if someone were trying to force his way in. Yet there was no one else in the house. I thought for a moment that perhaps it was the wind. But there was no wind that night and all the windows and the outside door were shut. I looked at Iacovos with puzzlement, wondering whether it was what people call a poltergeist phenomenon.

'Don't worry,' he reassured me, 'it is just the emanation from our etheric which is creating the vibrations on the door.'

In a couple of minutes the 'vibrations' ceased. I shook my head in disbelief and we continued our conversation as if nothing had happened. Iacovos talked to me of his out-of-the-body experiences and how he confirmed that they were not illusions.

'I woke up one morning and I was aware of an experience of a place that I had never seen before. I remember everything in great detail.'

'Perhaps it was an ordinary dream,' I suggested.

'No, it was not,' Iacovos responded emphatically. 'When I

visited Daskalos I asked him whether he knew where I had been the night before. He described to me in every detail where I had been and what I had seen the night before. I have had such experiences repeatedly and Daskalos has confirmed them. I cannot imagine that such experiences were coincidental. A lot of knowledge that I have now I bring from lessons I receive from other planes of existence.'

'Daskalos claims that he can get out of his body and travel to other parts of the world. Are you capable of doing so yourself?'

'Of course. For example, during the fighting in Lebanon we used to patrol the area and give encouragement to the wounded. One day I woke up very anxious. There was an earthquake, I believe it was in Romania, and I could see the bodies under the rubble. I implanted suggestions inside the minds of rescue workers to look under specific places and dig out people who were trapped. I also remember many cases when I was able to carry out healing on the psychic plane.'

'How could you do that?'

'Let us say that a sick person comes to me. I try to cure him. Later, during exomatosis, I visit him and continue the cure. The first time I had an out-of-the-body experience,' Iacovos went on, 'I trembled when I returned to my body.'

'Why so?'

'When the psychonoetic body returns to the material body, the nervous system is in a state of hypertension. The trembling is the result of the contact of the two bodies. With experience I managed to control my trembling.'

A 'silver cord,' said Iacovos, connects the material body with the psychonoetic body. One way of distinguishing whether a human being that one encounters within the psychonoetic planes has also a material existence is to see whether the person has a 'silver cord.' If not, it means that the person is 'dead' and lives only with the psychonoetic body. One's silver cord, Iacovos informed me, can expand as much as seven times the periphery of the Earth.

'You mean to say,' I asked, 'that you cannot travel with your psychonoetic body further than the distance equal to seven times around the Earth?'

'Correct. If you do, the silver cord will be cut and the material body will die. There are other ways of traveling into distant space but only the most advanced masters can do it.'

It was about nine o'clock at night and we felt hungry. We were getting ready to walk out of the house when Daskalos made his appearance. In spite of his insistence that we should stay and eat some of his village sausages that he had hanging from his kitchen wall, we went to a nearby shish-kebab tavern to eat and continue our conversation. Before we left the house Daskalos reminded us that the following day there was going to be a regular meeting of his students and he expected us to be there.

I continued questioning Iacovos about his life with Daskalos while having our dinner of *souvlaki* and beer.

'Talk low,' he warned me with a giggle and a whisper. 'If they hear what we are discussing, they may think we have just escaped from the insane asylum.' He went on to say that sometimes Daskalos gets forgetful and says things that can create problems. One day as they were riding to Larnaca in a limousine Daskalos, in a mood of nostalgia, began reminiscing of their past lives together. 'Do you remember when you were three years older than I?' Daskalos said in a carefree manner. Iacovos whispered to him to lower his voice because the other passengers could hear their bizarre conversation.

'Sometimes,' Iacovos added, 'Daskalos is so innocent.'

'Do you think I am crazy?' he asked suddenly after a few moments' pause. His eyes were shining and there was an inquisitive smile on his face. He must have thought that perhaps I was too scandalized by what he had been telling me.

'Not at all,' I reassured him, 'on the contrary. Please continue.'

'The matters we have been discussing tonight,' Iacovos went on as we were getting ready to leave, 'are not metaphysical. There is nothing metaphysical. We must study such phenomena scientifically. I find a lot of what I study in physics and mathematics similar to what Daskalos has been teaching us. I hope we can someday help develop a science which can save us from science.'

It was eleven-thirty when we walked into the street not knowing how to get home. I did not have my car that night and there was no bus service at that late hour. Iacovos lived in Aglantzia, a working-class suburb of Nicosia and about five miles from Daskalos' home. We needed a taxi. But there was no telephone around. Not knowing what else to do, we began walking. Suddenly a taxi, a black Mercedes, stopped next to us and the driver inquired whether we needed a lift. I looked at Iacovos with puzzlement. What a coincidence, I thought, a black Mercedes for hire in the middle of nowhere at such a late hour. For Iacovos there was no problem. The taxi had come because we had created a powerful elemental of desire.

When we met with Daskalos the following day I had more questions to ask on the topic of exomatosis. Even though I had discussed this issue with him on previous encounters there was always new material that would come up, information never before given to me.

Several days before I had been intrigued when I had overheard Daskalos talking to Kostas on the subject of exomatosis. I had been in the kitchen preparing coffee when I had heard Daskalos saying that when there is humidity in the atmosphere, it is much easier to leave one's body. Because of visitors seeking Daskalos' services I had been unable to ask questions on the subject that day. Now that Iacovos and Kostas were present I thought I could open the subject.

Daskalos first explained briefly that water is the dominant element in the various psychic planes and sub-planes. It is for this reason that a humid atmosphere is helpful during exomatosis. Iacovos added that he always has a glass of water next to his bed. The 'atomic emanations of water,' he claimed, help him get out of his body much more smoothly.

Daskalos went on to elaborate that exomatosis can be attained after a long training that involves special concentration and meditation exercises on the psychonoetic centers, the sacred discs. An initiate is taught these practices only after reaching a certain state of spiritual development and only after long training in more basic meditation exercises. Even after years of training there is no guarantee that one will be able to leave one's body. These special meditation practices are usually taught to those wearing the white robe and the members of the inner circle. Although Daskalos never taught me these esoteric techniques of meditation, he was not reluctant to brief me theoretically on whatever subject I was in a position to understand.

'Is exomatosis the same as telepathy?' I asked.

'No, it is not. We must distinguish between the two. Telepathy is simply the projection of an elemental, or the extension of an irradiancy, which will bring to the mystic, who remains within his gross material body, the desired experience. It requires intense practice and concentration so that one may become a master in the creation of powerful and solid elementals that can then be projected anywhere on the planet. To develop telepathy, the sacred disc that envelops the two eyes is awakened and the so-called third eye, which exists above the root of the nose, opens up. Exomatosis, on the other hand, is a state of trance which implies leaving the body. Once we are out of our body, we can go anywhere on the planet and be fully conscious as if we were there with our gross material body. When the mystic finds himself in the psychic worlds, he is still the same person, full and complete as a present self-conscious personality. When one is a very advanced Researcher of the Truth he can also carry out a second exomatosis. He may abandon his psychic body and exist only with the noetic, again full, complete and self-conscious. Let us remember that we must distinguish an individual as self-consciousness from his garments, the gross material, the psychic and the noetic bodies. When a person takes off one of his garments, the most external, he is still the same person. When he takes off a second and a third garment, he is still the same person. Likewise, when we abandon our bodies we are still the same self-consciousness, full and complete.'

'Does exomatosis take place within the etheric counterpart of the material planet or within a plane of the psychonoetic world?' I asked.

'Both are possible and can happen. However, when we are within the gross material environment, we are invisible to the people who live consciously in that environment. Unless of course we know the way to lower the vibrations of our psychonoetic body, which means to gather etheric matter, and make ourselves visible to ordinary eyes. This is not a phenomenon of full materialization, as I explained to you some time ago, and it cannot last long. The moment we shift our thought the materialization disappears.'

'How does one feel,' I wondered, 'in such a state of materialization?'

'It feels as if you are in a very hot climate and then you take a cool shower. It is a very pleasant experience. At that moment materialization begins. When materialization starts you hardly feel anything. You just find yourself back where you started, in this case on the psychic plane.

'When you remain within a psychic plane while in exomatosis, beings who reside within the psychic planes can see you. Suppose now you wish to have greater freedom of movement or become invisible to humans living within the psychic planes, what must you do? In such a case, not only must you come out of the material, but also out of the psychic body. This is what we call the second exomatosis, namely living only with the noetic body. It is much more difficult than the first exomatosis.

'When we exist only with the noetic body and we decide to materialize within the psychic world, we must lower the vibrations of the noetic body and absorb the etheric energy of the psychic world. When this type of materialization takes place, you feel as if you are covered with a cool aura, not a cool shower, in this case.'

'What happens to the psychic body during the second exomatosis?' Iacovos inquired.

'This has been a puzzle for many mystics throughout the centuries. Does it return to the gross material body? The answer is no. It gathers itself within the permanent atom which the present and permanent personalities take with them. The psychic body enters inside the noetic body like a microfilm. The entire psychic body shrinks and becomes a psychic atom within the permanent self-conscious personality. It is the permanent personality that looks after the psychic body now. Therefore, when the vibrations of the noetic body are lowered, the psychic body is right there, intact and complete. Nothing has been added to it and nothing has been taken away.

'So, when we abandon our gross material body in exomatosis, we leave behind intact the gross material body at the place where we left it and it is under the surveillance of the Holy Spirit. During the second exomatosis our psychic body, irrespective of what degree of perfection it reaches or as to what psychic subplane it vibrates, automatically gathers itself, and its image is transformed into a psychic atom inside the noetic body. We take with us in the noetic world our atomized psychic body and when we lower our vibrations it re-acquires its form and its life energy. This is beautiful.

'During the second exomatosis the Holy Spirit has no other task to perform beyond preparing the psychic and noetic substances. The task of caring for the psychic body is now in the hands of the self-conscious soul.

'At death our material body dissolves itself, along with its etheric-double. We have no relationship now with gross matter, which we have abandoned. It disintegrates and can now be used for the formation of new life. After the second death, which always follows the death of the gross material body, our psychic body becomes concentrated and enters the permanent psychic atom. A new incarnation then takes place. With every incarnation we bring along with us all the previous experiences of the self-conscious personality.

'At this very moment inside the permanent psychic atom, which is nowhere and everywhere within the present psychic body, there are all the recordings of all previous incarnations. Had this not been the case man would be dissolved, annihilated. His emotional life would be destroyed and no memory of past experiences would be possible.'

'Daskale,' I asked, 'is there any other kind of exomatosis?'

'Yes, through superconscious self-awareness. However, it is and it isn't exomatosis. When we extend ourselves and cover a certain space, large or small, outside of our material bodies and we receive impressions from many spots simultaneously, we acquire the so-called superconscious self-awareness. We are outside of our bodies while at the same time our bodies are within our sphere of receiving impressions. We can feel everything around us, including our bodies. We are no longer within the material body but the material body is within us. If we attune ourselves with the consciousness and self-awareness of the present personality, we can feel ourselves, not only as we are today but also as superconsciousness. Perhaps there lies the great joy of a Researcher of Truth, when he distinguishes his two natures as present personality and as a self-conscious soul. The two will be experienced as one and yet distinguishable.

'You see, the subject you have raised is not easy to comprehend as yet,' Daskalos continued with a lowered voice. 'But I believe that as a beginning, I have offered you a most faint picture of it.'

Daskalos then narrated an experience which he had not mentioned to me before on how through exomatosis and materialization he rescued a girl from being molested by an older man.

'It was eleven o'clock at night. I was reading in my study, the children were asleep, and my wife was knitting a sweater. "Nobody must disturb me this evening," I said abruptly. My wife wondered what was wrong. "In the nearby forest of eucalyptus trees," I explained, "a middle-aged man is about to seduce a young girl. I must stop him." His car was parked at the edge of the forest. He led the girl into the woods and was already at the point of deflowering her. He had taken her clothes off and was caressing her and biting her breasts. The girl was sobbing.'

'Was he trying to rape her?' I inquired.

'I don't know. She apparently had followed him. But she was only fifteen. I had to stop him. I got out of my body and materialized in front of him. When he noticed me he gasped. I grabbed his face with my materialized hand and pushed him towards the trees. He saw only my face, my chest and my hand. It was not a full materialization. "Take the girl home right now," I ordered him, "and leave her alone." I pointed at a path nearby and asked him to move on. "I shall follow you, be aware." The girl began to cry again. She saw my hand on his face and when she looked at me I felt that she was smiling. He followed my order to the last and left the girl near her home.

'This man was from Nicosia and he knew me. A few days later he visited me. He looked confused and was not certain whether his experience was real, or a dream, a nightmare. When he entered my house he said, "Friend, I want to ask you about something." "I am not interested," I said cuttingly. "Why did you interfere and stop me from enjoying myself?" "Are you not ashamed? Your own daughters are of the same age as that girl. You could have sent her to the whorehouse. Did I slap you that day?" "No." "Well, I do it now," and I gave him a slap on the face. "I find in your mind," I said, "that you still want to seduce that girl. You are a beast. Think of your daughters." He began crying. "My daughters are decent girls." "What do you think that girl was?" I said in anger.

'Sometimes, you see, we have to act in an almost savage way. This is not an easy Earth to walk on. In this case I had to materialize myself since there was not time to run towards the forest with my material body. But as far as I am concerned, I see no difference between exomatosis in the form of materialization

109

and the use of the physical body to accomplish the same task.'

'There are light years of difference between going to a place with your body or materializing yourself there,' I commented.

'You find it so? I don't,' Daskalos replied, feigning innocence.

'To accomplish what you claim you have accomplished, Daskale, violates all the natural laws that we common mortals are accustomed to.' Daskalos laughed and continued narrating yet another case of materialization from his apparently inexhaustible repertoire of exotic vignettes.

'I was passing by the coffee shop near my house when I noticed a heated argument going on inside. The subject was infidelity. The cousin of a married man had had an affair with the latter's wife. It so happened that the two men were sitting together drinking coffee that day. The husband discovered from their conversation that his wife had betrayed him with his cousin. He started to quarrel with him. The other customers added to the excitement with their comments. The cousin finally admitted to his illicit relationship but insisted it was not his fault. At that point the betrayed husband grabbed a sharp knife and got ready to plunge it into his cousin's chest. I was outside standing on the pavement. The scene moved so fast that it took everybody by surprise. Instantly I materialized a hand and grabbed the arm holding the knife.'

'Did you materialize an invisible hand?' I asked.

'Yes. However hard he tried, he could not bring his arm down. The others then jumped on him and took the knife away. The man looked at me and said, "Why did you hold my hand?" I told him that he should learn to control his temper because the hangman's rope was already around his neck. "Think of your child," I implored him. As for the cousin, I advised him to get a plane the next day and leave Cyprus. He took my advice and went to a relative in Africa.'

'Are there any dangers in exomatosis?' I asked after a pause.

'When a man enters into deep sleep,' Daskalos began to say, 'which often appears like annihilation, he is in fact in exomatosis. In that state the Holy Spirit looks after his body and repairs the damages done to it during the day. Even ordinary people experience exomatosis during sleep and they return to their bodies when the Holy Spirit has completed its task. When an individual is in a lethargic state he is receptive to experiences either of his present or past incarnations.

'Now, why do you suppose the Holy Spirit places the present personality in this lethargic state? Because whatever experience one has with his psychic body can be transferred on to the gross material body. If a man floating with his psychic body experiences a fall and actually hits the ground, upon awakening he will notice the bruises on his body. However, the Holy Spirit watches over not only the complete functioning of the gross material body but also over the tranquility and well-being of the sleeping personality. The Holy Spirit intervenes to protect the personality from unpleasant experiences that can afflict it during sleep. How often do you recall a dream where you are faced with danger but you are awakened just before the disaster? It is the wisdom of the Holy Spirit that sends you back to your material body before you receive the unpleasant experience. You must have noticed this from your personal experience.

'To answer your question then, whether there are dangers in exomatosis, I would say yes. There are dangers as we have seen both to the material body and also to the personality. During exomatosis the vibrations are much more powerful and if the individual could pull out from the permanent atom experience of past incarnations, he might awaken inside himself conditions that must remain dormant until they are transcended.

'In conscious exomatosis,' Daskalos added, 'one has to be extra cautious because the dangers are many.'

'In what way?' I asked.

'I'll give you an example from personal experience. During the civil war in Lebanon we were there trying to help the wounded, both Christian and Moslem. Some sorcerers realized what we were doing and were angry that we helped both sides. They wanted us to assist only Moslems. While I was in exomatosis these sorcerers came to my body, materialized a knife and stabbed me at the spot between the genitals and my leg. Then they dematerialized it. I immediately felt the pain and was back into my body. I grabbed a towel and stopped the bleeding. I called my brother-in-law who came and helped me out. The bed sheets were full of blood stains.

'You see, I forgot to create a guardian elemental before I left my body. Had I done so these sorcerers could not have harmed me. When we consciously leave the body we must always build an elemental to protect it while we are absent.'

111

'How do you do that?'

'By making a powerful auto-suggestion. I would tell myself, "No harm will come to my body while I am away." Incidentally, Theophanis got stabbed on the arm by these sorcerers. Fortunately the wounds were not serious.'

'I wonder what happened to those black sorcerers?' I asked.

'Indian brothers intervened and prevented them from returning to their bodies.'

'I am not sure I follow you.'

'When these masters, who were Moslem sufis, realized what the Lebanese sorcerers had done to us, they decided to stop them. With their thought they stopped their hearts and gently escorted them to the psychic worlds.'

'In common language,' I added, 'they just killed them.'

'I am afraid so. But I vigorously objected and implored my sufi brothers not to harm those Lebanese sorcerers. They wouldn't listen. "We are Moslems," they told me, "and we shall solve this problem the Moslem way. We must not allow them to continue their destructive actions."'

Daskalos strongly triggered in my memory a strange experience that an anthropologist had had while conducting a field research in Africa. At an unguarded moment he related to me his experiences which he had kept a secret for many years. When he went to Africa to study this particular tribe the local medicine man was hostile. Strange and frightful episodes were happening to this anthropologist. He realized that the culprit was the local sorcerer who felt that this European was a threat to his authority. Fearful for his life he approached and eventually befriended this local 'witch doctor.' 'You Europeans,' the native shaman said to the anthropologist 'are totally ignorant about hidden powers that we master here in Africa.' To demonstrate his power he boasted that he could, through magic, cause insanity to a high-ranking colonial officer of that region. To the amazement and dismay of the anthropologist that particular official 'had gone mad' and had to be hospitalized the following day. He had no prior history of 'mental illness.'

When my anthropologist friend had completed his field work and was about to leave Africa, the tribesmen were sad and implored him to stay with them. Trying to avoid hurting their feelings as much as possible he fabricated the excuse that the reason he had to leave for Europe was because he needed to go to a dryer climate. 'There is too much rain here,' he told them. 'If that is the problem,' they said to him, 'how about if we stop the rain falling around your tent but let it pour everywhere else in the forest.' The natives began a wild dance around his tent and started pulling plants right from their roots and then planting them upside down. He assumed that they were symbolically trying to reverse the process of nature. 'I just couldn't believe it, Kyriaco,' my friend said to me, 'the moment they started dancing the rain stopped falling around my tent while it was pouring everywhere else in the forest.'

This anthropologist had no doubt in his mind that his experience was genuine and that the rain did in fact stop falling around his tent. Yet he kept this and similar other 'exotic' experiences secret because he was concerned for his academic reputation. His colleagues might have branded him mad and might have discredited his field work. 'Besides,' he said to me, 'I have been trained all my life to think in rational terms. In spite of my experiences I cannot deal with such matters. I am too old for change now. You are young. Maybe in your lifetime these issues will be respectable for academics to study.'

'These stories should not shock us,' Daskalos said to me, as he did on many occasions. 'These are powers latent in every human being.'

Daskalos went on to say that we must learn how to use such powers the right way, only for healing purposes. 'Unless we evolve spiritually,' he was fond of saying, 'such powers should remain dormant. Unless we overcome our egotism we can become a menace to others and to ourselves.'

Our discussion on exomatosis was interrupted by a knock at the door. A forty-five-year-old man dressed in an elegant business suit was accompanied by an equally well-dressed woman who appeared to be his wife. They seemed intensely anxious and asked whether they could have a private audience with Daskalos. He replied that he was giving a lesson at the time and asked the visitors to contact him the following day if possible, unless it was urgent. It was very urgent, they insisted. A crucial decision affecting their life had to be made the following day and they needed Daskalos' advice. Iacovos, Kostas and I left the room as Daskalos spent the next half-hour conferring with the visitors.

After they left, Daskalos told us confidentially what the problem with the strangers was. He was a well-paid bank employee who secretly and illegally smuggled foreign currency out of the island. His actions were about to be discovered and he was afraid of losing his job. Daskalos knew some influential people in the bank and the man implored him to intervene on his behalf.

'I refused and explained to him that his actions were dishonest,' Daskalos said severely. '"Given the problems facing the country, some would call such action downright betrayal. We are carrying on a struggle for survival," I said to him. "Our island is half occupied by foreign troops and you undermine this struggle by sending foreign currency abroad. What kind of struggle do you think we could fight? With guns? Our only chance is to maintain our economy and pursue the struggle through political means." "I never thought of it that way," was his response.'

'Well, what did you advise him to do?' I asked.

'Under the circumstances I thought that the least painful alternative was for him to give his resignation. Otherwise he was bound to be discovered. If any compensation was given him, with that money he could start something on his own and have a new life for himself and his family. Actually there was no other choice for him. He could end up in jail.'

We spent the rest of the evening discussing politics. 'We'll have more to say on exomatosis some other time,' Daskalos reassured me before we dispersed for the evening.

'One last question,' I said in a playful tone as we were getting ready to leave. 'I read in the paper the other day that an English tourist in northern Greece burned his feet and had to be hospitalized because he jumped into a pile of burning coals. He wanted to prove that the *Anastenarides* were fake.'

The *Anastenarides* are a cult of fire-walkers who once a year, as part of their religious ritual, dance barefoot over burning coals. They first dance around the fire, holding in their hands the icon of Saint Constantine, and after they get themselves into a certain psychological state, they begin to walk and dance barefoot over the burning coals without suffering any injuries. This phenomenon has been well documented in the anthropological literature. Cases of this type have been reported not only in Greece, but also in Africa and Asia. To my knowledge there has been no scientific explanation of this strange phenomenon. The Greek Church denounced it as a satanic and pagan ritual. Its practitioners claim that it is the Holy Spirit that protects their feet because of their deep faith.

Daskalos went on to explain that the same principle that allows people to levitate is at work in this case also. Everything is done through the subconscious. With their yearly rituals they have created an elemental of Saint Constantine which they have imbued with protective attributes. This elemental enters into their subconscious once they begin the ritual.

'What they actually do,' Daskalos said, 'without their realizing it, is that they cover their feet and body with a condensed layer of etheric energy that acts as insulation between their feet and the burning coals.

'I want you to be in bed by midnight,' Daskalos said to Iacovos and Kostas as the three of us were leaving. 'We have work to do tonight.'

Such talk did not surprise me. When I first heard strange exchanges of this type I used to react by asking questions and probing for explanations. By now it had become a matter of routine. I knew what Daskalos meant. He needed his disciples for nocturnal journeys out of their bodies, something like 'astral patrols,' as it were, to be, as 'invisible helpers,' of service to whomever was in need.

Some time before I had overheard Kostas and Iacovos whispering and exchanging notes on their experiences of the previous night. They were checking the authenticity of their exomatosis and the convergence of their experiences and encounters.

'Was your experience identical?' I inquired. Both nodded in the affirmative and laughed when they noticed my apparently incredulous expression. This type of testing and checking on their part solidified their certainty that the world they lived in, and into which Daskalos introduced them, was not fantasy or make-believe but in fact a truer version of reality.

CHAPTER 7

Visitors

The meeting was over. Daskalos' lecture was a complicated discussion on the relationship between Christ's teachings, the sacred discs and the eastern concept of Kundalini. As on previous occasions I was given special permission to attend this gathering of the inner circle composed of the more advanced disciples. Permission was given to me with the understanding that I was not to tape or take notes of the content of the lecture or whatever else may happen during that period. The concern of Daskalos and particularly of Kostas was that certain truths that might be revealed within the inner circle might not be appropriate for the general public lest the uninitiated be harmed. But in the few times that I attended the inner circle, nothing had been revealed that at least I could consider potentially damaging to the uninitiated. I was not certain, however, whether during the times that I was present Daskalos was careful not to divulge secrets that had to remain in the privileged possession of advanced adepts. In fact on one occasion when the meeting was supposed to have taken place on the regular day, Wednesday at two in the afternoon, it was rescheduled for Monday of that week. I was not informed of the change nor of the reasons for the unusual rescheduling of the time. And on that day, I was told later, the Logos descended into the room while the lesson was in progress. Everyone kneeled down as the Logos in the form of vibrating white luminosity hovered over their heads. Kostas explained to me that perhaps it was not meant for me to have that experience. Not as yet. I asked him to explain what it means for the Logos 'to come down,' since the Logos by definition is within every human being anyway. 'In such cases the Logos descends in a more manifest, focused and concentrated form,' he replied.

Once the lesson was over Daskalos in his usual manner

moved to the living-room, sat comfortably in an armchair, and surrounded by his disciples indulged in casual conversation. Theano, Kostas and myself went into the kitchen to prepare the coffee and some pastries brought over by Aspasia who had become a new initiate into the inner circle.

While making the preparations I engaged Kostas in a debate on the significance of Christ's divinity as far as the research for truth is concerned.

'Some people assume,' Kostas commented as he began preparing the coffee-cups, 'that the birth of the Christ Logos took place only on our planet within a specific place and time. From our own temporal perspective this is true. But from the perspective of the eternal present there has been no time that has not experienced the birth of the Christ Logos. There are planetary systems within the boundlessness of space that experienced the birth of Christ perhaps millions and billions of years in the past and there are planetary systems within which the Christ Logos has not as yet expressed Itself.'

'When you say "birth" I presume you literally mean the incarnation of the Logos into a human form.'

'Yes.'

'Why do you suppose the Christ Logos was born on our planet at the time It was and not in previous epochs?' I asked as Theano listened with a broad smile.

'Perhaps because it was at that moment in history that human consciousness had reached a state of maturity that could have absorbed the light and the truth offered by the logoic expression. You see, it was the collective needs of human beings at this point in time that brought down the Logos in a human form.'

'Many people,' I went on, as I helped Kostas with the preparations, 'find it very difficult to accept that the pan-universal Logos came down as a common mortal who died on a cross like a criminal. I mean people who are very serious about their spirituality. They could accept Christ as a human being who had reached the highest states of consciousness but not as the incarnation of the Absolute Itself.'

'Christ,' Kostas said, who like Daskalos stressed that Jesus was not a man who attained Theosis through successive incarnations, but was God incarnate, 'came down as a human being in order to make Himself understood. And even now human beings have difficulty understanding. Can you imagine what would have happened had he come down in a different form?'

I went on 'debating' with Kostas the issue of Christ's incarnation until all the cups were prepared, each one individually according to specifications on the amount of sugar. We made certain that Daskalos' was *sketos*, no sugar. He is a diabetic. I then put the cups on a tray and brought them into the living-room.

'Daskale,' I said as I handed him his coffee while Kostas was still in the kitchen with Theano, 'I just discussed with Kostas the issue of Christ's divinity. In my opinion it seems that it really makes no difference for the spiritual path whether one accepts Christ as God incarnate or whether one accepts Christ as the expression of the logoic aspect of the Absolute. According to you, what is the difference as far as the evolution of the Researcher of Truth is concerned?'

'None whatsoever,' Daskalos answered without hesitation. 'However, sooner or later during the Researcher's ascent he will realize the truth.'

'Is it therefore necessary to emphasize this point? There is a danger that such positions can develop into rigid dogmas.'

'Of course it is not necessary. But when you proceed on your evolution toward enlightenment and you absorb this truth you will experience a greater joy,' Daskalos added. 'Either way you do not retard your progress.'

'I want Kostas to hear this,' I said self-righteously and called Kostas to come over.

'What is it, my dear?' Kostas replied as he entered the room with a plate of pastries in his right hand.

'Don't misunderstand me, Kyriaco,' Kostas said after I explained my exchange with Daskalos. 'Christ did not come into the world to destroy other spiritual systems or to change The Way. He came to fill the missing links, to offer more light. He came to disperse the darkness that the others were in, to liberate us from our illusions.'

'Exactly. Pay attention now. I see The Way ahead of me,' Daskalos added and went on pointing his right palm forward. 'Whether I have abundant light as I travel on that road or a few street lights that can help me proceed in relative safety it is the same Way. I can still reach my destination. Whether I can see more or less clearly during my travel it does not matter in the final analysis.'

'However, I am not able to observe everything in detail and with clarity,' Kostas added.

'Very true,' Daskalos said. 'My journey into the interior of myself becomes easier with greater light.'

'I can accept this,' I said. 'I may even accept Christ as the incarnation of the Logos Itself. But I can also accept with equal ease the others' argument that Christ is an expression of absolute wisdom, as a self-realized master. What difference does it make either way?'

'Just a minute now,' Daskalos said quickly. 'Both yourself who sees Christ in one way and the others who see Christ in a different way do so not through the inner light, as Saint Paul said, but through the medium of image construction, through reasoning and meditation. And thoughts are powerless wings for great heights. Let me explain. Whether you construct a monstrous-looking god, a dunce, or a beautiful idol of a god and you tell me this is God, I will say this is your god. Both of your gods are earthly. "But," you might say, "look how beautiful my god is." Look how beautiful is Hermes and Apollo and how ugly the other gods are, with hair, teeth, horns. As a mystic I will say to both of you that your gods are nothing more than idols, they are earthly constructions. I may appreciate your aesthetic sensibilities for constructing a beautiful image of a god but, like the monstrous-looking god with hair and teeth, it is not God. People fight among themselves based on the idols of God they have created. And I ask, how many of these people who throughout history have butchered one another defending their image of god really knew God? A mystic will search to find God inside,' Daskalos said and pointed at his heart.

'I understand what you are saying, Daskale,' I said, 'but my point is that when we emphasize too strongly whether Christ was God or not or whether He was an expression of godly wisdom it is an unnecessary exercise in dogma. I would like to know whether according to you it is in fact a significant distinction.'

'No, it is not significant because such arguments are focused on a god that has not been experienced. And when people have fights over such issues that is precisely when they don't know God in reality. Christ is Love, period.'

'In other words,' I proceeded, 'a Zen Buddhist may be closer to Christ and be more firmly on The Way than many devout Christians.'

'Absolutely,' Daskalos replied. 'A Zen Buddhist who is on what they call the "Eight-fold Path" and carries out his prayers and practices and tries to overcome evil, tries to cultivate tolerance and non-attachment and tries to make these attributes part of his consciousness, is much more firmly on the Christian path than dogmatic priests and theologians.

'I hear people say,' Daskalos went on, 'that God is light, or that God is superlight, and they have experienced neither light nor superlight. But unless you have the experience you don't know. I repeat what Father Yohannan said in a previous lesson, "Thoughts and beliefs are too weak as wings to help us attain great heights of knowledge,"' Daskalos concluded and sipped the last drop from his cup of coffee. Then he proceeded to describe an encounter.

'They once brought me a Lebanese boy. I asked him in English, "Are you Moslem or Christian?" "Moslem, *ishallah*," that is, "I am a Moslem with the grace of God." Notice how we are fanaticized very early in our lives. In the same way my grandson Marios prays and says the "Our Father who art in Heaven." Who is more correct now? I would say both are in their own way. It makes no difference that the Lebanese boy believes in Allah and my grandson believes in the Christian God. But what God now? Can Marios now explain what God is?

'When he was five years old,' Daskalos continued with a smile as he reminisced of his relationship with his grandson, 'he began to wonder about these matters. "Mister Daskale," he asked me one day, "where is God and what is God?" "God, my love? Come and I will show you." I took him by the hand and we went outside. "Look how beautiful this almond tree is," I said. "A few weeks ago, my love, it looked like dead branches of wood. Look at them now fully blossomed with so many flowers. After a while they will have leaves and later almonds. It is God who is going to do that. He is inside the almond trees." "Mister Daskale," he said again, "these are blossomed almond trees." "Come," I said, "I will explain to you. Do you see all these birds around? They sing so beautifully. They are life, my love, they are God." "Grandpa" he called me now and giggled. "These are birds that are singing and these are trees that are blossoming." "Come" I said again and we went inside in front of the mirror. I tickled him and he started laughing. "Now who is tickling Marios who is laughing?" "You," he said and went on giggling. "My love," I said, "if I bring here a dead person and tickle him is he going to laugh?" "No," he said. "But you laugh because you live. God, my love, is life, it is your smile, it is everything around us." "Grandpa," he said, "that one inside the mirror is Marios who is laughing." And then with a very serious look he said, "Listen, Grandpa. What is God and where is God? You know and I know. But neither you nor I can tell what is God and where is God." And he was only five years old,' Daskalos concluded with an obvious pride on the intelligence of his grandson.

'It does not matter,' Daskalos went on, 'whether we are Christians, Buddhists or Moslems. Our Master, with absolute wisdom, set things straight. He could foresee the confusion that was bound to develop and the fights among the other apostles. He could foresee his exile on the island of Patmos and before he wrote the Gospel he set down the foundations of Christianity. It was neither Paul nor Peter who established these foundations. "In authority," Yohannan said, "is the Logos. It is the light that enlightens every human being descending upon the Earth."

'Therefore the Christ that Christians believe in is within every human being and not just Christians. The Christ Logos is that force that at a certain stage of the evolutionary process awakened within the animal its self-consciousness. It is that which transformed the beast into a self-aware logoic being.

'Throughout the centuries,' Daskalos continued as everyone else was listening, 'we have abused the word God. One asks, "What is God?" But can anyone define what God is? They called Apollo God and Artemis and the jealous Hera and Zeus with his thunderbolts. They called criminal Kali God and also Circe. Should we start fights over something that we don't really understand? You cannot see God through thought but through the heart. For me, the question "What is the Absolute, the Holy Spirit and the Christ Logos?" – I would respond it is Love. If we are to perceive things rationally we must overcome our tendency to limit God from within our own idiosyncratic ways of understanding, from within our own idols of the mind, because people perceive both God and the saints in accordance with their level of understanding and level of spiritual growth and awareness. The Greek militarists, for example, perceive the Holy Virgin as if she was a general leading the troops. With their unbridled fantasizing they saw the Virgin Mary leading them against the Bulgarians and they saw her dressed up in military uniform.

'One of the best dialogs I had on the nature of God,' Daskalos continued after a pause, 'was with Jonathan, a Jew. Jonathan was one of our guides when I visited the Holy Land. He was a student at the university and worked part time as a guide. I remember when his director, a Jew from Salonica who spoke Greek himself, asked me to become the interpreter and help Jonathan whenever necessary to translate from English into Greek. We got into the buses. "This is Cana of Galilee," Jonathan explained, "a small town. This is where Jesus turned water into wine." I laughed when he said that. And then he continued, "This is Gethsemane. This is Bethany, the place where Jesus raised Lazarus from the dead." When he said that I stood still and stared at him. "Who then is Jesus Christ?" I asked. "A Jew," he replied.

'He was a very bright fellow,' Daskalos continued after we calmed down from laughter. 'I kept staring at him and said, "I will ask you a question. Jesus Christ said All Ye are Gods and Sons of the Almighty. All of you." "No," Jonathan interrupted me. "It was David who said it first after Revelation. Christ repeated what David said before." "All right," I said, "Christ repeated it. But do you think Christ was the son of God?" I asked. "Of course he was. As much as you and I are," he replied. "All of us," he said, "are sons of God. Only Jesus knew who He was while you and I do not know who we are." I looked at him with admiration.

'When we entered into the Sepulcher he followed us. "But you are a Jew," I said, "why are you following us?" "Don't forget, sir," he protested, "that you are in Israel. You are on my land." I laughed. Then I crossed myself and kissed the icon. He put his hands in front of his head as is customary in his religion. "All the nations," he said, "should worship God." I stood there looking at him. "I know I have puzzled you," he said, "but believe me you are my brother in God. You are God and I am God. And Jesus Christ is the God-brother of ours who knew who He was."

'Now tell me,' Daskalos said loudly as he leaned back on his chair, 'is this Jew not closer to the Truth than many fanatical, stupid and idiotic jackasses who call themselves theologians?'

'Daskale,' I said after we quieted down from laughter, 'a Jewish friend of mine who had some personal difficulties went to a Maine psychic to ask for advice. This well-known medium was a very religious and simple old man. The advice he gave to him was to sit down and pray to Jesus Christ and his problems would disappear. My friend reacted against this kind of advice, he was terribly annoyed and offended even though he accepted this Christian medium as one with authentic psychic abilities. . . . '

'They were both wrong,' Daskalos said before I completed my story. 'That medium had in his mind a christ of his own fantasy and your Jewish friend may have believed in the Christ Logos under a different name, as Love. The mind of human beings is in such great confusion today.'

'What kind of advice would you have offered to this Jewish friend of mine had he come to you?' I asked.

'I believe I could have complete understanding with your friend in the same way that I did with Jonathan. I would tell him, "God the father, yours and mine, endowed you with reason with which you can solve your problems. And there is no problem you cannot solve through the proper application of reason, through right thinking. Human beings have used their reason to get to the Moon. Are your problems," I would ask him, "more difficult than going to the Moon?"' Daskalos added and smiled with irony.

'Human beings today,' Daskalos went on, 'have either abused or discarded their divine inheritance of reason, of Mind. We must not blame God for that. And we should not expect God to solve our problems. From my own point of view I never ask God for help even in my difficult moments. I simply coordinate myself with Him and call on Him as "My Love." Must we bother God all the time with our petty problems?' Daskalos concluded with a laugh.

Daskalos then described an experience he had had in the hospital when he was undergoing an operation on his foot. While Daskalos was in intensive care he saw the vision of

Christ watching over him.

'"Thank you, my Love," I said. The nurse later asked me questions about who I was talking to. You see at that very moment Christ may have appeared to millions of other people in a manner understandable to them. He could have appeared as the Buddha to a Buddhist, as Krishna to a Hindu, as Moses to a Jew or as Muhammad to a Moslem. Christ appears to you in a manner which will be understandable to you. The Christ Logos is part of every human being descending upon the Earth and anyone can coordinate oneself with Christ whether one is a Christian or not. It is like a television station, let us say. You can get the same program no matter where you are on the planet, no matter how many television sets you may have. So, you see, it is not a question of Christians being more favored than others. Your religious beliefs are irrelevant. What matters is to what extent you are spiritually evolved, to what extent you are attuned with the Christ Logos which is inside you.'

'Are you suggesting, Daskale,' Chariklia, the third woman in the inner circle, asked, 'that prayer is unnecessary?'

'No, I am not saying that. Prayer may be a way for you to coordinate yourself with that which is inside you. But I am telling you that Christ is close to you and watches over you all the time. He is closer to you than your right from your left eye and before you think and become conscious of something He already knows it.'

Daskalos then spoke of several experiences he had had when he was miraculously saved from certain death or injury by the prompt intervention of higher forces.

'I was walking one day at Ledra Street, right where there used to be the club of the government employees. There was construction going on. Suddenly I felt Father Yohannan pushing me backwards. "Go back, go back," he ordered me. When I felt him pushing me I made two to three steps backwards. At that very moment a huge piece of glass, as big as a door, crashed in front of me. Had I not made those steps backwards I would have been killed for certain. I was not aware of what was happening. It was Father Yohannan who saved me that day. I just put my hand on my forehead and felt Father Yohannan holding it as I murmured, "Thank you, My Love." I have so many stories like that. I did not ask him for help. He wanted to protect me in order to torment me later with all these things that are happening today,' Daskalos concluded with loud laughter. 'When they need you for work they know how to protect you,' Daskalos continued humorously, and shook his head.

After he ended his story almost everyone in his small audience had a story to tell on how they had been rescued from an imminent danger that could not be explained in any other way except that higher forces must have intervened. Daskalos then proceeded to narrate another story from his own inexhaustible repertoire of experiences.

'When I was young I used to spend my summers at the Stavrovouni monastery high up on the mountain. The abbot, as I believe I told you before, was an uncle of mine. When the schools were over he would come to Nicosia, dress me up in black robes as if I were a monk and take me along. That was how I spent my summer months. At that time most of the monks at Stavrovouni were illiterate. They loved me and used to call me "little Spyraki." I used to help them in the fields and try to teach them how to read the scriptures. In fact one summer I managed to teach them how to recite the *Exapsalmos* by heart. They had Vespers all night long and would wake up before sunrise and continue the prayers and the chanting until the Sun was up.

'It was Christmas Eve. I went to the monastery to celebrate with my uncle. I put on the black robes and went to church. My uncle that day was at Saint Barbara's, the monastery just below Stavrovouni – which was also under his jurisdiction. That night there were only four of us at Stavrovouni, Fathers Savvas and Mattheos (they were like grandfathers to me), another monk, and myself. Most of the others followed my uncle to Saint Barbara's. While we were praying and chanting there was pandemonium outside. There developed a frightful storm, a real cataclysm. We made certain that the windows were firmly shut and went on with the Vespers. Suddenly a thunderbolt hit the monastery. The lightning rod pulled it but it was too old and faulty. The lightning entered through the window, shattered the glass and rushed into the church from behind me. I was wearing shoes with iron points underneath because we used to work in the fields. I was kneeling on the floor praying as the lightning passed in front of me and hit the icon of the Virgin – they still have it there half burned. At that moment I experienced a peculiar feeling of joy and pleasure. The church for an instant was filled with abundant luminosity. Then darkness, then the deafening noise. We could barely see each other in the light of the few candles burning in front of the altar. Father Savvas rushed towards me and grabbed me into his arms. I was no longer wearing shoes. They were burned, as were most of my clothes. Some of my hair was burned but I didn't feel anything.

'When I touched the clothes that remained on me they fell apart, yet they did not catch fire. I was barefoot, nothing was left of my shoes. Father Savvas' shoes were also gone. They disappeared. I am sure scientists can find all kind of explanations because such phenomena do happen with lightning. But why was I not hurt and why was I not afraid, but instead felt pleasure?'

After Daskalos' narration, I mentioned that a man in Maine had an even more shuddering experience with lightning. He was a blind man who got his sight when lightning hit him on the head. Daskalos then mentioned that we are not alone in the universe, that it is filled with life and with higher intelligence that oversees our material and spiritual evolution. He then asked Kostas to go into the Sanctum and fetch the Unpointed Sword, the sacred artifact with which Daskalos conducts initiation ceremonies for membership into the inner circle.

'Just look at this,' Daskalos said to me as he took the sacred object from Kostas' hands. 'As you know, several years back we had problems with the Church. An intolerable situation was created and Father Yohannan instructed me to temporarily suspend the activities of the circles.

'This Unpointed Sword,' Daskalos went on as he raised it in front of me, 'disappeared in a mysterious way from the altar. I suspected one of my students that I had problems with. My other students urged me to carry on an investigation and confront him with this issue. I decided not to. Let him keep it, I said. Perhaps it would enlighten him. But we were not in fact certain whether he actually stole it. This episode took place many years ago. Six, seven years have passed since then. Father Yohannan gave me new instructions to reassemble the circles and proceed with new initiations. He instructed me to initiate Theophanis into the inner circle and have him put on the white robe. I was trying to figure out how to carry on the initiation since the Unpointed Sword was indispensable for that ritual. "I'll wait until that moment," I said to myself, "and something will come up. Perhaps Father Yohannan will instruct me to carry on the ceremony with just my hands, I will give Theophanis the blessing that way." I left the Sanctum, locked it and kept the key to myself. I was concerned in case some curious students who had not been initiated into the inner circle entered the Sanctum.

'When the others came I explained to them that there was no Unpointed Sword to carry out the initiation ceremony but that I was not worried. Father Yohannan was bound to give us appropriate directions on how to proceed. We entered the Sanctum to put on our robes. I opened the door and what do you think we saw? The oil candle burning. It must have burned for some time since the oil was half way down. It was not lit when I locked the Sanctum. I looked around and I saw the Unpointed Sword on the altar.

'This,' Daskalos exclaimed with high emotion as he held the Unpointed Sword, 'was dematerialized during those six years and when the time had come for the initiations, Father Yohannan rematerialized it. I stood there stupefied and then all of us kneeled down and prayed. Then I heard the voice of Father Yohannan. "You did not need it those years. Now that you do I brought it back to you." I asked Theophanis whether he was afraid to be initiated with this Sword. He said, "No," and we then proceeded with the ceremony.'

'Are you certain, Daskale, that no one had actually stolen the Sword and then brought it back?' I asked.

'Yes, my dear, I *am* certain,' Daskalos replied with some exasperation in his voice as if my question lacked seriousness. 'The door was locked for days and I held the key. It was not the first time that we experienced such phenomena.'

Indeed. One of Daskalos' apprentices, a medical doctor, described to me in all sincerity how once in front of his very eyes Daskalos materialized a leaflet of a local extremist organization that had not as yet been printed. Through his special powers Daskalos allegedly 'saw' the leaflet on the desk of the individual who had already handwritten it. Daskalos that evening dematerialized it from this person's desk, rematerialized it in his hands, read it, took notes of its contents and then returned it to the place from where he dematerialized it originally. He then called a high official of the government informing him about the nature of the leaflet. Daskalos was concerned about possible political turmoil that could have led to violence. Two days later, according to this internist, the streets of Nicosia were filled with leaflets, the contents of which were identical to the one Daskalos materialized in his hands.

'The universe within which we live,' Daskalos repeated once more after a short pause and after inquiries on my part, 'is full of life forms and more intelligent than the ones with which we are familiar. We are not alone in the universe. Higher intelligences are overseeing the evolution of our planet. They are like guardians of our planet and some of us are in communication with them.'

In earlier encounters I had with Daskalos, he described to me at some length how he encountered such beings, that according to him were theosized beings unencumbered by time and space who were masters of matter and were able to materialize and dematerialize themselves. I confessed to Daskalos that I found such stories of 'extraterrestrials' too unbelievable for my humble brain and that in my mind I had difficulties reconciling the superb logical consistency and wisdom in his overall scheme of things and such 'wild' arguments about intelligent beings inside the Earth, inside the boiling sun, on Mars, on the moon and everywhere else in space.

Daskalos smiled as I was making these statements and so did the others. 'In comparison to the other planets of our solar system,' Kostas volunteered to add as if to shock me even further, 'the Earth is on a lower scale of evolution.'

'Now I am really puzzled,' I said. 'I find it very difficult to understand what you mean, Kosta. Science has proved that the other planets of our solar system do not have the conditions necessary to support life as we know it on our planet. Mars as well as other planets are for all we know dead matter. There is no water, no forests, no natural beauty as we know it. On what grounds then do you say that those planets are more advanced than our own? Tell me please.'

'By evolution, my dear Kyriaco,' Kostas responded as Daskalos shook his head laughing silently, 'we mean the psychonoetic development of the entities that have as their home base these planets.'

'Therefore, Kyriaco,' Daskalos added, 'we should not expect

to discover life in other planets the way we understand it and the way it is expressed on our Earth. Life is everywhere and not only in environments known to us. I tell you, even the sun itself is full of life, and organized life at that. Don't you think it is rather egotistical to expect life to express itself always in the manner with which it is expressed on our planet? Just keep in mind that orthodox science has yet to explain or cope with such simple phenomena as fire-walking, telepathy or even clairvoyance. They are beginning to acknowledge them as phenomena but they can't explain them. And they still cannot understand how so-called UFOs travel with such high velocity and appear and disappear instantly. If orthodox science cannot do that, how can we assume that, because the conditions as we know them on Earth do not exist on Mars, therefore there is no life there?

'Ultimately, in our own evolution, we will also become liberated from the necessity of gross matter and of the natural environment on Earth as we know it. Gross matter will no longer be an obstacle to us. We wouldn't, for example, need oxygen so that we could breathe. We would be able to travel instantly into the very depths of the Earth and inside the sun, if you will, without being affected by the element of fire. By then we would have become masters over the elements. Therefore, when we travel to the other planets of our solar system and we search for life as we know it, we will never find it. Those intelligences are more advanced, they are masters of matter. They dress themselves with gross matter at will. They have a shape similar to ours, they are human beings who have passed through the Idea of Man and, yes, they do have organized societies.'

'If so, where are their cities and their buildings?' I asked in jest and everyone laughed.

'Do you now see the buildings and cities that exist within the psychonoetic dimension of our own planet? Since common people cannot perceive them on their own planet how do you expect to find them on other planets when the entities there are more advanced?'

'What I don't understand is this,' I said. 'Since they are liberated from the necessity of gross matter why do these intelligences need to be identified with a particular planet, such as Mars for example? Since after all they live on the psychonoetic planes of these planets?'

'Because apparently they are fulfilling a divine purpose and because it was on those planets that they had undergone their spiritual evolution.'

'If that is so,' I reasoned, 'then it follows that in the past on those planets they had undergone a gross material existence in a similar manner as on our planet: birth, death, rebirth, et cetera.'

'Right. But they no longer need a gross material existence. They transcended the necessity of gross matter. It no longer serves them.'

'What do these entities do now?' I asked.

'They are assisting those of us who are at lower levels of evolution. Pay attention, not every being within our solar system is on the same level of evolution. Those who are at higher levels help those below to evolve. And when every entity attains the stage of Theosis then our solar system will have no purpose to exist. It will, sooner or later, disintegrate. Note that not all planets of our solar system are at the same level of evolution. For example, the entities on Mars may be of the highest stage of development. They may be residing within the noetic counterpart of that planet. Consequently, they could travel anywhere within our solar system and even beyond it into other solar systems and galaxies. Those extraterrestrials who visit us may be, therefore, from other solar systems and they visit us in order to challenge us and help us evolve. They appear like flying saucers as a way of expressing themselves to us in a material form that we can understand. When they enter our system they gather matter from our planet and appear with the known human form characteristic of our planet.'

At my probing Daskalos revealed that he communicated telepathically with beings that reside on Mars. Although, he said, it was possible for him to visit them he had neither the desire nor the reason to do so.

'You can go there,' Daskalos went on, 'by travelling with incredible speed, using only the noetic body. It takes about an hour to arrive there, but you can return in fifteen minutes. Your body draws you back much more quickly. Only a master who has gone beyond the noetic world and entered into the world of meanings and ideas can visit other planets. As for myself, it is here on this Earth that I have been assigned to teach, and here will I come to teach again.'

'You may get a transfer,' Kostas cracked from his corner and the rest of us laughed heartily. Daskalos added that although he had never visited Mars, he coordinated himself with beings on that planet and learned a great deal about them.

'You mean to say these Martians are human beings like us?' I asked.

'They are human beings but they are not like us.'

'Do they have a gross material body?'

'Sometimes they do, but it is different from ours. The human beings that live on Mars are much superior to ourselves. They are masters of matter. They can materialize and dematerialize themselves at will. Their material body looks like two triangles, of the head and of the chest. The waist is very small and the hands and legs resemble ours. Their heart differs from ours and their blood is very thick and has the color of honey. Their body is not complex and even though they have a circulatory system, they have few arteries and veins. Our blood takes thirteen minutes to circulate. In the body of a Martian it takes an entire day. The deterioration of their body does not proceed at the same tempo as ours. The body of a Martian is more like a house to him. As an entity he gets in and out with as much ease as we enter and leave our homes. His body makes very few movements and he uses it as if it were his workshop. Martians are not bound to a place nor are they enchanted by it the way we are.

'When a Martian comes to Earth he leaves his body behind. His blood continues to circulate but the tenant is absent. When he arrives at the ionosphere of the Earth he creates, by thought, whatever he desires. The objects created often appear to us as flying saucers. If he decides to materialize on Earth, he assumes the shape of a human being, sometimes wearing clothes that seem to be an extension of his body. What creates this impression is the concentrated etheric energy. He may also appear dressed like us, wearing a suit for example. He can shape matter at will. He can absorb ideas and meanings by coordinating himself with the thought of humans on Earth and, through the power of visual imagery, he can materialize and look like them. He may then sit in a coffee shop, have a drink and speak the local language. Since he can coordinate himself with human thought, he can know whatever humans know.'

'If that is the case,' I said, 'then they must know what is happening on Earth.'

'They certainly do. Why do you think they visit us?'

'Do they have any influence over our planet?'

'They must so that we may not destroy it again. They have always visited our planet through the centuries and humans have seen them as angels or gods. I would say they are eternal beings like ourselves but on a higher stage of evolution. They have transcended the idea of Evil.'

'How is it that we have not discovered them as yet?'

'Who told you they are not in contact with a lot of us?'

'But Daskale,' I probed with some exasperation, 'the instruments the Americans sent to Mars showed no sign of life there.'

'They avoided the contact themselves. Do not forget that they are masters of materialization and dematerialization and they merely do not have a gross material body. They could have created with their minds the conditions that prevented the instruments of the Americans from recording any information. These beings will eventually make their existence known to a wider audience.

'Do you think it is easy to discuss these matters publicly? But I am telling you that I have come into contact with such beings; that I am now in contact with them; that they are my friends; that I know a lot of things about them and there is nothing I know that they do not know through coordination. Who is going to believe me? Who is going to accept what I say?'

Daskalos then narrated an experience he had had with such beings. The episode took place in 1969.

'I felt them coming. I was out of my body and I came near their spaceship which was roving over my house. The beings inside sent me a message urging me to return to my body because the spaceship could burn my etheric. When I returned I heard a neighbor, an old woman, screaming that the Turks were coming. She saw the spaceship, which looked like an expanding and contracting ball of light, and assumed that the Turks were attacking. I tried to calm her down and explained to her, in vain, that it was not the Turks but a UFO with beings from outer space. I went inside and then the UFO disappeared. They returned late that night. Two of them materialized in my house. They looked like men. They explained to me that they

132

could take on the characteristics of the beings of the planet. They wore silvery suits and it was hard to distinguish their outfits from their skin. When I touched them I felt as if I had touched a snake. We communicated by thought. They entered into my aura and at that moment they knew everything I knew. My late wife, who was present, offered them some baklava which she had just baked. They spat it out the moment they put it in their mouths. It was too bitter for them. There was too much earth in what we gave them, they said. They then demonstrated for us how they nourished themselves. We turned the lights off and they drew cosmic light that brightened the entire room. They were absorbing it into their bodies. Before leaving they told us that it was their wish not to make their existence known to the public as yet.'

'Do these extraterrestrial beings have families like us?'

'I believe so.'

I then asked whether they bore children like humans, and whether they reproduced themselves through sexual contact.

'This I do not know. They may reproduce themselves differently. They act through thought and attract one another through love. That is how they are born. In our case the reproductive process is the domain of the Holy Spirit without our conscious participation. These Martian entities, on the other hand, are masters of their bodies. They know and control whatever is happening to it.'

'Do they die?'

'No. They dissolve their bodies and create new ones. They are eternal gods. Of course we are gods, too. But they have reached the stage of Theosis. They are Logoi who live an archangelic existence of their own. They can, for example, descend to the center of the Earth and acquire the appearance of the angels of fire. They can also penetrate another element and assume the image of the idea of that element.'

'Since they are capable of such feats, why do they need a material body?'

'Perhaps because it may so please them. It appears, however, that only a few have or use a gross material body.'

The sun was getting ready to set when we dispersed. Kostas drove to Limassol, Theano and Chariklia left for Larnaca, Theophanis drove to Paphos and Aspasia volunteered to offer me a lift home. I preferred to walk, enjoy the afternoon breezes, the colors of the setting sun, and contemplate the discussion I just had with Daskalos.

I began walking towards Acropolis, the suburb adjacent to Strovolos where we had set up our home for the year. I passed through the English School with its spacious grounds covered with eucalyptus trees, one of the few places in Nicosia that remained unspoiled by surrounding vulgarities brought on by the bulldozer and enthusiastic and overzealous 'developers.' As I slowly crossed the fields the divinity of Christ, UFOs and extra-terrestrials kept spinning in my head. Daskalos never failed to shock me with fantastic stories. But even ideas that seemed totally absurd and unbelievable at first under the weight of subsequent experiences and exposures rendered themselves less absurd, forcing me to re-evaluate my original skepticism. Months later, when I returned to Maine, I was in the university bookstore browsing through the science section. There I came across a monograph, *Life Beyond Earth* (Morrow, 1980) written by two no-nonsense, conventionally established scientists. The authors, Gerald Feinberg, professor of theoretical physics at Columbia University, and Robert Shapiro, professor of bio-chemistry at the City University of New York, advanced the thesis that

> life may be quite common beyond Earth but that its forms and habitats will be incredibly different from those we are familiar with on our planet . . . the interior of stars, and the clouds of isolated molecules in the interstellar space may each have their characteristic life forms. Within our own solar system the surface of Titan and the interiors of the sun, Jupiter . . . are plausible locales for life. Even the Earth itself may harbor undiscovered *living beings* [emphasis added].

Experiences and coincidences of this type which I have had routinely since I met Daskalos and began focusing my attention on them, have mercilessly assaulted the foundations of my rational skepticism, undermining further my Doubting Thomas status. It became increasingly problematic for me not to take Daskalos seriously even when he spoke of close encounters with entities from other worlds and other dimensions.

CHAPTER 8

Guardian angels

Rumors spread that two yogis from India had come to Cyprus to explore the possibility of setting up a center in Cyprus. They planned to offer a series of lectures on 'Nirvana' in the home of one of Daskalos' students. Daskalos was preoccupied with patients the morning that Iacovos and I decided to contact the newcomers. 'Besides,' Daskalos cracked, 'I don't believe in Nirvana. But you go ahead. Who knows? You may learn something.'

One of the attractions of Daskalos' teachings for the more educated among his students was the absence of restrictions for exposing oneself to other doctrines and beliefs. 'We are not afraid of comparisons,' he was fond of saying. 'Use your reason to be Researchers of Truth,' he would urge his followers. This position was very compatible and highly accommodative to me as a participant observer. I could ask any question, however challenging, without fear that I might jeopardize my relationship with either Daskalos or his associates. I was also defined by them as a Researcher of Truth and as such I had the freedom and the right to pursue my research in any way suitable to my situation and needs.

The bearded, turbaned yogis wore long rose-colored robes and sat cross-legged, an unusual sight in Cyprus. One of them whose complexion was quite dark, appropriate to the stereo-typed image of an Indian yogi, kept his eyes closed most of the time, while his younger companion spoke of the virtues of vegetarianism, mantra yoga and Nirvana. His English was devoid of an Indian accent and his complexion was light for an oriental guru. It turned out that our Indian yogi was in fact a Jewish lad from Santa Barbara, California.

Iacovos was not impressed. When they began arguing that the practice of healing was contrary to the law of Karma he shook his head in disbelief. Their credibility lost further ground in his eyes when he discovered that they were incapable of leaving their bodies. He realized then that the gurus were amateurs and we left. We agreed to meet at Daskalos' in the afternoon.

When I reached his home he was teaching Iacovos Sanskrit. 'Iacovos,' Daskalos explained to me, 'will have to learn how to keep his notes in Sanskrit.'

'What is wrong with Greek?' I inquired.

'In the event that his notes fall into the wrong hands those who get them will not be able to decipher them,' Daskalos replied and showed me his notebook filled with calligraphic Sanskrit letters written in red ink. Other symbols, including an outline of the human body and its various chakras, was also included. The language used was Greek but written in Sanskrit characters. To decipher his secrets one had to master Greek as well as the Sanskrit alphabet.

'Besides,' Daskalos said, 'Sanskrit is a sacred language and Iacovos has to learn it so that he can construct talismans.' Then at Iacovos' request Daskalos proceeded to elaborate on the construction of amulets and talismans.

'We always make talismans,' Daskalos said, 'by using the six-pointed star. Never the five-pointed star.'

'Why not?'

'The five-pointed star is earthly and symbolizes the human body. But when it is turned upside down it symbolizes the devil. When someone comes to me struck by black sorcery and I coordinate myself with his aura I always notice inside him the five-pointed star turned upside down. Then, as you have seen me do before, I start the procedure with the candles and order the devil to come out and pass through the fire so that it may get dissolved within the holyspiritual condition. When the five-pointed star is black, it is very dangerous. It means that someone through sorcery is trying to kill the person. Dark brown implies an evil influence but not death. Putrid green is the product of envy. Perhaps someday science will come to grips with these issues. They may come to understand them as forms of radiation.

'In excommunication proceedings that clergymen carry out, you can notice a blue five-pointed star turned upside down. It encloses within it the religious superstitiousness and aggressiveness of so many priests. This type of star cannot have any effect. It is basically harmless.'

Daskalos then proceeded to demonstrate how to make up a talisman which is always constructed with the six-pointed star. The upper part of the triangle, Daskalos explained, symbolizes the divine part in us, the higher self, which is triadic. The three sides symbolize the power, love, and wisdom of the Absolute. The triangle facing down symbolizes the descent of the lower self into matter. It, too, is triadic and has a common center with the higher self.

Iacovos suggested that the best way to demonstrate how to construct a talisman was to make one for the family. Daskalos agreed and began assembling the necessary artifacts. They included a white paper, markers, a candle, a glass of water and the Unpointed Sword. Daskalos put on his white robe and sat in front of the table while Iacovos closed the windows, lighted the candle and burned some church incense. Daskalos began as Iacovos and I looked on. He pointed his hands upward and murmured a prayer. Then with a black marker and the Unpointed Sword he drew the six-pointed star. He then asked whether we were baptized as Christians. I nodded affirmatively. Then with a red marker he drew the sign of the cross inside the topmost corner of the six-pointed star. On the right side he drew the symbol of masculinity, on the opposite side the symbol of 'motherliness and harmony.' Daskalos then fixed his gaze on the flame and, as I had seen him do in earlier cases of exorcisms, he moved his palm left and right from a distance of two or three feet as if communicating with the flame. Then he drew a snake over the six-pointed star, the tail beginning at the top and the head at the lower end. Over it he drew a zigzag red line like lightning hitting the head of the snake. I learned that the snake symbolized evil elementals and lightning the fire of Archangel Michael. Then inside the star Daskalos wrote in Sanskrit the names of all four of us, Emily's, the two children's and mine. At the bottom of the star Daskalos wrote in Greek, but in Sanskrit characters, 'The Power of the Lord Upon Thy Servants: Love, Wisdom, Health, Well-being.' He folded the paper in a triangular shape several times until it acquired the size of no more than three inches. He then covered it carefully and tightly with a blue tape.

'Sew it inside a piece of blue cloth,' Daskalos instructed as he gave it to me, 'and put it in a safe place, preferably in a family shrine if you have one. Never step on it. Your protectors are the Logos, Virgin Mary and Archangel Michael. You can call on them in time of need, particularly the Virgin Mary. This is a very powerful talisman,' Daskalos said and I noticed a serious look in his face. Then he asked us to drink the water in the glass.

When Daskalos ended with the construction of the talisman he expressed a desire to 'burn' a few elementals that were tormenting a family he knew. Iacovos helped him out through concentration while Daskalos forced the elementals into the flame of the candle.

'There you go, burn, burn,' Daskalos exclaimed as he moved his hand around the fire as if to prevent some insect trying to escape from it.

'Enough for today,' he said after awhile. 'We burned three of them. We can burn some more tomorrow.'

When I asked Iacovos what he saw in the fire that was so fascinating he replied 'elementals in the form of little devils.' He claimed that he also saw inside the fire the man-size face of Archangel Michael.

'How could you see a man-size face inside a candle's flame?' I asked with incredulity.

'It was not with the material eyes that I saw,' Iacovos said, giggling. 'The "screen" opened up in front of me and I saw.' Iacovos' favorite metaphor for clairvoyant sight was the television tube. 'When I "see,"' he said, 'it is as if my ordinary vision recedes and a screen opens up in front of me.'

'Is there any other way that one can protect oneself from psychic dangers?' I asked Daskalos as he took off his white robe and Iacovos placed the Unpointed Sword back in the Sanctum.

'Many, depending from which religious tradition you come from,' Daskalos replied. Then he showed me how a Christian can find protection against intrusions from the outside by making the sign of the cross in a special way and mentally stating 'the great truths.'

'You put your three fingers together – Catholics put four – it does not matter. The three fingers symbolize the Holy Trinity and the triadic nature of the Absolute. You stand and say "For Thine is the Kingdom,"' Daskalos brought the three fingers of his right hand to his forehead, '"and the Power," you come down, pass the heart and stop at the genitals. That's where the power is and, by extension, the Solar Plexus. Then, saying "and the Glory," you come up and stop at the heart. Then you move up to the forehead again, saying "of the Father," the Absolute, "and of the Son" as you move down and stop at the heart. Saying "and the Holy Spirit," you come down again to the genitals, the seat of the Holy Spirit. You then return to the heart in the condition of time. "Now," at the present, "and ever," you move your fingers to either one of your shoulders, "and to the Ages," again coming to the heart, "of Ages," moving on to the other shoulder, then "Amen," as you move back to the heart. So the heart is the Glory and the Eternal Present. Let us repeat it.'

I followed Daskalos' movements, trying to learn this method of creating instant protection against the dangers lurking in the netherworld. Daskalos went on:

'For Thine is the Kingdom and the Power and the Glory, of the Father and of the Son and of the Holy Spirit, Now and Ever and to the Ages of Ages, Amen.'

'Do you say these words, Daskale,' I asked, 'whenever you find yourself in danger?'

'You should say these words all the time. I, for example, say them every morning when I wake up and every time I eat. I say these truths at night before I sleep and even in the psychic plane. The greatest talisman for a Christian is not a golden cross hanging from the neck with a chain, but to harmonize oneself with the power of the Absolute Cross. For the Hebrews it is the Six-Pointed Star.'

Our discussion was interrupted by a phone call. I walked up the steps and picked it up. A female voice that spoke in heavily accented and broken English wished to speak to Daskalos. He came to the phone and spoke briefly. He looked pleased as he smilingly shook his head. In an effort to be discreet I silenced my curiosity and did not try to find out more about the foreign woman. But Daskalos must have either sensed my curiosity or simply succumbed to his own great weakness to talk.

The person on the phone, he said, was a tall and good-looking Arab woman from Iraq who had spent some time in Greece. She had visited Daskalos two days ago complaining that her period hadn't stopped for the last eleven months.

She had visited many doctors who could not help her.

'Did you cure her?' I asked.

'Apparently yes. This is what she just told me on the phone.'

'How did you do it?'

'I asked her to sit comfortably on the chair and reassured her that she would be fine. I told her she was going to feel a vibration in her vagina. I placed my hands there . . . my etheric hands, Kyriaco, my etheric hands,' Daskalos rushed to clarify, laughing as he noticed my eyes widening.

'With my etheric hands I spread a layer of etheric matter and told her that she would have nothing to fear from this problem any more. You see, in this case not only did I apply etheric matter, but I also made a powerful suggestion for her cure. I told her to go to the bathroom and change. She thanked me and left. She has not seen any blood since then.'

When Daskalos ended his description an English woman, her right leg bundled up and limping, came in accompanied by a Greek friend. Daskalos seemed to be expecting the two women. He escorted them into the living-room and asked Iacovos and myself to leave them alone for a while. We went into the kitchen, made coffee and sat in the hallway waiting. In a while Daskalos opened the door and motioned for Iacovos to go in. In five minutes he returned, sat next to me and continued quietly drinking his coffee. As they were about to leave the English woman stopped and thanked Iacovos.

'What did you do?' I asked him inquisitively.

'He made her toes move,' Daskalos volunteered to answer. 'She could not use them before.'

Iacovos explained that he concentrated and covered her toes with white light and made a strong wish that she might begin to use them. 'It doesn't take long to do that,' Iacovos noted.

'Daskale,' I asked after the visitors left and we were sitting comfortably in the living-room, 'is there a different way of offering protection to a beloved person other than designing an amulet?'

'Of course there is,' Daskalos replied, 'by constructing and bringing to life a guardian angel. But before I tell you more about this, how about if Iacovos makes us some coffee? I am really thirsty for it. What do you say, Iacovo?'

'I'll do it only on one condition,' Iacovos replied with a half-serious tone in his voice. 'You will have to promise me that you will never again do any readings from coffee cups. I don't want my master to gain the reputation of a fortune teller.'

'Okay, sir,' Daskalos said mockingly in English, with a strong emphasis on the 'sir.' 'But I am only doing it for fun with my friends,' he added almost apologetically.

I had witnessed this rather pleasant pastime on several occasions but only during light moments when Daskalos relaxed with some of his close associates. Iacovos had explained to me earlier that there is a rational explanation for how a mystic or a psychic can look at the dried leftovers in a cup of Turkish coffee and 'see' the probabilities within the immediate future. The subconscious of the individual, he explained, is imprinted symbolically within the coffee-cup. One can read these symbols and draw inferences. Iacovos, however, was concerned with Daskalos' reputation. Just the other day he had turned away two women who knocked at Daskalos' door asking to have their 'fortunes' told. In Cyprus coffee-cup reading is reputed to be the practice of 'superstitious old women.' Based on my personal observations, however, I had noticed that many of these women who are considered to be 'specialists' in reading coffee-cups are exceptionally talented and intuitive in human relations. It appears to me that this popular practice in that part of the world is more a form of folk psychotherapy than mindless superstition.

'Now, how about telling us the way you go about creating guardian angels?' I asked Daskalos as Iacovos handed him his cup. 'Are you saying that humans are capable of constructing angels?' I went on, not knowing quite how seriously I should have taken Daskalos' earlier contention about guardian angels.

'What have we said before about angels?' Daskalos asked rhetorically, and proceeded to answer his question. 'They are projections of eternal archangelic entities, correct? Man too is an archangel. Therefore, he has the potential and, as a Researcher of Truth the right, to construct guardian angels for the protection of beloved ones.'

'I would very much like to know how it can be done,' I said, and noticed that Iacovos shared my desire to hear what Daskalos had to say on this topic.

'Every human being descending upon the Earth,' Daskalos began without much hesitation, 'is accompanied by a guardian angel given him by the Absolute.'

'If that is the case,' I interrupted, 'what's the point in creating one ourselves?'

'I will tell you,' Daskalos answered confidently. 'The guardian angel that each human being brings with him is attached to his aura and is in a semi-hypnotic state. It is part of a man's Karma and it does not always intervene. Do you follow me? Our purpose is to awaken this angel so that it becomes a protection for the person. We do that by creating an angel ourselves. It is simply additional protective energy, if you prefer to put it in these terms. Since we know how to create such an angel, why not do so? Suppose I wish to create a guardian angel to protect, let us say, an infant. I must first seclude myself in a room, place a stool in the middle, burn incense, and light a white candle. With powerful concentration I will then create an angel with my mind. It must always have the image of a young girl or a young boy of about sixteen which will have the features of the person we want protected. In the case of an infant you must envision its characteristics as a grown-up girl or boy. It is not always easy.'

'How do you manage this?' I wondered.

'Look at my grandson. He is now almost ten. It is not that difficult for me to envision him as a sixteen-year-old.'

'What if the visual imagery you construct is not accurate?'

'It does not matter. It will acquire the identical appearance by itself. The same procedure must be followed when the person for whom you construct the guardian angel is an elderly person. I will again create an angel in the image of the person as he must have looked at sixteen or seventeen. In case I do not know how the individual looked at that age, I will not construct the details on the face. It will automatically acquire the missing details. I will learn in fact how the old person looked at a younger age. You will experience these phenomena yourself through practice. The accuracy of your visualization is not so important as the amount of energy you charge it with. Occasionally, for example, you will create an angel who will be more handsome than the person himself. However, you can never make an angel look uglier than the person whom the angel will protect. Through coordination the angel will take up the image of the individual to be protected. When I created an angel for Iacovos,' Daskalos added playfully, 'I made him much more handsome than he is.'

142

'Really now,' Iacovos giggled.

'I construct the angel,' Daskalos went on in a serious tone, 'either in the image of a girl or a boy, depending on the gender of the person to be protected. I construct this angel in every detail. I coordinate myself and envision this angel dressed either in white, white-blue or rose colors.

'I try to envision this boy or girl, at first, seated like a statue on the stool I placed in the middle of the room. I construct the guardian angel in a manner analogous to the way a sculptor creates a statue. I build it with a material that appears like a plastic sac emanating light. I place the white candle next to me and take deep breaths. I continuously envision the angel-elemental with my thought and with every inhalation I charge it with additional energy. I do that for fifteen minutes the first day. The second day I follow the same procedure at the same time. For five minutes I concentrate on the elemental, preventing any other thoughts from entering my mind. During this period the angel-elemental must be envisioned as real and this practice must be continued for ten more days, always at the same time. On the seventh day the elemental begins to acquire substance. It comes to life and begins to move. I continue giving it energy and encouraging it to come to full life. On the tenth day I build it to its perfection and it can now talk to me and acquire its own separate existence. At that moment it is ready to receive my instructions. I then assign it its name which will be that of the person it will protect. It smiles. I then say to it, "You are coming down to life. You have within you holyspiritual power and you are coordinated with me. I want you now to coordinate yourself with the person I have asked you to protect and report to me whether or not you accept my request to protect him." At once the angel-elemental will close its eyes and will begin deep breathing. If the person is too heavily indebted with Karma, the elemental will open its eyes and will tell me, "Dissolve me. I do not accept." I will then dissolve it. It means that the nature of the person's situation and his Karma are such that no other power must interfere beyond the condition of his guardian angel that may exist in a hypnotic or semi-hypnotic state. Therefore, I must stop at once for the time being and try again later. If there are egotistical tendencies in my character, the elemental will not obey me. I must dissolve it at once.

'If, on the other hand, I notice that it begins to smile at me, it means that protection is possible. The elemental will tell me, "Yes, I accept. He will be my love." Then I will proceed to set up a covenant with that elemental. "Good," I will say. "You shall protect him. However, I do not allow you to interfere with his personality. I do not permit you to interfere with his character, his psychic and noetic bodies, because then you will be tampering with his Karma and his spiritual development. Your role will be purely protective against material dangers. You will also intervene to protect him on the psychonoetic level against external dangers." I am the one who suggests to the elemental what to do. Therefore, when the person from within himself, through his thoughts and sentiments, acquires an experience, the angel must not intervene. I will instruct the angel, however: "You must help the person in moments of confusion of thought and sentiments to see more clearly and make his own decisions. You must never intervene dictatorially over the life of that person."'

'Daskale,' I probed, 'are there any dangers in creating such guardian-angel elementals?'

'Certainly. I must warn you that when an angel is created for the protection of a beloved person extreme caution is required. That angel will absorb from the quality and attributes of your own character elements which can have disastrous effects on the beloved person. The danger will exist that if there is the seed of egotism in the character of the mystic the elemental he created can gradually take control of the person. We must be very careful that when we build such an elemental we are completely at peace with ourselves and that we are not vibrating with feelings of jealousy and egotism. Otherwise the angel will be transformed into a destructive demon.

'The elemental must protect and not interfere with the character of the person who must follow his path in accordance with his Karma and the suggestions of his own God-given angel. To prevent the elemental from intervening with the character of the person, you should periodically bring the angel to you in order to inform you about its actions and to cleanse it from any accumulated egotism. In addition, after a certain period of time you must dissolve it completely. A new one can then be created. I am sad to say that a few Researchers of Truth have created, instead of angels, demons.'

'In what way, Daskale,' I asked, 'can a Researcher of Truth create destructive demons?'

'Through the imposition of his will on another person. Sometimes beloved ones will abandon the path that you consider the right one. It is possible that Karma will send them on that road to acquire certain experiences. You must not egotistically impose on them what you consider to be good. Do not assume that you have the right, once you have learned the way to project such elementals, to restrict the manner of thought and actions of a fellow human being. The construction of guardian angels is permitted only for the purpose of protecting loved ones, never for personal reasons.

'During the Middle Ages,' Daskalos went on to say, 'black sorcerers tried to create humanoid robots for their personal use. But the only thing they managed to attain was to create something which they would semi-materialize.'

'You mean it is possible for mystics to create elementals that can be materialized and behave as if they were living beings?'

'Yes, but it is a curse. We do not have this right. As Researchers of Truth we must never project and materialize elementals for any other purpose than psychotherapy, for purposes of helping our fellow human beings.'

Before the night was over I became a witness to another healing session. A half-paralyzed young man was brought in by his relatives. Daskalos asked us to remove every object from the long table in the living-room and Iacovos brought a mattress to spread over it. The young man was laid flat on the table. Daskalos, with the help of Iacovos, began stroking his spine. The treatment lasted for about twenty-five minutes. After it was over Daskalos instructed his visitors to bring the patient back in two weeks. Apparently this was not the first time that he had been treated.

'The young fellow had a car accident,' Daskalos explained later. 'His spinal cord was so crushed that when they brought me a picture of him and I felt his vibrations I suggested that he would be better off dead. Through a foreign embassy they took him to Eastern Europe for treatment. Nothing could be done for him. In fact his condition worsened. He has a strong faith that I can help him recover. I do what I can. But it will take a long time before and if he recovers.

'Karma,' Daskalos went on and shook his head, 'works in

such mysterious ways. That young man was the leader of a hostile tribe during one of my Aztec incarnations. He once seriously wounded me with an arrow right near the genitals. Now Karma has brought him to me for therapy. The day he saw me, he said, "You know, I have a feeling we have met before."'

When I visited Daskalos the following afternoon he was playing a Beethoven sonata on the piano while Iacovos and Kostas listened. The brand new piano was Daskalos' dearest possession. He had bartered for it recently with four of his paintings. He stopped playing and complained that his fingers were not as agile as during his youth. 'This has been a tiring day,' Daskalos murmured, as he sank into his armchair. 'More than thirty people have visited me in different groups, and they have exhausted me.'

Kostas sensed my reservation over what I thought a rather exaggerated claim and rushed to clarify that not only the living but also the dead come to Daskalos. 'Unless you are careful,' he told me once, 'it is easy sometimes to become forgetful and confuse the various levels of consciousness because they are so very much alike.'

'I'd like to know more about your dead visitors,' I asked Daskalos and he went on to tell me under what circumstances contact with the dead is permissible.

'There has to be a serious reason for bringing the living into contact with the dead.' The departed, Daskalos claimed, must not be distracted from their activities. Quite often, he went on to elaborate, it is the departed who seek the contact. He then proceeded to narrate a case.

'A man who had just died came to me. He wanted to speak to his wife and asked me to be the intermediary through which to convey his message. He was rich and married to a woman from a poor family. While he was still alive his wife started an affair with his chauffeur, his godson. He learned of the liaison after his death. His wife, dressed in black, mourned him in church and periodically placed flowers on his grave. In the meantime she carried on the affair with the godson.

'I decided to assist him fulfill his desire since I realized it was not easy for him to find rest and move higher into the psychic planes. He implored me that I should say exactly what he wanted her to hear without any interference on my part. I gave my word to him. I then contacted his wife who came along with her lover. The dead man addressed her through me. I was very embarrassed to hear the words that came out of my mouth. "You slut, you whore," he shouted. "I picked you up from the gutter and made you a lady and you betrayed me with my own godson." "Listen," the woman replied. "Try to understand. It is you I love but I like him better. He can satisfy me, you could not." She began to see her dead husband on her own and it was no longer necessary for me to be the channel. The godson kneeled down and started to cry, asking forgiveness from his godfather. He could not see the dead man, however. After this encounter the dead husband found rest and they went on having their affair.

'Here is another case,' Daskalos continued after a few minutes. 'Many years ago a dead father contacted me and implored me to save his son who was about to commit suicide. The father died when his son was six years old. It was the dead father who directed me to his son's home. I got on my motorcycle . . . '

'On a motorcycle? I can't imagine you riding a motorcycle,' Kostas exclaimed and shook his head laughing.

'I got on my motorcycle,' Daskalos went on, 'and rode to Trachonas [a section of the old Nicosia inside the Venetian Walls]. Following the instructions of the father, I rode straight to his house. I pushed the door in and found him sitting by the table writing a letter. "What you have in mind to do is stupid," I shouted at him. He looked aghast. "Who are you?" he mumbled. "Your father sent me to bring you back to your senses. He asked me to take the pistol you have under your pillow and throw it into the outhouse." "But mister . . . " he began to say. I took the pistol, went outside and threw it into the cesspool. He asked me not to leave him alone because he was afraid. He was not in a position to control himself. I asked him to mount his bicycle and follow me to my house. With our help he overcame his problem, got married and he now has two children. His dead father saved his life.'

Daskalos claimed that when you can 'see' it is possible to contact the dead. He personally is in continuous communication with his late wife. 'She even tells me that I should urge my younger daughter to quit smoking. But I just can't order her to do that. My wife does not realize that times have changed. It is not easy to make her understand. She sometimes visits Rea [the younger daughter], causing her great nervousness.'

'Daskale,' I asked after a break of several minutes, 'it is very difficult for me to understand how you can handle so many cases each day simultaneously, as you claim.'

'When you develop your superconscious self-awareness you will be able to understand. For the time being do not torment your brains. There are no words that I can use to make you understand.' Daskalos' words echoed Kostas' constant complaint that his basic frustration in life is that he cannot convey with words to his students his own experiences. 'Language is such a poor vehicle of understanding,' he would often say.

'To give you a faint idea,' Daskalos went on, 'I build powerful therapeutic elementals and direct them towards the persons in need of help. I let the elementals work by themselves. It is as if I am there. When the elementals need extension of life they come to me, draw new energy, and report on the patient's condition. It is like receiving a communiqué,' Daskalos said, laughing.

'I suppose when you say you build powerful therapeutic elementals for healing purposes it is equivalent or similar to the construction of guardian angels,' I said.

'Very true. And I should add that sometimes you may have to create such angelic elementals that may act more like policemen than angels.'

'What do you mean?'

'Let me tell you of a case I handled not long ago and then you will see what I mean,' Daskalos replied and proceeded to narrate his story.

'One day a villager named Maritsa came to me in great fear. "Mister Spyro," she pleaded, "our priest accused me of being crazy. He said I should go and see a doctor. I am not mad, my dear Mister Spyro." Her daughter had been engaged for six years but her fiancé refused to marry her. He died in a car accident in Morphou. "My dear Mister Spyro," she said, "he is not dead. He comes to her. I saw him with my own eyes in the yard. He slams the doors and doesn't talk. I am telling you he is screwing my daughter. She is possessed. I can hear her breathe and moan when he is with her. When I told the priest that I would come to see you he warned me that I would be damned."

'One evening at ten o'clock a car arrived with three persons inside. It was Maritsa again, with tears in her eyes. "My dear Mister Spyro," she said, "he did the act again. He was so mean. When he saw me he took a nail from the wall, one we use to hang photographs, and drove it into my hand." I looked at her hand and noticed that it was bleeding. I urged her to go to the hospital immediately and have a tetanus shot. I accompanied them to the hospital and later followed them to their house. The girl was nowhere to be found. Later we heard her screams. She was inside their water well. To our amazement, she was dry. I was never able to explain why. The girl told us that her dead fiancé grabbed her by the hair and threw her into the well in order to take her with him. She cried and begged that she wanted to live. That evening I stayed with them. I was sitting on a chair half asleep when I heard a crack on the window. That son-of-a-gun was semi-materialized.'

'Does that mean that anybody could have seen him?' I asked.

'I know that I saw him. I am not sure about others. When I noticed him entering the house, I asked, "Eh . . . mister, where do you think you are going? Come and sit here next to me." "Why should I? Who are you?" "Come and sit here," I ordered him and raised my voice. "Are you trying to force me to sit there?" he asked, and turned around ready to leave. "No, you are not leaving," I commanded. "You mean you are not letting me go?" he replied. "No," I said, "I will not let you go. What do you want from this woman?" "She was mine for six years," he replied. "Do you realize," I said, "that you go contrary to the Will of God? You must follow your own path and leave this girl in peace."

'He refused to listen to what I was saying so I had to resort to a different method. The invisible helpers taught me to handle such situations. I immediately created two elementals, one on his right and one on his left. I assigned them the task of escorting this man to the psychic plane where he should have gone in the first place. I constructed these elementals in the image of two handsome angels. He saw them, however, dressed like policemen. "Eh . . . mister," he said, "who are these cops you have sent here?" I told him that if he was good when they were with him they would not harm him. In two weeks' time these angelic elementals reported to me that he had found relatives and beloved persons in the psychic worlds where he was now living in peace. His fiancée was then able to live a normal life again.'

A few days later I had the opportunity to witness the effects of Daskalos' intervention on a forty-five-year-old woman who was becoming, according to the psychiatric lexicon, schizophrenic. Daskalos diagnosed it as a case of black sorcery.

I was personally involved with this episode because Stella, the woman who was going mad, was an old acquaintance. It was through me that the contact with Daskalos was made. Stella was married to a successful businessman. After the 1974 invasion of Cyprus by Turkey the couple, including their three sons, moved to Athens. Her husband started a new business there while at the same time they maintained their household and businesses in Cyprus. Meanwhile Stella and her family made frequent visits to the island and planned to return permanently as soon as their sons completed their university education. They were quite wealthy by any standard.

Stella complained to me, during a visit to the island, that for the last fifteen days she had been hearing a voice coming from within her that incited her to quarrel and fight with her husband and sons. Each time the family was together she had a strong desire to attack them. She could not resist the power of this voice. Life in the family became a nightmare and she was afraid that her marriage would collapse. She visited several psychiatrists and their diagnosis was that there was nothing wrong with her. Yet the voice was persistent.

'I would start a fight,' she told me, 'for no apparent reason. But I am fine when away from my family. I have terrible headaches and pains in my stomach, in my bile and in my intestines. These symptoms have been confirmed by my physician. I feel I am going crazy. Someone within me tells me that I am not going to live long enough to enjoy my children. Last night I felt something in my stomach like a bird that was moving up and down. I could even grasp it with my hand.'

Stella mentioned that the thought had occurred to her that someone might be practicing black magic on her because she had repeatedly found strange objects in her yard. A few days before she had found a white veil tied with white ribbons and pinned on it there were paper flowers like the marigolds people used to make wreaths for funerals. Another day she had found on her doorstep a plastic bag with a liver in it. The liver was pinned with a needle and inside the bag there was a piece of blue cloth cut in the shape of a forehead, just like the halo painted on icons over the heads of saints. Only the previous day, she told me, she had found another plastic bag with chicken livers tied with a blue ribbon. She kept the bag in order to take it to Daskalos. Stella's house was only two miles from his and she knew of Daskalos' reputation as a specialist in the occult. Yet she was not aware that he dealt with questions concerning black magic. It was after my sister's advice that she decided to seek his help.

I drove with her to Strovolos the very day I was informed of her problem. We first went by her house and got the chicken livers. On the way Stella, while driving her Mercedes, further explained the situation. Her husband was a non-believer, but he did not object to her visiting Daskalos since the situation in the family had reached breaking-point. She had found out from her husband that a few years previously, when their house was under construction, he used to find a variety of strange objects that he had destroyed without mentioning anything to her. He used to find in the foundations of the building such objects as bars of soap with, presumably, Stella's hair pinned on them.

Daskalos greeted us in his usual friendly manner. He was in the yard watering his plants.

'Daskale,' I said, 'I have brought you a customer,' and introduced Stella. 'Look, I even brought you some chicken livers,' and raised my hand so that Daskalos could see what I was holding.

'Oh . . . that looks bad,' he murmured and shook his head. 'Leave them out there and I'll take care of them later. Come on inside,' and he waved us to follow.

Stella explained her problem. Daskalos then took a piece of paper and a pencil and asked her to spell the names of all the members of her family including her own. He wrote them down in Sanskrit characters.

'You have been hit very badly,' he said. 'Someone cast black magic on you and your husband but not on your children. You have been hit in the stomach, the chest and the head. They are not devils but elementals which actually inflict the same damage. These Lebanese sorcerers,' Daskalos turned to me, 'are creating so many problems for us.'

Daskalos had mentioned to me earlier that since the start of the Lebanese civil war magic had begun flourishing in Cyprus. With the influx of thousands of Lebanese to the island there were among them several 'powerful' sorcerers who made a living by practicing their black art.

Daskalos asked Stella whether she suspected anybody but before she had a chance to reply he quickly pointed out that it was immaterial to find out who the culprit was. What was important, he said, was that she should eliminate any traces of hatred against that person. He urged her to reach a reconciliation with whomever she suspected. He then reassured Stella that she had nothing to worry about from then on and that he was going to start working on her problem right away.

'Go downtown now and fetch me seven white candles, some incense and charcoal. Tonight it will be full Moon and it will be easy.'

I felt that it would be inappropriate, at that moment, to inquire about the meaning of the seven white candles and the full Moon. Instead I drove with Stella downtown in search of a shop that could provide us with what Daskalos ordered. Iacovos explained to me later that the seven candles were used for the seven major sacred discs or chakras of the individual, one candle per chakra. He said that black sorcery is directed against the chakras of a person. Spirits or elementals take possession of the person's sacred discs and, through them, assault the psychic and gross material body of the individual. A clairvoyant can see the elementals or spirits glued on the chakras of the person. Under such circumstances exorcism is facilitated when the psychic body of the Moon touches the psychic body of the Earth, that is during full Moon. Entities that reside on the psychic body of the Moon can then assist in the process.

Upon our return we found Iacovos waiting for us. Daskalos asked him to take the seven candles to the Sanctum. He then asked Stella to wear a cross.

'A small crucifix pinned inside your clothes will do,' he said. 'From now on you have nothing to fear.' She thanked Daskalos and we left.

I visited Stella in her luxurious home three days after the encounter with Daskalos. Her mother opened the door for me and guided me to the living-room where Stella was sitting comfortably in an armchair. She was wearing a long white dress and hanging from her neck was an oversized crucifix. She was all smiles.

'You remind me of the Archbishop,' I chuckled as I pointed at the huge cross. Then Stella explained to me that she had not heard the voice since the meeting with Daskalos. Her relationship with her husband also had improved. On the second day after her meeting with Daskalos there was yet another sign of black magic in her yard, a three of spades pierced with needles and dirt presumably picked up from a cemetery. However, she was not disturbed physically or psychically. Stella planned to return to Athens in a few days and was concerned that her problem might begin again since she would be so far away. I reassured her that, on the basis of Daskalos' teachings, distance is of no consequence.

The last I heard of Stella was when she called me up from Miami Beach where she was vacationing with her husband. I was by then back in the United States. She informed me that she had not been afflicted with her problem since her encounter with Daskalos. But when her older son was about to get married, he suffered, on the eve of his wedding day, from an excruciating headache that doctors could not explain or do anything about. Stella suspected black magic again and visited Daskalos. His intervention worked once more and her son found immediate relief. The headache never returned.

I have witnessed Daskalos handling cases diagnosed as black sorcery on several occasions. The method he used and the procedure he followed in the exorcism varied in accordance with the nature of the case.

One day I was chatting with Daskalos and Kostas when a distressed-looking woman in her late thirties stepped into the house asking for Daskalos' help. She suspected that someone had applied black magic on her husband because his actions were bizarre and aggressive. Daskalos confirmed that indeed the case was one of black sorcery.

'You and your husband,' he said, 'have been hit six times. Someone is trying to separate you.' The woman began crying and said that she had been feeling it all along. She revealed that for the last month she had been finding strange objects in her yard. She burned everything she found. Daskalos commented that what she did was not very wise and that she should have brought those objects to him. Then he asked her to give him whatever object she had with her that belonged to her husband, such as a photograph. He also asked her whether she had a handkerchief. The visitor very nervous and with a trembling hand she searched in her purse and took out the objects Daskalos asked for.

'I want you,' he said, 'to take a deep breath and exhale right into the handkerchief.' After she complied with his instructions, Daskalos took a piece of white paper and wrote in Sanskrit her name and those of her husband and children. He then placed the handkerchief on the paper and folded them together in the form of a triangle.

'Now you can go home and everything will be fine. We shall dissolve the spell.' The woman sighed, thanked Daskalos and left. When she was out of the house Daskalos whispered that he 'saw' that her husband had had an affair with another woman some time ago. When he terminated the relationship, his ex-mistress wished to get revenge on him and employed the services of a black sorcerer.

Half an hour had passed since the woman left. Daskalos continued chatting with Kostas and myself. Suddenly he stopped. 'That woman is really suffering,' he said. 'We should proceed with the exorcism right away.' Kostas assembled the necessary paraphernalia. He filled a glass of water, lighted a white candle, got a piece of white paper and markers, and fetched the Unpointed Sword from the Sanctum.

Daskalos put on his white robe and sat in front of the table. He made a short prayer and then took a black marker. By using the Unpointed Sword as a ruler, he drew a six-pointed star. At each one of its corners he inscribed the sign of the cross, using a brown marker. He also drew inside the star certain symbols the meaning of which I could not understand. Kostas then handed him a green marker and Daskalos drew over the six-pointed star six snakes, presumably symbolizing the evil elementals bequeathed by the black sorcerer. Then with a red marker he drew over each one of the snakes a zig-zag line symbolizing lightning and fire. At that point he asked Kostas to begin chanting a certain mantra while concentrating on the flame. Daskalos pointed his palms upward and murmured a certain prayer. He then moved his hands near and around the flame as if to seize it with his palms. Then he opened them over the markings.

'She is crying now,' Daskalos said in a low voice to inform us of the current psychological state of the patient. After he finished working with the flame he placed the handkerchief of the woman over the paper with the markings. He folded them together in the form of a triangle and then placed the edge of the packet over the flame. Kostas took it outside in a container to burn.

'They will be fine now,' Daskalos said confidently and took his robe off. 'Someday,' he said, 'you will be able to understand the meaning of what I have been doing.'

CHAPTER 9

The Initiation of the mystic

'So you claim you have spent ten years in London studying mysticism. Tell me, have you learned how to leave your body?' Daskalos asked his visitor with a piercing look.

'No,' Stephanos replied softly.

'Can you diagnose an illness by examining the etheric-double of a person?'

'No.'

'Can you at least heal a wound with your thought?'

'No,' said Stephanos as Daskalos threw his hands up feigning exasperation.

'What in the world have you learned all these years in London?' Daskalos added, and in his voice there was a mixture of despondency and irony. 'What a pity. You have wasted ten precious years of your life.'

I was taken aback by Daskalos' aggressive disposition as he continued to roast Stephanos whose only crime was his desire to meet him and explore the possibility of joining his circles. Theophanis, Daskalos' close friend and associate, who was present, seemed undisturbed by what appeared to me an unnecessary and unjustifiable attack on my friend. I was ready to come to Stephanos' defense and point out to Daskalos that his attitude made no sense to me. I wished to indicate that his stand was contrary to his teachings. Had it not been for Stephanos' ten-year quest in London, he would not have been in a position to discuss the possibility of joining his circles. But then it dawned on me that perhaps Daskalos was testing Stephanos for some reason that I failed to comprehend. Stephanos, I noticed, was sitting quietly and stoically listening to Daskalos' provocative language. He maintained his serene composure and with a mild tone tried to defend himself.

He was a forty-five-year-old man, a teacher of 'practical philosophy,' a spiritual organization having its central offices in

London. The teachings of this group were based on the works of Gurdjieff, Ouspensky and a Hindu master. Stephanos learned of my research and inquired whether it would be possible to arrange a meeting with Daskalos. He confided in me that he had reached a deadlock in his spiritual path and that he felt the need for a master to guide him. He suspected that Daskalos might be this master, even though he had never met him. Stephanos had spent twenty years in London where he received his university education. He had then made sufficient money to permit him an early and modest retirement in his native Cyprus. Transcendental matters were his central preoccupation. During the last ten years of his stay in England he had devoted most of his time to moving from one spiritual circle to another in search of answers to his existential problems.

The circles for 'practical philosophy' had no direct link with Daskalos' groups. It was not until I began my research that I discovered the existence of such circles thriving in Cyprus with membership drawn as a rule from the more educated urban classes.

Daskalos continued his aggressive interrogation of Stephanos for more than half an hour. It was clear to me by then that Daskalos was staging a theatrical act and for this reason I had to accept what he was saying, tongue in cheek.

'What do you say, Theophani?' Daskalos said abruptly as he turned towards his old friend who had been sitting quietly without saying a word during the entire encounter. 'Should we accept him in our circles?'

'I guess so,' Theophanis, who seemed unprepared for Daskalos' question, replied with a shrug of his shoulders.

'You are accepted in our circles, with our love, as a brother,' Daskalos said softly and with a smile as he addressed his visitor. Stephanos looked pleased. The grilling he had undergone apparently had had no effect on his readiness to become Daskalos' disciple, even though it had caused his face to flush several times. I had the impression that Daskalos' forcefulness towards Stephanos had somehow established the master's legitimacy in the eyes of his prospective disciple. It appeared as if Stephanos were undergoing an initiation rite before he was to be fully accepted as a brother.

My friend indicated that he was prepared to withdraw from

157

the other circles if need be. Daskalos, however, advised him to maintain his position so that he could be of service to others. 'You are doing important work there,' Daskalos added with seriousness. What a change, I thought. Only a little while before he had announced in categorical terms that Stephanos' ten-year spiritual odyssey in London had been a waste of time. He now became fully supportive and accepting of Stephanos. So much did Daskalos appreciate Stephanos that he invited him to join us the following day when he planned to discuss with Iacovos and me the issue of the initiation of the mystic to the four elements. It was a topic for 'advanced' students.

I asked my friend later on what he thought of Daskalos. 'Why,' I asked, 'did you maintain that serene look in the face of so much provocation?'

'I knew,' he replied with confidence, 'that he was testing me. He wanted to see how I would react, how my ego would respond.' He then went on to say that on the basis of his studies and experiences he knew that masters as a general rule behave in a similar manner when they first encounter a serious prospective disciple. Was that the reason, I wondered, why Daskalos made me feel so uncomfortable when I first asked to become one of his students and write a book about him?

After the encounter my friend had no doubts of Daskalos' authenticity. 'It does not matter,' he stated, 'that Daskalos may have some rough spots as a personality. When you have only one pipe which can provide you with water it is of no importance whether the pipe is a little rusty.' 'What a metaphor to characterize him,' I marveled, and we both burst into laughter.

At ten o'clock the following morning we set off for Strovolos. We had to wait in Daskalos' small hall for about half an hour until his visitors left. Unlike professional therapists, he did not work through appointments. Whoever needed his services simply went to him, even at odd hours of the day and night. Visitors often had to come repeatedly until they found him home. He kept his telephone number unlisted so that he could be spared constant phone interruptions. Yet I do not recall a time when I was at his place that he did not receive several phone calls from all over the island and from Greece.

We entered the living-room after the visitors departed. Iacovos was with Daskalos. I assumed he had assisted him with the therapy just completed. I volunteered to make four cups of coffee before we started our conversation. I then checked my tape recorder to make sure it was working. Daskalos made himself comfortable in his armchair and began the lesson on the initiation of the mystic to the four elements. First he elaborated on the nature of the four elements, the material with which the universes are made. The goal of the mystic, he said repeatedly, is to attain mastery over the elements. It presupposes the overcoming of one's enchantment with them. It is a process that can take centuries, or thousands of years.

'On the gross material plane,' Daskalos began, as Stephanos, Iacovos and I listened attentively, 'we can observe the existence of four elements: earth, water, fire and ether. The aim of the mystic is to become initiated into these elements, that is, to master them. It is not accidental that God was called by the Hebrews Yahweh or Jehovah. In ancient Hebrew the word Yahweh was a derivative of the initials of the four elements. God Jehovah was perceived by the ancient Hebrew mystics as the master of the four elements.

'The cross,' Daskalos went on as he drew the sign of the cross on a piece of paper lying in front of him, 'symbolizes the four elements. From the center upwards it is ether. The horizontal lines represent water and fire respectively, two elements close to each other. The down part of the cross symbolizes the material plane, earth. All four meet at a central point. The cross signifies the synthesis and balance of the four elements and for this reason it is a great symbol within Creation.'

Responding to my question, Daskalos claimed that it was not accidental that Christ was crucified. The cross is the symbol of the pan-universal Logos, the master of the elements.

'The cross was a symbol of many ancient civilizations including the Aztecs, Incas and Egyptians. In these civilizations they had the symbol of the cross as motion, that is the swastika, which was corrupted by the Nazis when they used it as their party emblem. The swastika symbolizes destruction and dissolution. When the projections are pointed in the opposite direction, it is a sacred symbol of creation. It means right motion through the balancing of the elements. Whatever exists within creation, the worlds of forms, implies movement, balance, dissolution and recomposition.

'The four elements can be classified into two general categories, the active, generating energy, and the acted upon. The active elements are fire and ether and the acted upon, earth and water. On a higher level both earth and water are fire.'

'In what way?' I interrupted.

'If you split an atom of earth, what will you get? Fire. If you split an atom of hydrogen, namely water, what will you get? Again, fire. Do you follow me?'

'What is it,' I probed further, 'that provides the characteristics of the four elements?'

'It is the frequency of vibrations and nothing else. Let us assume, for the sake of illustration, that the frequency of vibrations one to ten is the element earth, ten to twenty, water, and from twenty to thirty, fire. Beyond that there are the vibrations of ether. I cannot put any limits there.

'Earth and water can be seen with the naked eye. The vibrations of the active elements as energy are invisible. They cannot be seen but can be felt. For example, you feel the air only when there is movement. Take a piece of paper, move it in front of your face, and you will feel the air.'

'Can you feel the ether?' Stephanos inquired.

'Of course. Later on when you advance with the exercises, not only will you be able to feel it, but you may reach the point when you will be able to solidify it.'

'What is beyond the four elements?' Stephanos asked.

'Mind as supersubstance. It is the source, the womb from which all the other elements spring. It is there that we will find the laws, the causes, and ideas that underlie all Creation. The Researcher of Truth will enter there after he exhausts all the necessary experiences he can have over the four elements.'

'When you say Mind, do you imply God?' Stephanos probed.

'No. Let us not confuse the Creator with the substance with which the phenomenal world is constructed.'

'What, then, is God? I mean how do you perceive God?' Stephanos persisted.

'The moment you create in your mind an image of God, that image is not God but fantasy. The only thing you can do is to accept that God is an expression of total wisdom, goodness and power. I understand God as Life and Love. Beyond that we can say nothing of God. We will know God only when we become gods ourselves, in Theosis.' Daskalos then resumed the discussion on the four elements.

'The material world is composed of the four elements in different combinations and syntheses. Examine for example a seed of an eucalyptus tree. That tiny seed encapsulates within it certain possibilities and probabilities. It will become a tall tree when the appropriate composition and synthesis of sunshine, water, earth and air are present. When the tree dies the element of water will begin to evaporate. There will remain primarily the elements of earth and fire. The tree, as dead wood, has within it the vibrations of fire that can bring about the phenomenon of heat and combustion. Heat itself is not an element, but the effect of the element of fire, which, like all the elements, is a vibration within the void. Heat is generated when something or someone vibrates at a certain frequency. At higher levels of vibrations of the element of fire the object will get increasingly heated. At a certain point ignition will take place which means there will be a dissolution of the elements. At that critical point the substances subjected to the vibrations of fire will not tolerate the generated heat. Some objects can absorb only low levels of the vibrations of fire before ignition will result. For example, dried wood can easily get ignited because the proportion of the element of water is very low whereas the harnessed element of fire is very high. An object made of earth, water and little fire, such as iron and other metals, will need high levels of vibrations before the critical point is reached for its dissolution. On the other hand, for substances such as wood, olive oil, and gasoline, the ignition point is very low. In reality gasoline is liquid fire, just like oil. We find in these substances the element of water, very high levels of fire and little earth. These examples that I have given you suggest that whatever exists in nature is composed of the four elements in varying proportions. These are physical laws that a mystic must observe and study.

'Try to understand that the four elements do not represent dead matter. The universe within which we live is not a dead machine of atoms hitting atoms. It is for this reason that the ancient mystics and the church fathers gave names to the intelligences that govern these elements. They called the lords of fire the Michael and gave names like Gabriel, Rafael and

Ouriel for the other elements.'

'Why was it necessary to give them such anthropomorphic names?' I asked.

'Perhaps in order to emphasize that in reality these elements are intelligent entities. They are not blind, lifeless laws. It is intelligence that keeps nature in balance. Some day when you advance as masters you will be able to verify this principle with your own experience.'

I was getting ready to ask about the nature of such experiences, particularly Daskalos' own, but Stephanos fired his own question.

'Do the four elements exist only on the gross material plane?'

'No. They are pan-universal. They exist in all the planes of reality, in the gross material, psychic, lower noetic and higher noetic. In each of the universes one of the four elements is predominant but it encompasses the other three. In the gross material universe there exist all the elements in different combinations, but it is the earth element that is dominant. In the psychic world the dominant element is water. Similarly, within the lower noetic world, the dominant element is fire and in the higher noetic, ether. It is for this reason that we call thought forms "elementals." They are made up of the four elements.'

'I find it difficult,' I remarked, 'to imagine in what way the earth element is present in the other dimensions.'

'I will explain. The four elements within the psychic world have different properties than the ones on the gross material level. There is, however, a common point. When you find yourself within the psychic world you perceive yourself as if you are walking on solid ground. The vibrations, however, of the earth element in those worlds are very different. You move about within the psychic planes and subplanes, walk, touch furniture. In short you carry within you the sensation of solids, of earth. This is how we notice this element in the psychic world. Even though the earth element in the psychic world is very different from that of the gross material, the two dimensions share a common point of convergence, that is, the conception of earth, of solids.

'In a similar manner we can observe the other elements within the psychic world. The element of fire, for example, is a vibration widely dispersed within the void. It is the dominant element within the lower noetic world. In the psychic world, fire, in combination with water, makes possible various types of sentiments such as anger, aggressiveness, jealousy. You may ask what proof do we have that such sentiments are related to fire and water? We can observe the results of such sentiments on the elements that make up the material body. Under the spell of severe anger we say that one's blood is "boiling." Anger results in raising our body temperature, which is a manifestation of the element of fire. At the same time, our hearts begin to pulsate violently and our blood circulates faster, a manifestation of the element of water. Fire also makes possible the phenomenon of spontaneity which is a form of creative energy.

'Let us now examine fire within the lower noetic world. Sit down, think and concentrate. What do you think will happen? The temperature of your body will rise. Thought is a combination of fire and light. The element of fire in the noetic world enables us to reason and concentrate. Just like the sun can dry up a swamp in the material world, thought, as the expression of an inner sun-fire, can neutralize thoughts destructive to oneself and to others.

'Thought means fire and ether. When I say "thought" I do not only mean the creation of noetic images, but also the knowledge of meanings, of conditions, of ideas and phenomena of ecstasy. All these are expressions of ether and fire that have an effect on the human body.

'As Researchers of Truth we must examine the elements and ascertain their power and value and the manner in which they can be utilized creatively. We must also be aware of the damage they can cause and try to avoid it. For example, a certain combination of the elements of water and fire in the noetic and psychic worlds generates the phenomenon of egotism and narcissism. We must study, analyze and know such situations. And through knowledge we will be able to transform the energy of these elements into something productive and beautiful. All the elements within the world of opposites provide two situations: creation and dissolution. The rays of the sun offer us life and health. They can also cause burns and sunstroke. In reality, however, the dissolution of the elements exist in order to create new conditions for new creations.

'The real mystic,' Daskalos went on, 'must reach a certain point where he has transcended the enchantment of the elements. He must become master over them, not only on the material level, but also on the psychic, the noetic and beyond. Without mastering the elements the mystic cannot move freely inside the various planes and subplanes of the psychic and noetic worlds.'

'Daskale,' I interrupted, 'you mentioned some time ago that a mystic undergoes certain tests or experiences which help him overcome the limitations of the elements and acquire control over them. What are these experiences?'

'The masters will often subject the neophyte to various tests in order for the latter to familiarize himself with the nature of the elements. He may, for example, be subjected to various experiences relating to the element of fire. He will have to pass through that element and discover that he cannot be burned. The mystic will have to master fire within the other dimensions before he can master fire on the material level. Unless he can control and master noetic and psychic fire a material flame will not obey him.' Daskalos then proceeded, at my probing, to narrate an intense personal experience he himself underwent when his master, Yohannan, took him on a voyage to the center of the Earth.

'One day Father Yohannan took me to the center of the Earth so that I could have the experience of fire and meet the archangelic entities in charge of this element. I saw huge yellow and orange odorless flames, as well as an unusual nuance of red that one cannot find anywhere on the planet. Within those colorful chambers glowing in flames I saw some absolutely magnificent entities. I want to paint them but the masters do not give me permission. Perhaps this may be allowed one day. When I noticed them Yohannan remarked, "These are your servants that work within you overseeing to the proper circulation of your blood. They enable you to live within a material body." They are the emanations of the archangel Michael. Their work and domain are within the largest as well as the smallest aspect of matter. They live on the sun, inside the planet and within our blood·corpuscles. "You are one of them," Yohannan said to me. "You are an archangel." "Master," I said, "I wish to know what I look like at this very moment." The master motioned to me to follow him and then, with a movement of his hand, spread in front of him a huge wall of fire. "Look," he commanded. I looked and noticed that

I was inside and outside of that flaming wall. I had the appearance of the archangels of fire as if I were one of them. At that very moment I understood why Yohannan, during the lessons of the inner circle, addresses us as "Children of the Spirit, of the Light, and of Fire." I also understood what John the Baptist meant when he said, "I baptize you in water but He who follows me will baptize you in Spirit and in Fire." How many understand the meaning of these words? What does "in Spirit and in Fire" mean? It is only now that I am beginning to understand. In the inner circle we undergo, step by step, the baptism of fire. One has to work gradually to understand these truths. The initiation of the mystic is not a ceremony whereby the master places the sword on the head of the initiate and mutters a few words. Initiation is a process that could last years and even centuries of spiritual development.

'Today,' Daskalos said, after a few seconds of silence and with a low voice, 'we have talked about matters that perhaps should not be discussed outside. But because you have such a thirst for knowledge it is better to know the way and to proceed. Iacovos already thinks that I am talking too much.'

'Is that what he is telling you?' I exclaimed, and gave a sharp glance at Iacovos who had been looking on with an innocuous smile.

In response to a question Daskalos went on to say that he had already undergone the initiations of all the elements in previous incarnations, although the experience he had just narrated took place in his present life.

'Iacovos probably remembers similar experiences himself.' The latter nodded affirmatively as Daskalos continued to give examples of how masters train prospective mystics in the various elements. 'Some night you may find yourself in a cave during an earthquake, while dirt covers the entrance of the cave. There is no way out. You feel trapped and desperate to get out. Suddenly you find yourself out of the cave. The masters give you such an experience to show you that you are not bound to the earth element. In regard to water they may place you in the depths of the ocean and then let you find your way up. How else can you learn to accompany people when they go down with their boats and drown? You want to be in a position to console them and then escort them to the psychic worlds.'

'When I first had such an experience,' Iacovos remarked, 'I froze with fear, thinking that I was going to drown.'

'He has already undergone the experiences of earth and water and, to some extent, of fire,' Daskalos added as he pointed at Iacovos. 'But he is still afraid of fire and of ether. When we are in exomatosis with our etheric bodies floating in the sky and the boats below looking like little match-boxes, Iacovos is terrified so he comes and covers himself under my arm. I keep urging him to look down to overcome his fear. There is no way I can convince Theophanis and Kostas to look down. They are too scared. Only my little grandson is not afraid and plunges playfully all the way down to the sea level. I am not sure why he is not afraid. Perhaps because he is small. I can hardly control him. It is really difficult for them not to experience apprehension. They are afraid they may lose their balance. What I usually do to calm them down is to create a very bright five-pointed star and put them inside. It gives them a feeling of security and they forget their fears. Is this not perhaps the reason why mystics through the ages have considered the five-pointed star the symbol of exomatosis?

'Now,' Daskalos continued with a low voice and smile on his face, 'you have entered into the mysteries of the inner circle. Permission is given to Iacovos to show you how, through image construction, you can create the five-pointed star at the various parts of your body for protection. He will then teach you how to abandon the form of the five-pointed star and remain only inside the meaning of the five-pointed star. Sit down with him to discuss these matters. Even though he has not yet been taught these issues through a living voice, he knows them. He has been taught about them in exomatosis through me and through Yohannan. When we have a lesson in the psychic world, he already knows certain things that he has never heard on the material level.'

'That is true,' Iacovos added in all seriousness.

'A real mystic must eventually transcend the enchantment of the four elements and become master over them,' Daskalos repeated. 'He therefore is not someone that people consider as such and give him titles, but one who has attained a certain level of spiritual advancement through his personal efforts.'

'When you say a mystic should master the four elements, do

you imply subjugating the senses?' Stephanos inquired.

'No. I mean he should cease being a slave to the material body. Subjugating the senses means opposing the power of the attraction of the elements. A mystic is not someone who fights the four elements, but one who has disentangled himself from their charm. Liberating one's self from the enchantment of the elements is a precondition for becoming master of matter. The mystic may eventually order the elements to obey him. Matter is like the goddess Circe that transforms humans into swine.'

Daskalos proceeded to argue that the mystic has physical needs like any other human being but, whereas the ordinary person is under the spell of desires and bodily pleasures, the master has transcended these needs. 'For example,' he said, 'for the advanced mystic food is nothing more than a necessity in keeping the body alive. Sexuality, too, is not an end in itself, but a means for cooperating with the Absolute in the process of creation.'

I pointed out that to me what he had said about sexuality sounded like a doctrine for the ascetic life.

'Not so,' Daskalos insisted. 'The ascetic aims to subdue his desires, whereas the advanced master has transcended his desires.'

In an earlier conversation Daskalos had confided to me that he never felt the need for sexual pleasure. His body, he explained, did not produce the amount of hormones that normally generates sexual desires. He married and fathered two daughters for no other reason than procreation.

'I am not at all suggesting,' Daskalos went on to clarify, 'that sexual desire should be suppressed. It is a need for you. I cannot demand that you abstain. You are at a phase of your existence when sexual pleasure is a necessity. I am not urging you not to cook delicious gourmet food which you have a craving for. In my case I can meet my nutritional needs with bread or boiled wheat. For me food is what is necessary to keep my body alive. Do you understand now? You may say that pleasures of the flesh are illusions. For those who need them, however, they are good and beautiful illusions that can create harmonious relationships between human beings, men and women. I am not underestimating physical desires. But as for myself, I am not enamored of them.

'A true mystic,' Daskalos then continued, 'must overcome the illusion and passion for ownership. Our real possessions are not the amounts of material things we own, but what we have stored within ourselves. Attachment to material objects, therefore, is an impediment to one's spiritual advancement. I do not have to own flowers in order to enjoy them. When I enjoy beautiful flowers, the gardens of the whole world are mine. I need not own them. What I possess in reality is what I can behold, not what I own. The moment that you grab something and call it "mine," you are a very poor man. The moment you open your palm and say, "everything is mine," without restricting what is yours to what is in your hand, you are truly a rich person.'

Daskalos went on to say that for each of the four elements there are several initiations. The first series of initiations pertains to the earth element. The vow of the seven promises made by the Researcher of Truth upon entering the circles is the first initiation. It focuses on the development of one's character, the acquisition of virtues and the first serious attempt at transcending the enchantment with matter. It further involves the realization of the existence of an Absolute Intelligence behind the phenomenal world and of one's own self-conscious soul.

During the first initiation the mystic learns various virtues such as tolerance, patience, mastery of body and personality, and the overcoming of anger. Furthermore he becomes conscious of the need to be of service to others. The earthly master helps the neophyte acquire these virtues through appropriate exercises and self-analysis. Subsequent initiations are usually handled by masters who do not live on the earth plane. The decision, for example, as to who will be initiated into the inner circle usually 'comes from above.' It belongs to the second series of initiations pertaining to the element of water which is the dominant element of the psychic world.

'Is it possible for someone to embark on the second initiation without a ceremony performed by the earthly master?' I asked.

'Of course. The second initiation involves the first step in the acquisition of powers. The mystic realizes that he can live fully conscious outside of his material body. At first he may not have the experience of exomatosis but subconsciously he knows that he can live outside of his body. He will begin to experience vivid dreams which he will be able to recollect in great detail.

Furthermore he begins to reason within his dreams and be conscious while still in the dream state. He can then express the various virtues he acquired during the first series of initiations. On the psychic plane these virtues are expressed with greater intensity. Tolerance is greater and concentration is more complete. During the second series of initiations the mystic tries to bridge the gap between his present and permanent personality.'

'What happens during the initiation in the lower noetic world, I mean the initiation into the element of fire?' I asked.

'You begin to express to a greater extent these virtues and in addition your psychic powers expand. You develop greater abilities of concentration, of thought, of understanding and of will power. Let me explain what I mean. On the material plane, through my eyesight, I have the ability to concentrate over a landscape. I absorb certain impressions but only a small portion of them will be retained in my consciousness. After the first initiation I am able, through psychonoetic exercises, to retain in my memory experiences derived from the gross material plane. During the first stages of the second initiation, on the other hand, while in exomatosis, I cover a greater field of vision and begin to receive more experiences and impressions. I am not limited to the five senses. I also have a greater awareness of existing conditions. When I undergo the second series of initiations I can move freely within several planes of the psychic world and simultaneously be of assistance to more than one person without being restricted within the different psychic planes. Yet even these abilities are limited. In my third series of initiations in the noetic worlds, I can expand my powers. At the early stages of the third initiation I develop the abilities of my mind. Furthermore I develop abilities such as the expansion of my consciousness over a great area in order to experience everything and know everything. When you reach the higher levels of the third series of initiations, you are at the doorstep of Theosis.'

'What is beyond the third series of initiations?' I asked.

'Enlightened ascent towards infinity.'

'Has Christ undergone these initiations?' Stephanos inquired.

'No. Christ was not a man that attained Theosis. He was God incarnate,' Daskalos responded categorically as he so often did on this issue. Unlike the Buddha and other great masters who attained perfection through repeated incarnations, Christ as the embodiment of the logoic part of the Absolute incarnated on the earth plane only once.

'Must all the disciples go through these initiations in the same manner?' I asked.

'No. Quite often one can work through all the initiations simultaneously. It is imperative, however, that one go through the initiations of the earth element first and then proceed with the rest. Some may move from the first initiation to the noetic and then return to undergo the initiations of the psychic world, of water.'

'Would you say, then, that the third series of initiations, the initiations of fire, are superior to the initiations of water?' I probed.

'What did Christ say? "Blessed be the meek in spirit." By that He did not mean the fools and idiots as some naively assumed, but those who are innocent of slyness and knavery. It is neither cleverness nor the accumulation of knowledge that will lead us to self-realization, but a clean heart. "Blessed be the pure at heart," He said, "for they shall see God." Christ does not place sentiment above reason, as some have argued. "Pure at heart" refers to Love which is our nature. Without the actualization of the heart's purity, which is done through the third initiation, you cannot know God. You must reach a state whereby you are aware of the cleanliness of your heart. For the heart to become aware of itself, of its own godliness, presupposes the ability to know and understand. Take note, however, that in the third initiation right thinking has nothing to do with cleverness or cunning. Rather it encompasses a love for knowing the Truth. The intelligence of many scientists who, for the sake of their personal aggrandizement, are ready to sacrifice thousands of human beings is nothing more than an expression of the satanic in man. This type of knowledge has nothing to do with the third series of the initiation of the mystic.'

'Is it possible for a human being to undergo these initiations without becoming a member of the circles for the Research of Truth?'

'Each human being has inside him the light that enlightens every human being descending upon the Earth. Whether he knows it or not, he has his master and guide inside him. The daily life of every human being is an exercise leading him towards the three initiations.'

'You mean it is possible,' I probed further, 'to attain godliness without the help of an earthly master?'

'Why not? Did the great masters of humankind have earthly teachers? Once you are coordinated with the Logos you are in no need of an earthly master.'

'Is corporeal existence an obstacle to entering into the world of ideas?' Stephanos asked after a break of half an hour while Daskalos advised a couple having marital problems.

'Naturally it is. The mystic, however, must become master of his material body. He must learn how to leave behind at will, not only his material, but also his psychic and noetic bodies so that he may enter into the higher noetic worlds of ideas and laws. To attain that stage, a single lifetime is not sufficient.

'As an advanced mystic,' he went on, 'you will attain a certain state when, not only will you remember who you were in previous incarnations, but also you will know what the purpose of your existence is. Your goal was set aeons back and with every incarnation your way was patiently and calmly paved without haste, without delay. You must become, yourself, The Way. As Christ said, "I am the Way, the Truth and the Life." That is how to become master over spacial-temporal events and know what the purpose behind these events is. You must know and trust yourself and prevent doubts from obstructing your path. Unless you become master of yourself and of the phenomenon of life, you cannot become an advanced mystic.'

'What kinds of doubts are you referring to, Daskale?' I interrupted.

'Doubts about your own abilities and healing powers. Many mystics, not the advanced ones, often wonder whether what they accomplish in a healing session is real or not. "Can I do it? If I do it again will I succeed?" These are questions that often come to their minds. The advanced mystic does not have doubts because he knows. That is where his power lies. He knows who he is. He knows what life and the phenomenon of life are. He knows where he is going and the purpose for which he came to this Earth. He will be in a position to ascertain the difficulties.'

'When one remembers who he is, is he continuously aware of it?' Stephanos inquired.

'Certainly.'

'Is it not possible,' Stephanos went on, 'to know who you are but to let oblivion cover your self-awareness?'

'No. Oblivion means you do not know. A real mystic remembers even his first ascent into matter, thousands of years back. Some mystics begin to remember fragments of past lives and get excited. But they are still at the infancy stage of mysticism.'

'Daskale,' I asked, 'if one has powers to create phenomena that appear extraordinary or supernatural, does it imply that one is an advanced mystic?'

'Not at all. I have known many such self-proclaimed mystics. In fact only recently I was visited by such an individual who wanted to impress me with his powers. With his thought he raised a glass of water from the table and brought it down on the floor in front of me. I asked him to take it back to the table. He complied with my instructions but spilled half of it in the process. I asked him to repeat it once more. He tried hard but to no avail. With my mind I created the opposite power and he could not move the glass. Then I let him bring it in front of me again. He became like a vegetable from exhaustion. "My dear friend," I said to him, "why are you tampering with your etheric body like this?"

'He boasted that he had spent several years with a yogi and was able to acquire these powers. I then posed the question to him, "Who are you?" "But haven't I introduced myself to you?" he replied. "I remember what you told me," I said, "but your name is of no interest to me. I repeat the question, who are you?" Again he began to exalt his present personality, trying to impress me with his knowledge. He went to India, to the Himalayas, and spent six years with the yogis. He took out a card with his name and his titles and gave it to me. "Is that who you think you are?" I asked. "Yes," he replied. I tore the card apart and threw it into the waste-basket. "Do the same with all the other cards you have," I urged him, "so that you may be able to find yourself because you have no idea who you truly are. These powers that you have demonstrated today are childish. What you have accomplished lacks seriousness."

'I wanted to test him and find out to what extent he managed to transcend his fascination with his present personality. My ceaseless probing enraged him. He went on boasting about himself. "My dear friend," I replied, "your words are the cry of someone enamored with matter. Come to your senses." He was offended. "I made a mistake. I should not have come here," he shouted angrily. "How about a cup of coffee and then we will continue to talk." I made him the coffee and returned. I touched his head with my hands. He looked at me in the eyes and started crying. "Don't you realize that I understand you? What do you want me to do, grab my idol and break it into pieces?" "If you have the courage," I answered, "do it in order to find yourself." "I am afraid," he said. "Afraid of what? To smash an idol and discover who you really are?" "I am not ready yet," he murmured in all sincerity. "Let me go," and he went on crying. "I love," he said. "Love what, your shadow?" "Yes, my shadow." "When you are ready come and together we will break that idol of yours which torments you so much and keeps you from moving forward." "I feel that we have met before and that, like today, you gave me the same harsh lesson." "The lesson will be harsher the next time around," I promised, "because I love you." Some day he will be able to break his idol. It is such a pity to torment himself with illusions. He sees the light but he does not have the courage to move forward towards it. I invited him to stay with me for a few weeks so that he might be able to break his idols and put on the white robe. He entered the Sanctum, took a white robe, kissed it and wiped his tears with it. "I am not ready, master, to break my idol," he sighed.'

I asked Daskalos to clarify his notion of the 'idol' and how one goes about breaking it. 'To smash our "idol,"' he said, 'we must first find ourselves. The present personality as material body, thoughts and sentiments represents those mirrors that reflect back to us our "idol." If these mirrors are dusty, the reflection will be nebulous and misty.

'Suppose we stand over a peaceful, clean lake,' Daskalos said. 'We can see clearly our image in the water. With the slightest disturbance we can no longer perceive the reflection of ourself.

'Our aim as mystics,' he went on to say, 'is to bring about a balance in our thoughts and emotions, to calm the waters and polish the mirrors so that they will reflect our true self more clearly. The ultimate goal is to break the mirrors that distort us and balance the triangle.'

'Balance the triangle?'

'Yes. We have said before that the Absolute can be symbolically represented with an isometric triangle. Each side represents one of the three attributes of the Absolute, total wisdom, total power and total goodness. In the macrocosm, within Nature, the triangle is always balanced. Within ourselves, however, it is in the process of becoming isometric and balanced. Let us examine this. When there are only knowledge and power in an individual, but no goodness, a satanic condition prevails. A demon is, after all, an incomplete god. When there are love and power but no knowledge, again the triangle is . nbalanced and can lead to misery. A person with power and goodness but no knowledge can create, out of ignorance, confusion and tragedy around him. When one has love and knowledge but no power, it is a benign condition, yet the triangle is still incomplete. The individual cannot accomplish much. The closer one is towards balancing his triangle, the closer one is towards self-realization, towards becoming a god.'

The metaphor about isometric triangles generated a lively discussion between Stephanos and Daskalos which I interrupted by asking a prosaic question about 'idols' again.

'Must one break one's idol before one wears the white robe?' I inquired.

'Not necessarily. I can initiate someone and dress him with the white robe as a way of placing him on the right path so that he can gradually discover himself. But when someone comes to me and tells me he spent six years in the Himalayas and demonstrates such powers, I have greater demands and expectations from him. You cannot have the same expectations from someone who has just finished elementary school as you do from a college graduate. He was exceptional. You must bear in mind that the higher you are the more you understand and the greater your responsibilities.'

'Is it not gradually that one will break his idol?' Stephanos asked.

'There are some who break their idols without being aware of it and they hold them like a mask so that they can live within time and space. They are at a stage when they at least know

174

that beyond the mask there is something else, their true selves. When you become conscious of this reality then you will become conscious of the necessity to be of service to your fellow human beings. It is not paranormal or psychic powers that make a mystic, but the level of his spiritual growth. It is very easy to train people to develop their psychic abilities and become powerful mediums. But what's the use if their spiritual growth is stunted? The acquisition of psychic powers must parallel one's spiritual growth. Otherwise one can easily fall into black sorcery.'

'As a human being are you not influenced by temporal considerations yourself?' Stephanos probed.

'Naturally I am influenced since I live within time and space. But I see further inside. I cannot be motivated by anything other than love even if that love is very earthy. Nothing else can influence me. I can tell you that when I say love, I don't mean only the very beloved ones in my personal life, but even those that are considered to be my enemies. The aeons have rendered me incapable of hate. Even if I wanted to hate I could not, for I know who I am and what I can and cannot do.'

'Are you suggesting that the question "Who am I?" is answerable?' Stephanos inquired as he looked somewhat perplexed.

'Certainly it is answerable. I know who I am but how can I tell you who I am? There are no words to make you understand. I am neither a name nor a title.'

'I presume,' Stephanos went on, 'understanding is possible only when two people are at the same level.'

'Precisely. Very few know who I really am. These are people that I have lived and worked with for thousands of years. We have a common name and address one another by that name.'

'What name is that?' I wondered.

'Love. Can you truly understand what this word means? When we call each other by that name we are often misunderstood because ordinary people imbue this term with earthly meanings. Perhaps one of the few who was capable of understanding the nature of love was Saint Paul and I am always moved by his exposition on the subject.'

'Daskale,' Stephanos interjected, 'isn't there a danger of strengthening one's idol of himself when one says "I know"?'

'No. When you really know yourself you are not interested in the mask.'

'But that is possible,' Stephanos added, 'only when one reaches a perfect state of "I know" which for us is unknowable. Is it not better to begin with an overall "I do not know" and avoid the dangers?'

'Fine. You start with an overall "I do not know, but I have faith that I will know," rather than "I will never know, period." I know that the Sun rises from a certain direction because I saw it the day before. Right now it is dark, but I have patience and conviction that the Sun will rise again. Knowing is an experiential certainty.'

'To me,' Stephanos remarked, 'knowing oneself seems to have nothing to do with categorizing. It is enough to say I simply am without the epithet.'

'It is not enough,' Daskalos responded. 'You must analyze this "I am," get to know it. This is the purpose of self-analysis.'

'But who is going to decide this? One's own inadequacy?' Stephanos retorted.

'No. The person himself will decide. He must become a Researcher of Truth.'

'Truth,' Stephanos reacted, 'is not to add a superlative on your "I" when in fact you are not. I have met so many who say "I am" and you realize that there is a falsity there. You feel it, that is.'

'Good. I can accept this falsity, this illusion. I will urge him to proceed. I will then pose the question, "Are you sure that what you think is you is in reality you?" I will not shock or surprise him. Do you understand?'

'You said before that you are against idols. Therefore it necessarily follows that you must also be against categorizing,' Stephanos replied.

'No. Categorization is the process which will provide me with the power to gradually destroy the idols. There are idols and idols. There is the good man, the better man, et cetera. These are conditions that are inside the idols and which one day will be swept away by the wind of knowledge. Do you understand what I want to say? I have mentioned to Kyriacos before, suppose I climbed up the ladder and reached the top. I needed all the steps to do that. Just because I reached a certain level I am not going to destroy the steps behind me. There are others who need them so that they can climb up. And I am happy to see my brother, who is at a lower step, struggle to climb a step higher. I appreciate his effort, his seriousness and his purposefulness.'

CHAPTER 10

Right thinking

There was a certain heaviness in the air when I visited Daskalos the following Monday. He looked somber as he introduced me to his three guests. In an armchair next to Daskalos a slender, frail-looking man in his fifties could barely breathe or keep his head upright. His wife and father-in-law sat on the couch facing the patient. They were gloomy and silent. I sat next to the patient while they continued their conversation.

'Like I said, your problems are in your mind,' Daskalos said as he addressed the patient. 'Do not indulge in morbid thoughts.'

'Yes, yes,' his wife joined in so as to reaffirm Daskalos' diagnosis which I found preposterous given the physical condition of his visitor.

'Yes, it is in my mind,' the man sighed as if to convince himself of something that he knew deep down was not true. 'Bad thoughts come to my mind. What can I do? I get upset.'

After a few moments of silence the patient asked for a glass of water which I readily offered. Unable to handle the cup by himself I had to help him hold it close to his lips. I knew Daskalos deliberately avoided revealing the patient's real condition.

'My advice to you,' Daskalos said as the man drank the last drop of water and sank back into his chair exhausted, 'is to regularly take the medicines the doctors prescribed. And don't indulge in negative thoughts.' Daskalos then reassured his patient that he will soon be fine.

'Time to go,' his wife said after a few minutes of nervous silence. They thanked Daskalos for his advice and I helped the woman hold and guide her husband into the car. Daskalos remained seated and looked pensive.

'Daskale, how could you tell that man that his problem was

in his head?' I said in protest after I returned. 'To me he looked as if he already had one foot in the grave.'

Daskalos shook his head with sadness and said that the man was covered with cancer 'from top to bottom' and that his days were numbered. Daskalos could do nothing for him except 'in his own way' reduce the amount of suffering that he had to go through. Daskalos claimed that he could not reveal to him the reality of his condition because the patient was not ready to face the truth. Without further elaboration on this issue we proceeded to talk about other matters.

I met Daskalos again in the evening in more relaxed and congenial circumstances. My friend Neophytos and his wife Katerina invited us for food, drink and conversation. Katerina, a practicing clinical psychologist at the local mental hospital, repeated how she was looking forward to our encounter in the evening. She had so many things to ask Daskalos, she said, particularly those pertaining to her profession.

Unlike the morning encounter Daskalos was jovial. The fact that local intellectuals were beginning to get interested in his teachings made him particularly happy.

In addition to Daskalos, Emily and myself, Neophytos invited Stephanos and his wife Erato. After we all assembled in their living-room Daskalos, in his customary manner, started a discussion sparked by a passing comment of Katerina's related to her work. 'You can't avoid a certain amount of nervousness,' she said, 'when you are dealing with the problems of your patients.'

'Let us examine this,' Daskalos responded. 'If by nervousness you imply the conditions that induce you to focus your attention, I accept it. However, if by nervousness you mean to lose your self-mastery then I would call it a character flaw. In the first case when I maintained my self-composure, my coolness, a certain nervousness would help me study better certain conditions that I would not have studied under a normal state of mind.' Then Daskalos leaned back on his chair and after a few exchanges with Katerina went on to discuss the relationship between a therapist and a prospective patient.

'First of all we must never discriminate in terms of who we choose to help. Whether the person who comes to us is a great scientist or a long-shoreman is irrelevant. This is what we must have in mind if we are to help anyone. Whoever comes to us we

179

must first psychoanalyze him. By that I mean we must get to know him, feel him out. We must do that before we are in a position to help. Many psychoanalysts and therapists have a single method which they apply to all their patients. And based on that method they ask their patients some standard questions which then lead them to draw certain conclusions.' Daskalos then raised his voice and thundered that this is idiotic and disastrous for therapy.

'You will never find two persons that are alike,' he went on as he extended his two fingers. 'When you are about to help someone you must first determine which stage of intellectual and psychic development that individual is at. This requires great patience and serious study. But that is the way to be successful. One must never employ the same method for everyone because each person is unique and therefore only a method appropriate for that individual must be employed.'

At this point the doorbell rang and Daskalos interrupted his narrative. Neophytos introduced the newcomer, Yiannis, a forty-three-year-old businessman who belonged, like Stephanos, to the school of 'practical philosophy.' Yiannis expressed his pleasure at meeting Daskalos for the first time after hearing 'so much' about him. Once the commotion was over and after our host generously poured local beer into our mugs, Daskalos continued.

'The psychoanalyst should not only ask questions but must train himself or herself to listen to the patient's story and understand what kind of experiences the person had in life, what pains, what reactions, et cetera.'

Daskalos then, after answering several questions, went on to criticize the tendency of therapists to have their patients 'let steam out,' as he put it. This could be very harmful, he instructed, because conventional therapists are not always aware of the great power of auto-suggestion. Through this lack of awareness, Daskalos pointed out, therapists quite often are responsible for letting certain morbid ideas get rooted within the subconscious of their patients, ideas from which they supposedly try to liberate them.

'A psychologist must learn to listen without reacting. He must examine how the mechanism of suggestion and auto-suggestion works in each case and make use of them.' At this point Neophytos, who like the others was listening quietly, interrupted.

'I have a question, Daskale, about what you said earlier about auto-suggestion. You mentioned that you should not let a patient "let steam out" because he may make negative auto-suggestions. From my understanding one who wants to help someone should approach him in such a way as to let him talk about his problems.'

'No, not always,' Daskalos replied in a low, soft voice. 'Just be aware of one thing. There are people who tend to indulge in morbid thoughts about past and unpleasant experiences. They would, for example, exaggerate the pains of an operation. This is a morbid form of auto-suggestion. Do not allow them to indulge in such negativity. I knew of a doctor who had undergone a simple operation and he kept describing it, and describing it. One day I got impatient, "Doctor," I said, "for God's sake, are you a masochist? Do you get pleasure by talking like that? What are you trying to provoke? Pity?" "You are right," he replied, "I never thought of it this way."'

After further clarification on this issue, Emily, who was listening attentively, interrupted Daskalos and asked whether it was advisable to lie to a patient for therapeutic purposes. She referred specifically to patients suffering from terminal diseases.

'In fact,' Daskalos responded, 'I had such a case today when your husband was present. Let us examine this. A few days ago a woman visited me. She brought a picture of her brother and through psychometry I tried to find out what the problem was. She did not tell me at first. In fact she said she believed there was nothing serious but that she wished to make certain that there was nothing wrong with her brother.'

Daskalos had said to me on another occasion that this was a common trick that people played on him in order to check his clairvoyant abilities. It was an attitude that deeply annoyed him.

'When I took the picture into my hands,' Daskalos went on, 'what do you think I saw? Cancer all over his body, in his liver, lungs, arteries, pancreas, and moving up to the brain. He was so weak he could hardly walk. "Tell me," I asked her, "did you take him to the doctors?" "Yes," she said reluctantly. "And what did the doctors say?" I asked her again. "Well, we are waiting for you to tell us," she said. "I'll tell you," I said to her. "Have you taken the doctors for fools? Why are you so naive?

Do you think they could have made a mistake after so many tests, so many analyses and biopsies? Listen," I said to her, "he has a few more days to live, perhaps weeks. The only thing I can promise you is that in my own way I will stop the pains so that he does not realize what is happening to him. Nothing else, nothing." As if that was not enough, she sent him to me the following day accompanied by his wife and father-in-law. Now tell me, what should I have told him? Do you think I should have said, "Yes, my dear friend, you have a few more days to live?"'

'Don't you think you should?' Emily responded as if muttering to herself, not knowing what the correct response under those circumstances should have been.

'No,' Daskalos said loudly.

'Don't you think a patient has a right to know if and when he is dying?'

'Listen, listen,' Daskalos replied. 'Had he been a mature person and I sensed from his thoughts that he was going to patiently and beautifully accept his fate I would have revealed to him the reality of his condition. At that moment you must figure out what the consequences will be if you tell the truth. I realized that had I told him the truth he would have started screaming hysterically and would have become desperate. He would have demanded to have his son brought to him from America and the other one from London and until his last breath he would have tormented everybody around him.

'Just tell me,' Daskalos said to Emily as he gesticulated with his hands, 'what right did I have to tell this man the truth? I would have made him more miserable than he was.' Then after a pause Daskalos changed the tone of his voice and went on. 'In fact I did tell him the truth. I said to him "Listen, friend. You will become completely well very soon. Your pains will go away and your weakness will disappear."

'Did I lie?' Daskalos continued as the rest of us laughed nervously about a matter that ordinarily should have caused somber contemplation. 'I did not lie. His pains will go away. Why should I tell him the truth that would have generated so much unhappiness? Be aware. Truth is fire and sometimes we have no right to burn our fellows because we must tell the truth.'

Daskalos then turned towards Katerina and continued his

instructions on being a therapist.

'How are you as a therapist going to handle so many diverse cases? You must first of all learn about certain laws that govern human nature, such as the law of repetition. No one is exempt from this law, neither the scientist nor the peasant, neither the saint nor the criminal. For example the saint with the repetition of his mantras indulges in continuous auto-suggestions that reinforce the power of his faith. The criminal with his daily manner of thinking and acting also makes auto-suggestions to himself that tend to reinforce his criminal lifestyle.'

'Is the law of repetition the expression of Karma?' Stephanos asked.

'In a way, yes. The law of repetition is expressed at each moment when we construct a thought. You believe in something. Automatically this thought will leave and then return to you and it would tend to become part of you. These are the elementals we create every moment.'

'And the repetition in the opposite direction can help you liberate yourself from these thoughts?' Stephanos asked again.

'I have studied this problem very extensively. Depending on your attitude you either inject more energy and life to this elemental or you de-energize it. It is the latter that we must learn how to do in order to help ourselves and others in therapy. I have pointed out in a lecture I gave that we cannot dissolve an elemental by fighting it. It will defeat us. The best approach is through indifference, through a certain apathy.'

'When you say indifference do you mean we must transport our attention elsewhere?' Stephanos inquired.

'Be careful now. You may transfer your attention somewhere else but after a while the elemental will return and hit you on the head.'

'Exactly,' Stephanos nodded. 'Then what is apathy and indifference in such cases?'

'What is apathy?' Daskalos repeated and got ready to answer Stephanos' question. 'The only way is through *orthologismos*, through right thinking. We must analyze through the use of right thinking,' Daskalos continued, 'our specific desires and thoughts around those desires. And then we should ascertain to what extent the thoughts we have are harmful or benign, what purpose do they serve, or what damage they inflict. After analyzing our thoughts through right thinking we should draw the analogous conclusions. Is it better to allow these thoughts to get energized through the law of repetition or is it wiser to generate the opposite thoughts and again through the law of repetition to consciously de-energize them? If we decide that a thought which we repeat in our head is harmful then we must, through auto-suggestion, instruct ourselves that such thoughts are harmful.'

'The law of repetition works 'in both ways,' Stephanos observed.

'Definitely. I will now use the law of repetition for my own benefit. And when I have convinced myself I will have already de-energized the elemental which I decided to get rid of.'

'This de-energizing will leave some leftovers. Is it not so?' Stephanos asked.

'Let it be so,' Daskalos replied. 'It is better that way than letting an elemental destroy us.'

'Earlier you talked of *orthologismos*, of right thinking. But how do we know, Daskale, that at any given moment we employ right thinking since one imagines that one's way of thinking is right?' Neophytos asked and the rest of us laughed heartily with the inherent irony of his question.

'Pay attention,' Daskalos responded, 'because on this very point Jesus Christ pointed the way. Let us not ignore the Great Teaching. Now, what does right thinking mean? It means a law-cause, a rule which is the same for every human being, not an idiosyncratic measure that is elastic and is applied in accordance with one's preferences. What did Christ say? "That which you hate do not do unto others," or "do unto others as you would have liked them to do unto you." This is a steadfast and reliable rule that we can use in order to ascertain whether we are on the right track. We can determine then whether what we consider as right thinking is not in reality a cover-up of our egotism which hurts others. The Turkish-Cypriot leaders, for example, claim that it is their right to occupy the north and expel the Greek Cypriots from their homes. According to their "right thinking" it is their prerogative to do so because the Greek Cypriots abused the Turks before the invasion of 1974. Everybody has a tendency to find rationalizations for egotism. Everyone has one's own notions of "right thinking."'

'I understand what you are saying,' Neophytos continued, 'but I still cannot see how you can escape from the trap of your own notions of right thinking. For example, in sociology it is taken for granted that special interests construct entire systems of thought that can rationalize whatever people are doing.'

'We cannot call that right thinking. It is not within laws-causes but a way of thinking based on personal interests. That is why social life today is so chaotic.'

'The individual, Daskale,' Neophytos continued, 'may wish to escape from all that but he is powerless to do so. He would not know how.'

'What Neophytos is saying,' Stephanos tried to clarify, 'is that right thinking becomes entrapped within subjectivity.'

'It must not,' Daskalos stressed, and raised his voice.

'Had it not been entrapped,' Stephanos went on, 'humans would have already been at the highest level of spiritual evolution. We are talking now about common people like ourselves who are subjected to this entrapment.'

'Just a minute now. Is there anybody, regardless of status and education, that does not know that if you grab something from someone else it is stealing?'

'Such a case is very clear and simple, Daskale,' Emily pointed out. 'But there are certain things that are much more subtle, which makes it difficult to determine . . . '

'I will come to that,' Daskalos reacted before Emily completed her sentence. 'We should begin the process of right thinking neither with masochistic tendencies to blame ourselves, nor with its opposite. Rather we should keep in mind that what we go through are experiences that will offer us certain lessons for clearer thinking in the future. Beyond our actions and thoughts there is someone else called conscience.'

'But conscience, Daskale,' Emily said quickly, 'presupposes an elaboration, a process . . . '

'Conscience means conscience,' Daskalos said cuttingly. 'You may do something wrong. Then you invent all sorts of rationalizations and excuses and you are convinced that you are right. When you sleep at night you will hear someone inside tell you that you are wrong. Believe this. I have very carefully studied the phenomenon of conscience. It is our conscience which we must have as a criterion of our actions.'

'Daskale, I still have some problems with what you just said,' Neophytos added. 'Suppose an industrialist who has worked hard in his life and employs over one hundred workers believes

185

that he is doing good because he feeds one hundred families.'

'He is right,' Daskalos responded, as if it was self-evident.

'Twenty of his workers,' Neophytos continued 'are communists and believe that this industrialist is exploiting their labor.'

'They are also right,' Daskalos said loudly with laughter and quickly went on to elaborate on his contradictory statements. 'Let us see what I am driving at and explore what true right thinking is under the circumstances. We must examine the real motives of the industrialist as well as those of the communist. The communist cries out that he is exploited by the industrialist and from his point of view and that of Papaioannou [the head of the communist party of Cyprus] he is right. Is it not so? He feels oppressed. The industrialist tells himself, "My intelligence created all these employment opportunities and had I not done so these families may have starved." He is also right from his point of view. Therefore, I observe two different circumstances in life that could potentially offer valuable lessons to each one of them. What valuable lesson you may ask? The communist could say to himself, "Fine, my employer is a millionaire and he owns this factory. He too will sit in a room and so will I. He could not possibly sit and enjoy fifteen rooms at the same time." The communist could use his right thinking and realize, "Okay, I too have two eyes and enjoy the world. I too will live a few years and so will he. Then we will both leave this Earth." If the industrialist is focused on what he has, he cannot avoid hearing Christ's admonitions inside him on the vanity and mindlessness of what he is doing. His inner voice will tell him, "Where are you going to take all that? You're leaving this Earth." As the years go by the agony and anxiety of the industrialist will be more intense. Therefore, both of them must begin to exercise real right thinking,' Daskalos said and stopped for a few seconds. Then he proceeded with a soft tone in his voice.

'And do you know where right thinking begins in order to be right thinking? With the power of Love. The communist,' Daskalos went on and raised his voice, 'must love his employer. He has the option to tell himself, "Yes, our employer looks after us, he pays us well." The communist must see things this way for the sake of his own inner peace, so that he is not in a constant state of psychic turmoil. And the industrialist for his part must truly see his role as one that cares for his workers and that he pays them well. He should do that for his own inner peace. Therefore, is there a potential for psychic turmoil for both of them? Yes. From where? From within themselves,' Daskalos said softly and pointed at his heart.

'From someone,' Daskalos continued, 'who judges more clearly on what genuine right thinking is, not the human type which is colored by earthly circumstances and conditions. And that is none other than that of Reality, of Love.'

'But for one to think that way,' Stephanos asked, 'does it not require tremendous preparation?'

'Yes. This tremendous preparation will come sooner or later, either through ordinary right thinking or through the whip of Karma. In life we receive lessons in two ways, either through right thinking, even the ordinary one which with time will become clearer, or through the law of Karma. Christ taught this to us when he said whatever you have sown so shall you reap. He told Peter after he cut the ear of the Roman soldier, "Be careful, for if you live by the sword you shall die by the sword," regardless of the fact that you are my pupil. No one can escape the law of Karma. Therefore, whether you know that you cause injustices or whether you do not, you will bear the consequences of your actions. When you open your eyes and look clearly you will arrive at true rational conclusions. For the world is not governed by an irrational Absolute.'

'Had we not had the possibility for right thinking,' I volunteered to add, 'there would have been no point in researching for Truth.'

'The world would have been a jungle, my dear,' Daskalos said in earnest.

'We start with the assumption,' I went on 'that we are all more or less irrational because we are ignorant of right thinking.'

'But why say that? Why not say that we must try to think more clearly after we carefully study the impulses that block our way to right thinking?' Daskalos added. He then proceeded to elaborate on a theme that Daskalos never tired of indulging, that every Researcher of Truth must make it a daily habit to observe with objectivity and detachment his or her thoughts and actions.

'We are all subjected to the same laws. It does not matter whether we are great scientists, philosophers or garbage collectors. For example, we all have a material body which at a certain temperature begins to sweat. If we leave our body unwashed for a few days it will begin to smell. A higher agent, in this case water, is needed to cleanse our material body. All human bodies need that. Our psychic body has similar needs,' Daskalos added with his voice raised. 'We must regularly cleanse it of the low vibrations of egotistical desires. In the case of our material body we cleanse it with a higher agent, water. Likewise we must cleanse our psychic body with a higher agent, in this case right thinking, with *orthologismos*. As Researchers of Truth we have given a promise to ourselves to "check our desires from their very birth." This is exactly what is needed in order to keep our psychic body clean. Ordinary people who are not Researchers of Truth allow whatever base desires they may have to get rooted into their subconscious through the law of repetition. This is what the Research for Truth trains us to do, to habitually cleanse our psychic bodies through self-analysis by using right thinking. I am telling you that the stench of psychic conditions, the result of unbridled desires, is worse than the smells of the unwashed body. And that is why the ancients at the entrance of Saint Sophia in Constantinople inscribed 'ΝΙΨΟΝ ΑΝΟΜΗΜΑΤΑ ΜΗ ΜΟΝΑΝ ΟΨΙΝ' (Wash away evil not only from your face).

'Right thinking,' Daskalos went on, 'is analogous to the maturation of the noetic and psychic bodies, that is to the maturation of thought and sentiment. Often human right thinking is a form of irrationality from a higher state of awareness. Similarly, higher forms of *orthologismos*, of right thinking, appear irrational from more human levels of consciousness.'

'Can you give us an example of the latter?' I asked.

'Jesus Christ taught that one should "turn the other cheek. . . . " From the perspective of Hebraic law of "an eye for an eye," "turn the other cheek" was sheer nonsense. Correct? In what way, you may ask was Jesus' admonition a form of right thinking?

'During those times,' Daskalos continued, 'people used to carry arms, knives, daggers, et cetera. If an angry man slapped you in the face and you reacted in a similar fashion the chances were that he would have drawn his dagger to kill you. From a practical point of view it made more sense not to counter-attack. "Turn the other cheek" was no advice for passivity for its own sake. To have right thinking you must balance thought with sentiment. In the case of Jesus' saying the two are balanced. In regard to thinking, "turn the other cheek" is a superior way to put down the fires of hatred that lead to more hatred and violence. In regard to sentiment, this admonition is consistent with Jesus' teachings of "love thy enemies." But what enemies in reality? My brothers who are under the spell of irrational impulses? True *orthologismos* is grounded on universal love as taught by the Logos. Nothing less.'

After Daskalos finished his sentence there was a few minutes' pause until Neophytos refilled our beer mugs. Then Emily reopened the conversation.

'Daskale,' she said, 'a major critique against metaphysics is that it perpetuates conventional viewpoints. Modern psychology, as I understand it, would say that one should discover what one's desires are and that part of the oppression of the individual is that one is never allowed to learn what one's real desires are.'

'But what have I said a while ago? By suppressing or fighting your desires you will not benefit anything. They will eventually subjugate you. You must get to know them and then ignore them if you are to succeed. And when you speak of metaphysics what do you really mean? Within what context do you place this word? To tell you the truth I do not accept the word metaphysics.'

Daskalos has repeatedly pointed out that what we call metaphysics is that which we do not understand through conventional science. In reality everything is part of Nature. The divisions between physics and metaphysics, religion and science are artificial constructions resulting from human ignorance of the true nature of reality.

'The problem that I have, Daskale,' Emily went on, 'is this. When Neophytos raised the hypothetical case of the worker and the industrialist you responded that in reality there is no fundamental difference between them. You said that by both knowing love the social injustices would somehow disappear . . .'

'The social conditions and injustices cannot disappear. What I have said is that they change their perceptions for the time being by accepting one another.'

'When you talk of acceptance,' Emily went on, 'don't you imply at the same time the perpetuation of these conditions? In other words when I tolerate an unjust system don't I somehow encourage its continuation?'

'But where do you see the injustice,' Daskalos responded with a puzzled look on his face, 'when people learn how to love one another and those who are gifted with special skills are ready to help those who are not?'

'But don't you think this is utopia Daskale?' Emily reacted as Katerina was about to join the argument but was pre-empted by Daskalos.

'Just a minute,' he said loudly and stretched his right hand forward. 'Which situation can you offer me which is better? So far we have had a French Revolution, injustices, guillotines. We have had a Russian Revolution, a Hungarian Revolution. What have they brought about? Tell me, please.'

'Does it mean, Daskale, that we must not fight for change and social justice? Does the fact that these revolutionary movements have not brought about the desired results make the prevailing conditions the right ones?'

'I have never implied such a thing. Change comes about every moment,' Daskalos responded and then with a raised voice he continued. 'It is love which is going to bring genuine change. Violence and wars and so-called struggles – all they manage to bring about is more violence. I believe that it is only with love and spiritual evolution through the aeons that authentic change can come about. Of course we want change, and change is inevitable. And in the example I gave change comes immediately when the employer and the worker begin to love one another and be of service to one another. This is exactly the secret and the true code to bring about change.'

'But are things that way, really, Daskale?' Emily added. 'Perhaps we can see that in some isolated cases of employer-worker relationships love indeed can work and hope that finally the conscience of the employer will be awakened and that right thinking will prevail. But if we examine this issue from the perspective of social realities, from the perspective of social structure, we'll see an entrenched injustice. We see for example the great powers exploiting and oppressing smaller states.'

'Okay, but what do you suggest?' Daskalos said and with

folded hands leaned back on his armchair waiting for Emily's reply.

'The only thing I can say is that if we accept what you said earlier we must accept things as they are. Are we to believe, for example, that the superpowers will ever reach a state of love and understanding in their relationships to the smaller states?'

'But why not?'

'Because, my dear Daskale, we know how politics work,' Emily responded again and everybody seemed amused with this debate.

'For me,' Daskalos went on, 'so-called politics is nothing more than immorality, egotism and stupidity.'

'But this is your personal opinion.'

'No. It is the truth. Listen. Whether I observe the egotistical behavior of two persons or two nations it is the same thing. The results are alike. I personally see no change beyond love and understanding.'

'What Emily is talking about, Daskale,' Neophytos volunteered to clarify, 'is cases such as Nicaragua. The Nicaraguans got rid of the dictator Somoza, and the Reagan administration decided that Nicaragua is threatening the United States. Nicaragua is a country a little bigger than Cyprus. And what do the Americans do? They mine their harbors, and they pay a lot of criminals to go around killing the people and burning their villages.'

'This is bad,' Daskalos noted as if to underscore the understatement of the night, and the innocence with which he said it made us all chuckle.

'Can the Nicaraguans now correct this situation by loving the Americans?' Neophytos asked.

'For the time being perhaps no. But sooner or later both the Nicaraguans and the Americans will resolve their problems only when they learn to love one another. You know, this new doctrine of human rights is a very positive development in history. I see in this dogma a new factor that can help towards the resolution of problems. This is progress.'

'Someone who is born in a place like Nicaragua,' Katerina stated, 'will have the choice of sitting down and waiting for the day justice will come to his country while seeing his children hungry and unhappy, or he will get organized with his fellows to react, resist and revolt.'

'In such cases,' Daskalos added, 'he has no choice. He will have to submit to the circumstances that he finds himself in and are beyond his power to change. He will react, resist and revolt. However, this does not mean that he should not eventually realize the truth. That someday it is the other way, that of love and understanding which will correct things. Do you understand what I want to say? It is not the struggle itself which will bring the desired effect. You may have to carry on a struggle. You may have no choice. I also took part in such struggles. Do you think that I enjoyed the fight? Do you think I enjoyed going around Omorphita trying to defend our positions from Turkish attacks? But I did it in spite of myself. I did it to prevent further bloodshed. Sometimes you are forced to plunge into a hurricane to rescue people in danger and to prevent worse things from happening. But there is one thing that I am happy about and thank God for,' Daskalos said and brought forward his hands. 'I have never stained my hands with blood except that of my own when I got shot. I insist, with violence and guns we can solve nothing. You may with force prevent a greater evil from unfolding, an invasion for example. You are inside the turmoil and you have no other choice. But you should know that such conditions must not last, they must not and they cannot be perpetuated.'

Daskalos told me once that evils like wars, revolutions and other forms of social calamities always have benign consequences. Historical tragedies are often stimulants to awaken sleeping humanity to the nature of Reality. It is the way Karma works on the historical vista, to offer incarnated entities experiences and lessons for their spiritual evolution.

'I have a question about this issue of love, Daskale,' Stephanos interjected after a pause of a few seconds. 'Do you see it as a form of exchange or simply as giving of oneself?'

'It is human nature pressing for self-expression.'

'But is it a matter of exchange in order to bring about an equilibrium or is it simply giving of oneself?'

'If you think of it that way it is a form of calculation. I do not want that. I want the spontaneous expression of the heart. Do you understand what I am driving at?'

'I think so,' Stephanos added. 'Under such circumstances you will never feel that you are being done an injustice.'

After nodding affirmatively to Stephanos' last remark

Daskalos proceeded to point out that in spite of all the problems with the Turkish Cypriots he still loves them and those who know him reciprocate that love.

'Would you mind if they did not love you?' Stephanos asked with a hint of irony in his voice.

'No. But when you love people it is natural to be loved by them.' Daskalos then described a case in which a Turkish governor of the occupied town of Kyrenia, who knew Daskalos from before, sent a message through a third party to inquire of his sister's health. Using a photograph of the Turkish woman, Daskalos carried out a diagnosis of her problem and urged the Turk to immediately send his sister to England for a mastectomy.

'All I could see in that case,' Daskalos concluded, 'was a human being concerned with the health of his sister. Nothing else.'

When I first heard Daskalos speak of his relationships with the Turks the thought crossed my mind that perhaps he was exaggerating. But as in other cases when Daskalos' claims appeared to me too far-fetched, later events corroborated his earlier claims.

I discovered the fondness of the Turks toward Daskalos in a most unlikely set-up. At a very rare get-together between some Greek and Turkish Cypriots who have been separated since 1974 as a result of the Turkish invasion, one of the Turkish Cypriots mentioned to me that until recently he had assumed Mr Sathi was a Turk. The reason why he felt so, he said, was because Daskalos was so popular among Turkish Cypriots. In fact, he said jokingly, he was disappointed when he discovered that Daskalos was in fact a Greek. Another of the Turkish Cypriot participants who overheard our conversation informed me with excitement how he himself had once visited Daskalos, who told him 'everything' about himself including a detailed description of a scar on his right foot which was hidden under his pants. He too vouched for Daskalos' fame among Turkish Cypriots and that he in fact was 'the only Greek the Turks loved.'

'Is love something that we learn, Daskale?' Katerina asked after we had spent some time discussing the disheartening state of affairs between Greek and Turkish Cypriots that have been separated since the 1974 invasion of the island by Turkey.

'No,' Daskalos replied. 'Love is our nature. It is inside us. All we need to do is allow it to express itself.'

'How do we learn to do that?' Katerina asked.

'Again, with right thinking,' Daskalos answered after pausing for a few seconds. 'What right thinking, you may ask. Let us say Ahmet, a Turkish Cypriot lad, and Andreas, a Greek Cypriot, learn through the law of repetition to consider each other enemies. They assume it is very natural to kill one another. And although this is irrational they themselves consider it the proper thing to do. When, however, they allow themselves through right thinking to express their feelings as love, then these two good boys could be playing soccer and tennis with one another and not shoot at each other.' Then Daskalos talked of some prominent Turks who were friends of his and sat in on some of his lectures given in the Turkish quarter of Nicosia.

'One day I gave a talk on the Turkish side. It was before the troubles. After I finished I said to them, "I would like to ask you a question. Suppose I destroy the corner of a mosque and then I gather all the sufis of the world and kneel and pray together day in and day out, will the mosque be rebuilt by itself, without human hands and effort?" Of course not, they replied. "Okay, Daskale," someone clever reacted. "What if we destroy the corner of a church and then gather all the bishops and archbishops of the world to kneel down and pray, will the church be rebuilt by itself?" "Of course not," I replied. "But let me now proceed with my questions. Suppose in an accident both Ahmet and Andreas injured their legs. The doctors made certain that there were no infections. Will their wounds be healed?" "Yes of course," said someone in the audience. "Very well," I said. "Therefore, neither the mosque nor the church will be repaired by God. But the body of Ahmet and the body of Andreas are temples of God. The Divine is inside them regardless of whether one is called Ahmet and the other Andreas. What right, therefore, do they have to shoot and kill one another?" Ali Bey, a notable, stood up and said, "You are absolutely correct Daskale. Please teach this to the Greeks." "Fine," I replied, "but can you promise me that you will teach this truth to the Turks?"' Daskalos' remarks brought hearty laughter to all of us.

'This is right thinking,' Daskalos continued, 'but how do you teach it to people since you have in front of you such a curse which people call patriotism?

'People do not realize,' Daskalos went on after a few seconds, 'that their patriotism nourishes the patriotism of their so-called enemies. Patriotism is an elemental that magnetizes the atmosphere. When the Greeks celebrate the 25th of March [Greek independence day] with the marches, the drums and the flag-waving, their patriotic excitement creates an elemental which, let us say, embodies the character of the Greek Cypriots. But parallel with the Greek form of this elemental there is also its aura which is then absorbed by the Turkish Cypriots. Then they become patriotic and copy step by step what the Greek Cypriots are doing. Therefore, when people indulge in these patriotic frenzies which one side assumes serves its own interests, in reality it has opposite consequences. It is us who have made the Turkish Cypriots Turks. The patriotic feelings of one group are etheric vibrations that tend to awaken and nourish the patriotic feelings of other groups. And this principle is true not only of patriotism. It is the same with religion. People pray in churches and mosques and get fanaticized with their gods. Do you know how many monstrous elementals get created daily, elementals of "faith and country"? When people understand the law of elementals, of how noetic images are constructed, they will realize that whatever they do it is on their heads that it will ultimately land. You cannot abuse the law of cause and effect, of Karma. You cannot abuse without consequences Mind, this infinite ocean of vibrations within which we all swim. The moment you create these vibrations of patriotism everybody will be exposed to their influences. For me there is nothing more stupid and criminal than militaristic marches, parades and celebrations.

'Every day,' Daskalos went on, 'we struggle to neutralize these monsters that people incessantly create with their fanaticisms.'

'How do you do that since these monstrous elementals are so powerful?' I asked.

'You project analogous elementals of love and understanding in order to bring about the balance.'

'But are the elementals of love you create as powerful as the elementals of hatred and violence created by tradition and history?' I asked again.

'Fortunately it is in the nature of things that good fights evil. And evil fights evil. In the process they become mutually exhausted. Also, the good supports the good and they become mutually strengthened. One who hates generates in the other similar feelings and both suffer, they punish each other. It is the law of Karma at work. Love strengthens love. Hatred exhausts hatred.'

'In our case here in Cyprus,' I probed further, 'evil elementals are created on both sides preventing a peaceful resolution of the conflict. Should things continue the way they do I am afraid a military confrontation is very probable.'

'In the meantime,' Daskalos responded, 'we neutralize as many evil elementals as we can on both sides. One of the duties of the inner circle is to create on a routine basis elementals of love that we project over the entire island.'

'How is that done?'

'During exomatosis we spread out over the island and we cover it with the white-rose color of love. When we generate these vibrations a fanatical Turk, for example, will be affected subconsciously and will calm down without knowing why. A Greek fanatic will become similarly affected. I believe the inner circle has contributed decisively in the maintenance of peace in spite of the stupidities and idiocies that go on. As I told you before, our work as invisible helpers is beyond ethnicity, religion or race. We do not discriminate. When you let water flow so that a thirsty person may drink you are not concerned whether that person is a Turk, a Maronite, a Greek, an Armenian, or an American. You are not concerned whether he is a bandit or a saint. It is Karma which will judge them, not yourself. The love you spread out is for everybody.'

'You mentioned,' I pointed out, 'that an evil elemental fights another of its kind and they destroy and neutralize each other. These fights, however, lead to wars down here on this planet. So, who gets destroyed in reality?'

'It is evil that gets destroyed. I am telling you that you may find yourself in the very heart of a battle and if Karma will not permit it nothing will happen to you. It is the wisdom of the Absolute that protects you. He who must pay must pay.'

Daskalos then mentioned that the wars on the gross material level are reflections of wars that go on on the psychonoetic levels. It is for this reason, he said, that in the Greek Orthodox liturgy the ancient fathers of the Church, who according to Daskalos 'knew about these matters,' chanted 'We pray to Thee O Lord for peace in the higher spheres and for the salvation of our souls.'

'Evil,' Daskalos continued, 'predominates everywhere at all levels, both on the psychonoetic as well as on the gross material level. But at the end it is the good which will triumph. This is the law. It is always like that.'

'Because of the reasons you have just mentioned, Daskale,' Neophytos commented, 'I still cannot see how one can arrive at right thinking.'

'I don't know either,' Daskalos replied with a smile and shrugged his shoulders, 'but just because we don't know how to make others see this truth it does not follow that we should not express this love ourselves, regardless of whether others will do so or not.

'If we Greeks,' Daskalos added, 'had some brains in our heads, we would have related to the Turkish Cypriots like brothers by now.'

'I suggest we stop the discussion for a while,' Neophytos announced, 'so that we can eat.'

The table was already set with a cornucopia of local delicacies. We followed his suggestion without protest and we all began to fill our plates.

'The way things are,' Daskalos began after we served ourselves and started eating, 'even though you may be aware of the truth you may not be able to overcome the obstacles. Regardless of how much you may be into right thinking, time is needed for the attainment of maturity.'

'This is the tragedy,' Neophytos added. 'This is true in our personal relationships as well as in politics. What puzzles me is how do you overcome the obstacles of the prevailing conditions? How do you transcend subjectivity and arrive at this expression of love which is also right thinking?'

'We can now perceive love and right thinking,' Daskalos said slowly, having a full mouth and focusing on his plate, 'as a truth inside a sun which is behind the clouds. Let us hope that these clouds will soon disperse. Now we do not feel warm because of the clouds. It does not mean, however, that we should lose our faith in the reality of the sun.'

'At first I had my doubts about whether love can solve our

social and international problems,' Neophytos added. 'But I have realized that although love may not solve all our problems, the other methods of struggle and fighting are capable of solving even less. I doubt, however, whether love as a method by itself can solve all our problems.'

'I was at a party where it so happened that a high-ranking member of the Russian embassy was present,' Daskalos said as he continued eating. 'He was quite an intellectual and spoke fluent Greek. We started chatting and a few people gathered around us listening to our conversation. "In Russia," he said, "nobody is hungry and no one is dying from starvation. Our system," he said, "is better than that of America and England where, as they say, people sleep in the streets in the cold of the winter. Through force," he said, "we have brought about a better society. Doesn't that satisfy you?" I said, "No. I do not accept violence as a method of changing the world. In your Russia today," I told him further, "you assumed power and imposed conditions which do not spring from the heart. If in your Russia I could see a doctor or an engineer with two children making less money than a worker who has three children, I would applaud. In such a case there would be no discrimination over the value of work. The doctor would have different responsibilities than the plumber. The plumber would look after the houses of his brothers and sisters and the doctor the health of his fellow human beings. And I would see the doctor considering both his own children and those of the plumber as his and loving them all without discrimination. And I would see the plumber relate to the children of the doctor in the same way. This I would applaud. But the system you have in Russia now, my friend," I said, "is in reality a capitalism of the state rather than of the individual."'

'You are more radical than the communists, Daskale,' I mused.

'"Jesus Christ," I said to the Russian diplomat, "showed us the way with the communal feasts. This is what He meant when He said, Love thy neighbor as thyself."'

'What did the Russian say?' Neophytos asked.

'"You are right," he said, "but this will take time." The following day,' Daskalos claimed, 'I found an anonymous letter full of curses and accusations that I was a communist. It was apparently from someone who overheard my conversation with that Russian diplomat. Poor me, what did I say?' Daskalos mused as he put his plate away and shrugged in a gesture of innocence.

'I presume,' Neophytos added laughing, 'that had Jesus come to the world now He would have been sent straight to jail by the bishops and archbishops.'

'No doubt about that,' Daskalos responded. 'Had He come today He would not have been able to recognize the religion He offered us.'

'Daskale,' Stephanos interjected from his corner as he placed his empty plate on the table while the rest of us kept eating, 'I still have some difficulties on the issue of love. I still wonder whether it is possible to have love without it being a form of exchange, a balance sheet. For if it is an equilibrium, a balance sheet, it is not true love in the last analysis. Right?'

'Right.'

'I recognize this,' Stephanos went on. 'But given my limitations I am unable to put it into practice. In ordinary people like ourselves there smolders the desire for reciprocity when we extend ourselves toward others. To be honest with you, I quite often wonder whether we are capable of knowing either the self or love. Let us take you as an example. Don't you have in your mind the image of yourself as one who loves?'

'It is not a question of experiencing satisfaction,' Daskalos replied. 'I simply feel that this is how I am and express myself without expecting recognition or rewards.'

'Therefore,' Emily added, 'if that is the case we must love everyone the same way, to the same degree. Does it mean that love has a scale or is it something absolute in the final analysis?'

'Now, just a minute. We must love everybody the same way, of course. But even Christ loved John more than the other disciples. That was fair, correct? You cannot avoid this. It is fair and understandable that you may be especially affectionate to a particular person, perhaps because that person may have a greater need for your love. I have studied these phenomena, but to tell you the truth I have not reached in my mind any definite conclusions.'

'Is it not that the love for someone,' Emily asked again, 'is the result of the fact that you are vibrating at the same wavelengths?'

'Love means that you vibrate at all the wavelengths,' Daskalos replied.

'Don't you love some people more because they have certain attributes that you love in yourself, such as common interests?' Emily added.

'No. For me all human beings have God inside them. And it is the God inside them that I love, "the light that enlightens every human being descending upon the Earth." I do not and I must not make comparisons between human beings. I must love the hobo the same way that I love my best friend.'

Daskalos' statement brought to my mind an encounter I had had with a Maine psychic healer. He had described to me how one day he went to a garage to have his car fixed. As he was waiting for the mechanics to complete their job he had an ecstatic experience that changed his life. All of a sudden, he said, he saw everybody that was walking around covered with intense white luminosity in the shape of an inverted egg. It was such a tremendous feeling of exhilaration and beauty, he claimed, that since that day there was no human being he met that he did not like.

'But are you sure, Daskale,' I asked, 'that you do not discriminate in your loves? You must discriminate.'

'I try not to.'

'I find this hard to believe. Are you telling us that you do not love your grandson more than other children of his age?' I asked again.

'I may not always be successful, but I do try.'

'Therefore,' Stephanos jumped in, 'you do discriminate,' and all of us roared with laughter at Stephanos' syllogism.

'Okay, of course I do,' Daskalos admitted. 'I do live inside matter. I have no choice. The conditions around me, those I find myself in, do affect me. I am not perfect, nor is it possible to attain perfection and be within gross matter. The vibrations of the environment, whether I like it or not, do have their effect on me. But someday we must liberate ourselves from these vibrations. I cannot say that I am now free of them. It does not mean, however, that we should allow today's prevailing conditions to affect our capacity for right thinking.'

'Why must we love only one person with whom we have decided to spend our lives and not love everybody the same way?' Yiannis, who until that point was silent, asked, provoking a lively debate.

'I can only speak for myself,' Daskalos went on. 'As far as I am concerned, based strictly on my own understanding and experience, one must love all the women that are older than oneself as one's mothers. One must love all the women of one's same age as one's sisters, and one must love all the women younger than oneself as one's daughters. Love them all. But you love only one woman with whom you will bring children into this world. Alas, if we related to any woman we fancied as if she were our wife, where then is the harmony within nature? Yes, do love all the women alike, but love them with your heart. The other form of love which leads to sexual union cannot be had indiscriminately. For example, do you think I love sister Theano any less than I love my daughters? Had my wife still been alive, my love for her would have been no different than the love I have for Theano. But my wife is my wife. My relationship with her has brought into this world two daughters. It is a different relationship,' Daskalos concluded and leaned back on his chair. Then after a few moments he continued.

'In my way of thinking you marry in order to develop between men and women that special kind of love so that they may cooperate with the creative force of the Universe, to bring up a family. You cannot do that with ten different women or men. At least this is how I understand this issue. Now, whether present conditions permit this is a different story. We in this age have dismantled every ethical standard. We needed to abolish some oppressive rules and in the process we abolished just about every rule. I do not accept social conventions as they are today but at the same time I cannot advocate to abolish them. Whenever we do we have chaos all around.'

Daskalos then went on to clarify that he would not exclude the possibility that within the infinity of time, at some future point, different alternatives may emerge in the relationships of the sexes when polygamous arrangements may truly express genuine love. So far, however, he argued, he had not seen or experienced such cases either in this or previous incarnations. It is only through monogamous relationships, he insisted, that he had noticed what to him was authentic love.

'What is your view of marriage as a sacrament?' Stephanos asked after a few moments of silence.

'It is sacred,' Daskalos responded with emphasis. 'But when I say that I don't mean the marriage ceremony in church. It is not the chants and alleluias of the priests that make up a marriage.'

'Can you tell us more about what you mean?' Stephanos asked again.

Daskalos went on to explain that for him 'marriage' means the closeness, love and commitment that two people have for one another, something which develops through repeated incarnations. The ancient fathers of the Church knew about this truth, he claimed, and it is for this reason that during the marriage ceremony in the Greek Orthodox Church the priest chants 'Bless them O Lord in their comings and goings. Bless their wreaths O Lord in Heaven and unto the ages of ages, Amen.'

'Since a couple could live a maximum of thirty, forty years in one lifetime, what does this mean,' Daskalos asked, 'other than repeated incarnations through the centuries?' He then went on to point out that in the eyes of God two people are 'married' if they live together and love one another. It is not social conventions and customs that bestow sacredness in a marital bond, Daskalos insisted. In fact two persons may be married in a conventional sense but not married from the perspective of the Divine.

'Daskale,' Katerina asked after further discussion about this issue, 'what is erotic love?'

'I wish I knew,' Daskalos chuckled and there was thunderous laughter by everyone.

'Is it a fantasy, an illusion, something egotistical or is it, as Plato said, something greater and more profound?' Katerina asked again.

'As I see it practiced in society today,' Daskalos answered, 'a society dominated by illusions and self-interest, the meaning of erotic love has lost its color and significance. But true love exists and you must search to find it.

'Men and women,' Daskalos went on, 'got spoiled in our times. They live within their illusions and self-indulgences, and this is the crux of the problem. Men and women have reduced everything to their own measure, to their own human measures.'

'Did you experience the great love of your life?' Stephanos asked and after a few thoughtful moments Daskalos answered softly. 'Yes, in my wife who gave me my children. I lived ten happy years with her and then she got seriously ill. With great efforts I helped her stay alive for another ten years. She left. In a manner of speaking she left. So many years now since then. I have not replaced her. I did not fall madly and idiotically in love with another woman. I love my wife.'

'But Daskale,' Emily pointed out, 'you did divorce your first wife.'

'Yes, but the first one was not *my* wife,' Daskalos explained and with his finger pointed at his heart. 'I was seventeen at the time and I got a few slaps from my father before I would accept and get married to her. It was an arrangement between my parents and hers. I cannot say that I could not have learned to love her like my wife. But she disappointed me. She said she loved me and adored me like a god and then went around with other men. I could not stomach all that. I got divorced six months after the wedding. It was only after seven years had passed that I met and married my real wife. She was not pretty like the other. Nor was she wealthy. But I loved her and she loved me. She suffered a lot during her illness. I stood by her side. That is how I understand love. And when the doctor after an operation told me that from then on I could relate to her only as if she was my sister, I accepted it. I never let her out of my embrace until the last moment. We never had any sexual relations during the ten years of her illness because she constantly hemorrhaged. But,' Daskalos added with high emotion, 'she was never deprived of my love and my care. That is what love means to me. I love her. I come into spiritual contact with her. I have kept our marital wreaths and I will take them along when I depart. She was my companion in this life who gave me my children. Sexuality was never the central focus of my life. That is how I see things and that is how I personally understand love, which is something powerful and great. And I do not speak on the basis of what I have learned from books. It is on the basis of what I have experienced and what I am living. Don't I love women myself? Many. And they love me. And I stand by them in their difficult moments and during their illnesses. And as I told you before, I relate to these women as if they were my mothers, my sisters and my daughters. When I relate to these women I never focus nor do I care to focus anywhere lower than my heart. When a woman comes to me, one that I have never met before, and tells me her problems and I take her hand into mine and call her "my daughter," what I tell her that moment she accepts and she trusts me. And really I do feel as if she were my own daughter. This is how I understand love, without second thoughts, without calculations. For me my greatest reward is the realization and the satisfaction that I express myself as love. Tell me, Neophyte,' Daskalos asked with emotion as he turned to our host, 'is there a greater reward in life than to be given the opportunity to express yourself as love? What other satisfaction must anyone desire?'

'You have said before,' Neophytos said slowly and in a low voice, 'that love is the natural expression of the soul. Most people, however, find it difficult to do so.'

'They have covered and suppressed their love-nature with the conditions under which they live and with calculations. And that is why they are unhappy,' Daskalos added forcefully.

'But my question,' Neophytos asked, 'is how does one uncover this love?'

'Again, through *orthologismos*, through right thinking,' Daskalos answered. 'To truly realize that all around me at this very moment there are men and women like myself. And just as the sun caresses my face and that of every other human being, so also the sun of my heart must caress every human being. Just as the sun does not discriminate on who absorbs its warmth, so also the warmth of my heart must be given freely to every human being that crosses my path. Since Christ is inside me, the light that enlightens every human being descending upon the Earth, why should I not express my love freely? Then you will truly experience peace and tranquility. Whether you want it or not you will experience satisfaction. You love.'

'And not to be concerned with the attitude and calculations of others,' Neophytos added.

'Definitely not. Even our children sometimes make their calculations. Are we to deprive them of our love? Or to love them unconditionally? We must love, period.

'Some time ago,' Daskalos continued, 'a person close to me had done, judging on the basis of human values, gross injustices and errors against me, accusations, even curses. Many in my life, including students, began to dislike him. They called him ungrateful, idiot, a liar, et cetera. Later on he began suffering as a result of his past actions. He felt the need to come to me. He

said, "I am dishonest, I am a bad person, I am a beast. . . . "
"Are you going to continue?" I asked severely. "That is because
you don't know," he said. "Are you sure?" I asked. "Why then
don't you give me a couple of slaps in the face and a kick in the
ass. Or at least, do you have the power to forgive me?" I stood
up, I took him into my arms and kissed him. "There is no need
to forgive. I love you,"' Daskalos said softly and then
continued his narration.

'He began crying. And do you know who that person was?
The husband of one of my closest students. They got divorced.
He used to beat her up. The other day he came over and I made
coffee for him. "I was so dishonest," he said. "Stop torturing
yourself unnecessarily," I told him. "There is no need to ask for
forgiveness." I advised his wife not to poison her heart with
hatred of what he had done to her. "He," I said to her, "is still
the father of your children."'

'In reality you have forgiven this person," Neophytos pointed
out.

'It is not a question of forgiving him. I love him.'

'Okay, but he has shown remorse for his past errors,'
Neophytos added.

'Not necessarily,' Daskalos replied. 'When he comes to his
senses that is the time when he will truly suffer. Deep down he
has not repented. He continues to behave like a fool. He has
done horrible things. He now has a mistress, the ex-wife of a
former friend of his. He became the cause of another divorce.
And he runs around with his lover provoking everyone. It
became a major scandal. Everyone was going out of their
minds. This is tragic, right? For me what he had done was quite
human,' Daskalos went on. 'He will come to his senses sooner
or later and he will suffer the consequences of his actions. One
day he passed by my house with his lover next to him in the car
as if to provoke me. Instead of getting angry I laughed. "You
fool," I said to myself.'

'Why did you not feel angry?' Neophytos asked.

'Because I love him. When I said "you fool" I meant that he
was suffering unnecessarily like an idiot. Tomorrow he may
visit me and have coffee with me as if nothing had happened.
That is how I understand love. From the moment you start
calculating and discriminating you do not love in reality. From
the moment you feel hurt and you demand of the other to ask

for forgiveness you do not love.'

'But what about the victim, his wife?' Emily asked with a mild tone of protest in her voice.

'But why see things in terms of victims and victimizers,' Daskalos responded, 'and not see human beings that are not aware of what is happening to them, who are irrational. Now let me ask you a question, Emily. This moment we consider his former wife as the victim, right?'

'Isn't she?'

'And we consider him the victimizer. Who do you think suffers most at this point in time, his ex-wife or himself?' Daskalos asked and after a few seconds of silence he continued.

'When their daughter was about to get married, the other relatives were wondering who should escort the girl to church. Was it proper for him to do so since he was in the process of getting the divorce? They had a family council to discuss the matter and arrive at some resolution. They invited me to participate and offer my opinion. I suggested that since he was the father the proper thing to do was that he should be asked to escort his daughter to church as it is the custom. Everybody agreed. They invited him to come to the house before the wedding to have coffee with the rest of us while the bride was getting ready for church. While he was at the house I felt heavy at the heart. No dislike, or anger. Nothing like that. When I saw him sitting by himself in the other room I felt such a pain. Theophanis came at that moment with another brother from Paphos. "Please, Theophani," I said, "go to the other room and kiss him like we used to when he was a member of our circles." "I'll do it only for your sake, Daskale," he said to me. "No, please," I said, "it is not good to think that way. I don't do it myself because I can't bear it." Not because I didn't want to but because I felt I couldn't. I am a human being too,' Daskalos pleaded and his voice almost broke with emotion as he described the scene.

'I am not sure how he took it,' he went on, 'but when we were getting ready for church he began banging his head on the piano crying. I tried to calm him down. Then his wife approached him and very coolly said to him, "Stop the crying and the theatrics. Our child is getting ready for the church. Let's take her there."'

'Now tell me, Emily,' Daskalos said and raised his voice.

'Who suffered more, his wife or himself? Why do you call him victimizer? Why not call him a victim of his weaknesses and stupidities? During the ceremony in church he looked at me with such profound sadness as if to tell me "What can I do?"

'In life we must learn to love people unconditionally. We must not be judgmental, we must not feel hurt and resentful, we must just love. This is the power of love as I understand it. Do you think that this man is not paying dearly for his weaknesses? Must I hit him on the head on top of that? Do you consider it right to awaken in him more guilt than he already has? Would this not be somewhat sadistic? And is he at this moment ready for his conscience to awaken even more? Would it be for his own good?'

Daskalos ended the discussion on love and right thinking and it was decided that we should continue some other night. It was already close to midnight. One by one we left the apartment, thanking Neophytos and Katerina for their generosity and Daskalos for his lesson. Everybody seemed uplifted with Daskalos' spirited exposition on the meaning of altruistic love. Yiannis murmured that we need periodically to hear such messages because the routines of daily life pull us in opposite directions.

CHAPTER 11

Dreams and fantasies

I started my project with Daskalos several years ago on the assumption that I would employ his own language and framework of understanding as a research strategy in order to penetrate his world. In the process of doing so, however, I often asked myself whether I was able to maintain the objectivity and detachment expected of my profession as a sociologist. Quite frankly there were moments when I wondered myself as to whether the real me was a mystic wearing the temporary cloak of the sociologist, or whether I was primarily a sociologist temporarily playing the role of the mystic in order to cope with the exigencies of my research. I confess that the more I associated with Daskalos, the more my original posture as a skeptical, detached and objective observer was shaken. I often wondered whether the objectivity, as narrowly understood by empirical science, is in fact a smoke screen that obscures our field of vision and prevents us from acquiring a better and more profound understanding of reality.

I have no way of evaluating the validity of Daskalos' world beyond my own personal experiences. I have no way of knowing whether there are higher intelligences overseeing the evolution of our planet, or whether Daskalos was the reincarnation of Origen, Spyridon and others. On the other hand, I cannot deny the authenticity of the healing sessions I witnessed, nor can I ignore the stunning coincidences I reported elsewhere that forced me to question whether they were in fact coincidences. Most importantly my relationship with Daskalos had a profound effect on my dream life, so much so that once I mused to Emily that no matter how much I struggled during the day to remain a sociologist, by night I was transformed into a mystic.

I once confronted in my dream the devil himself. He was dark, with red eyes, green tongue, horns, the works. I was terrified. Immediately Daskalos' instructions came to mind. I created with my thought a white cross, held it firmly in front of the devil's face and repeated breathlessly, 'Jesus Christ saves, Jesus Christ saves,' a phrase that my aunt who raised me used to say as she was pouring water over my head when giving me baths as a child (did I perhaps 'regress' in my dream?). The moment I said these words the face of the devil melted and disappeared. I felt elated with my accomplishment in defeating Satan and woke up. When I mentioned it to Daskalos he laughed in his customary manner and said that all I had to do to chase away the satanic elemental was to just order it to go away and it would have done so.

One night I was angry with Constantine, my son, for being cranky. He would not sleep and let us sleep. I had a frightful nightmare that night. A huge monster in the shape of a whale was about to attack my son while asleep. The moment the creature was attacking Constantine, his screams woke me up. We rushed to calm him down, not knowing what had happened to him. Never before had he behaved in such a manner. The child was in hysterics. I felt guilty and thought that in my anger I might have, in some mysterious way, created the monster that attacked him. Perhaps he saw the same dream, I thought. On the other hand, a more conventional interpretation would be that he began screaming, and then I created the dream of the monster and woke up. My experience, however, suggested otherwise. Daskalos reassured me that I could not have created the monster. Rather, we 'fished' together the monstrous elemental floating within the psychic realms and saw the same dream.

Some of the most enchanting and most extraordinary dreams that I have had so far, however, since I met Daskalos, are the following.

I dreamt that I was somewhere in Latin America walking by the waterfront. I turned into a dead-end street. At the end of the road there was a high wall with a door. Without any hesitation I opened it and entered inside a narrow corridor. At that very moment I became aware that I was in a dream – the door, Iacovos told me later, symbolized the gateway to the psychic worlds. I was terribly excited, breathed heavily and my heartbeat accelerated. It was an experience of peak intensity. I felt that every cell in my body was alive. Is that, I thought,

what Daskalos means by exomatosis? I walked slowly, trying
to figure out where I was. The corridor was painted with a rose
color and was dimly lit with reddish lights. A short distance
away there were several doors lined up on both sides of the
corridor. I clearly noticed several half-naked women with their
negligées open moving in and out of those doorways. 'Darn it,'
I thought and began laughing. 'Of all places, I got myself into a
psychic whorehouse. I wonder what Freud would have said.' A
girl standing in front of one of those doors noticed me and
waved at me to follow her. I entered into her room and she
began taking off the little she was wearing. She stood there
waiting for me. The excitement of finding myself within a
psychic plane was so cataclysmic that it overshadowed every
other trace of desire and concern. She had a very beautiful body
but a sad and pale face. 'Do you realize,' I began saying to her,
'that you are not alive?' She looked distressed and covered her
face. I started talking to her about the nature of the psychic
world and the freedom human beings have to shape their own
psychic environment. I felt in a hurry as I was fully conscious
that my time was limited and that I was bound to wake up at
any moment. I was standing in the middle of the room fully
dressed while carrying on my monologue, while she lay in bed
on her side facing and staring at the wall. Apparently my
lecture was annoying to her, or so I thought. Suddenly I felt the
presence of a huge bearded man of Orson Wellesian dimensions
getting ready to enter the bedroom. I assumed he was looking
around for some prostitute. 'How can I get rid of him?' I
thought. I knew that since I was fully dressed and had no
intention of sleeping with her he would want to come in.
'Daskalos taught me,' I thought, 'that in the fourth dimension,
if we consciously focus on something, it happens. I will appear
naked in front of the door and then he will go away,' I said to
myself. The moment these thoughts crossed my mind I found
myself standing in front of the huge man without any clothes
on. 'Pardon me, Sir,' he said, and moved to another room. I
turned around, went near the girl and resumed my lecture
about a subject that she apparently was not interested in. Yet I
persisted because I felt I had only a short time to help her get
'enlightened' and move out of her misery, a life in a
whorehouse. Suddenly I woke up. My heart continued to
pulsate rapidly for a while. Waking up filled me with a sense of

loss and disappointment. The dream experience somehow seemed to me at the time more real than the world I had awakened into.

On another occasion I dreamt that I was flying around people I knew walking in the street. I was fully aware that I was in a dream and was telling everybody that they did not have to walk, that they were within the psychic world and that it was much more enjoyable to fly. I demonstrated the fact with spectacular acrobatics. I then noticed a door and planned to open it to find out what was on the other side. 'Just a minute,' I thought, 'this is a chance to test Daskalos' claims about the psychic worlds.' He repeatedly taught that in these worlds objects are no real obstacles and that one can go through them if one decides to do so. I closed my eyes and with a great deal of fear I ran into the wall. For a few seconds I was in a panic. I felt that something terrible must have happened to me, that I was not going to be able to return to my body. I could see nothing in front of me except a heavy, bright, white mist. Suddenly the foggy mist began clearing up and I found myself inside a courtyard filled with lemon and orange trees, a typical Cypriot scene, a place very congenial to my soul. The walls surrounding the yard were whitewashed. It was a sunny day and I could see through the leaves a bright blue sky. At one corner of the courtyard there was a bright spot where an old couple sat in the sunshine. The man wore grey pants and a white shirt. He had grey hair and seemed to be quite fond of his oversized mustache. The old woman was dressed in black like any typical traditional Greek grandmother. I introduced myself and began asking questions to find out whether they were aware of their condition. 'There I go again,' I thought to myself and began laughing. 'I am carrying my field research into the psychic realms.' The moment this thought crossed my mind I regrettably discovered that I was back in my body.

In another dream I found myself on a brilliant day walking happily in the streets of the neighborhood where I grew up. I was totally conscious and exhilarated that I was 'outside of my body.' 'I can return any time I wish,' I thought. 'To prove it I will wake up.' Before I ended my thought I woke up, annoyed at myself for doing so.

Another dream of this type occurred just as we were getting ready to leave Cyprus. I saw myself inside a university library. I could clearly see students studying everywhere. It was a familiar scene. To my great surprise I came face to face with someone I knew to be dead. At that moment I realized that I was inside a psychic plane. I became fully aware that I was in a dream. I was all the more surprised as the person I met was a former neighbor of ours. He died from a heart attack while having coffee with my father. As a child I used to play with his son but other than that I had had little contact with him. In the dream he looked quite young, in his early twenties, even though I had known him only as an older man. I was fascinated to recognize him even though it was not possible for me to have known him during his youth. He smiled and began to pace quickly away from me. 'Wait, wait,' I shouted, 'I want to talk to you. I want to ask you many questions about the world you live in. You have a lot to teach me. Of all the people, why am I meeting you here?' 'We were room-mates at Leeds,' he replied as he continued to walk away from me. At that moment I did not realize what he meant. Later I found that there is a university in England at Leeds. I tried to run and catch up with him but I felt something holding me back. I breathed heavily. 'Just a moment,' I thought. 'Why do I have this problem? Daskalos said that when you find yourself within the psychic world you can literally create with your mind your own reality.' At that moment the memory of how I had coped in the earlier dreams came to my mind. I was fascinated that I could think, within my present dream, of an earlier dream. 'I am going to walk straight without any difficulty,' I said with determination. The moment these thoughts crossed my mind I walked without any difficulty and began breathing normally, but I lost the person I was trying to follow. I then walked around the library and came in front of a door. I opened it and went inside a small amphitheater. Some students were about to see a movie. 'The last thing I want to do,' I thought, 'is to waste my time watching a movie in the psychic world. My time is short and I must hurry.' I knew I was going to wake up soon and I wanted to talk to people and find out how they felt about being dead. The lights went off and the projector started to show a color movie. As I was about to leave the room I noticed a strange-looking man sitting in the last row. On his right shoulder there stood an awesome-looking large black bird that resembled a crow. 'Is that for real,' I thought, 'or did I create the bird myself?' 'Mister, what kind of nonsense are you telling us now?' the man with the bird said to me. 'You say we don't exist. Are you some kind of nut?' In fact I said nothing to him but I felt that he was picking up my thoughts. 'Buddy, if I sit down to explain where you are now, it will be such a waste of time for me. Besides it would take hours and I am about to wake up in a few minutes,' I mumbled to myself and walked out of the room. I was eager to move around and begin to interview what I thought were humans who lived on the psychic level. I approached a girl who was staring at me. I introduced myself and extended my hand for a handshake. Before I could touch her she pulled her hand back with a terrified expression in her face. 'You are not of our world,' she said with panic. 'Don't be afraid, love,' I said softly, trying to calm her down, 'I am not going to hurt you.' In the meantime several others gathered around, curious to find out who I was. At that moment I woke up. I sat in my bed all shaken up. My heart was still pulsating fast and I found myself in a pool of sweat.

The dreams I described above and others that followed are as vivid in my memory as the nights when I experienced them. The identifying characteristics and quality of these dreams, in spite of the differences in content, are essentially identical. Below I summarize what I consider to be their similarities.

First, they were peak experiences, to borrow Maslow's terminology. In general they were intensely pleasurable and radically different from anything else I had experienced up to that point. Either because of the nature of the experience itself, or because of its novelty, in all such dreams my heartbeat soared and my breathing was heavy. I felt as if I had an oxygen mask in front of my face.

Second, in all four dreams I was totally conscious of the fact that I was dreaming. I had a clear notion of the difference between the dream state I was in and the state of waking consciousness. In all the dreams I was in a position not only to think and be conscious of the fact that I was thinking, but also to guide my experience within the dream state. I was able to do that by bringing to my consciousness the lessons of Daskalos on the nature of thought and the psychic worlds. Once I had the first dream experience, I transferred the memory of my experience from the first dream to the subsequent ones. In this respect the encounters of the first dream, to some extent, set the tone for at least some of the experiences in the subsequent dreams.

Third, in all four dreams I had the intense feeling that the world I had entered was somehow more real than the waking state. Every cell of my body felt alive. There was, therefore, the desire to prolong the dream state for as long as possible, but not to remain in the dream state on a permanent basis. I never wished to remain there indefinitely. At one instance when that thought crossed my mind, I panicked. The persons in my life close to me numbed any desire for a more permanent residence within the psychic worlds, no matter how pleasurable they appeared. My desire was limited to prolonging my stay so that I might be able to gather more experience and transfer it back to the waking state. The return trip, however, was always disappointing. By comparison, the waking state lacked the intensity of experience of the dream state.

Fourth, I had no doubt that my recollections were accurate. The experiences were so vivid that I had no trouble remembering all that I had experienced with considerable clarity.

Last, unlike Daskalos and his close associates who claim that they can enter such states at will, my dream experiences were totally unplanned and unexpected. I presume that had I been able to enter into such states at will, the temptation to consider these other worlds more real, or at least as real, would have been irresistible. But, alas, my consciousness is hopelessly grounded within the three dimensions and I have no choice but to play, or pretend to play, the role of a Doubting Thomas.

Soon after I experienced the last dream I went with Emily to spend the evening with Daskalos and have a free-floating conversation on the nature of dreaming. It was to be one of our last encounters before I returned to my teaching post in Maine for the fall of 1986.

After I finished describing my last dream to Daskalos he shook his head and laughed heartily. 'You remind me of a toddler,' he chuckled, 'making his first steps and getting excited. Some day you will be able to attune yourself with any world you choose and come in contact at will with beings who live in different dimensions. You will then be able to converse with them in the same way you are conversing with me right at this moment. Then you will realize that all the dimensions are rooms of the same house. What you have experienced are not just dreams. Why not call them psychical experiences? You entered inside a subplane of the psychic world and you were given certain experiences. But the imprinting of these experiences was done in a way that pleased you. It was your own creation. You placed them in a sequence of your own. You most probably broke the experiences into several parts and you reassembled them in accordance with your wishes.'

'Are you suggesting,' I asked, 'that the persons I encountered were not real but the fabrication of my fantasy?'

'They were very real but the way you presented them in your brain was your own. This is what usually happens to beginners. What you have experienced others have experienced. They are real experiences but not properly recollected.'

'Why were they not properly recollected?' I wondered.

'I just told you. Because you are a beginner and beginners usually mix things up. When you practice extensively you will be able to recollect more clearly and you will have such experiences at will. Anyhow, even these limited experiences should have convinced you of the reality of other dimensions.'

I admitted that for the duration of these dreams I had had a feeling of total certitude about the reality of other dimensions that Daskalos had been mentioning all along. But when I 'returned to my body' the weight of the three dimensions forced upon me the skepticism of the 'Doubting Thomas.' Yet the intensity of those dream experiences remained vivid in my mind with the greatest clarity and detail. It was obvious that the way I experienced the dreams and the type of reasoning or dialogue that I carried on within myself during the dreaming could not have taken place without the exposure to Daskalos' teachings. I have often wondered whether I would still have experienced similar dreams regardless of whether or not I had ever met Daskalos.

Daskalos explained that the persons in the dream were most probably real. When one encounters, he said, entities who live within the psychic planes, their appearance is always youthful. When an old man dies he will acquire the appearance of a younger age. The fact that I recognized my father's friend when I had known him only as an old man was a sign that there was contact with the real person. The reason he had run away from me, Daskalos explained, was because I was not fully attuned to him. In the case of the girl who experienced terror when I extended my hand to her, a thirst for the material plane could have been prematurely awakened to her detriment.

Another crucial test of the reality of my psychic experience was my ability to reason and guide my dream experiences. Ultimately a Researcher of Truth will learn how to fully live within what people call dreams.

'Advanced masters,' Daskalos said, 'live consciously and continuously within all dimensions of existence. A dream, therefore, is not something unreal. In fact, all human experiences in all the dimensions, including the gross material, are forms of dreams. What people call 'reality' does not exist anywhere. Everything is a dream.

'To understand the nature of dreams,' Daskalos went on, 'we must study the nature of fantasy and how the human subconscious is being formed. I explained to you before that the present self-conscious personality, both in past and present incarnations, incessantly projects elementals. The sum total of these elementals is the present personality. When a human being is born he brings with him from previous incarnations the material upon which he builds his new personality. By that I do not mean that he brings the elementals of the past in terms of details, images, and ways of life, but rather as a sum total of experience, or propensities.

'Within our subconscious we have myriads of elementals that remain in a dormant state. They are ready, however, to become activated at any moment. Within our subconscious there is, as it were, a microfilm of innumerable elementals, each one enclosing within itself the nature of the energy and power that created it. It is the quality of the energy of the elementals that is being imprinted on the subconscious of the individual, not the details of events and images that prompted their creation. Under appropriate circumstances in the new incarnation, the energy of these elementals gets activated and analogous psychonoetic images are created. Once our attention is attracted by something related to the elementals inside us they are set into motion and reach the surface of our subconscious. It is our attention and focus that activate these elementals. Fantasy then begins. Let us take the example of someone listening to music. Let us assume that inside him there are many

216

elementals related to this musical composition. The resonance of the sounds may generate within his mind memories of journeys to distant lands where he had experiences associated with this music as well as others that have nothing to do with the music.

'When fantasy begins to gallop it may lead to regions hardly imaginable at the beginning of our reverie. What is the motive of fantasy, you may ask? Usually pleasure.'

'What about unpleasant fantasies?' I interrupted.

'Yes. One can also have nightmarish fantasies. Someone may witness an accident. Within his mind it may bring up the memory of a similar experience he had had in the past. Fear will now enter his mind that a similar accident may happen to his family. In this case fantasy becomes a tyrannical state of mind. Fantasy may awaken within an individual feelings of anger, confusion, all the base sentiments. A Researcher of Truth must become conscious of these feelings and try to eradicate them through self-analysis.

'Human fantasy has often led to the creation of deleterious and irrational elementals that do not exist on the material level. The ancients created several monstrous fantasized creatures such as the Pegasus, the Cerberus and many others. Man could never create anything which does not already exist within his subconscious. Take for example Pegasus. Everybody has seen horses, fire, white color and wings. Combine the four and you create a flying white horse that emits fire from its nostrils. Let us take another example. Snakes exist, so do dogs, fire and teeth. Human beings mixed them up and created Cerberus. Such a creature does not exist except as an elemental within the psychonoetic worlds. The mythical monster of Loch Ness is an elemental of collective fantasy which is so powerful that it acquires substance whenever there are electrical charges in the area. It becomes semi-materialized. Man has fantasized and created innumerable such nightmarish elementals, demons, evil spirits, hells made of boilers filled with burning tar and monsters that have never existed. Yet they do exist as elementals within the psychonoetic worlds.

'I ask you now, since in both fantasy and creative thought we construct mental idols or thought forms, what is the difference between the two? In fantasy our will plays hardly any role. We cannot concentrate and control in our minds the mental images that we create. We cannot focus undistractedly on the object we create. In fantasy the mind gallops from one experience on to another leading us nowhere in particular. When we fantasize, the most minor distraction will bring us back to what people call reality.

'Creative thought on the other hand is purposeful. The exercises we offer for the construction of noetic images help the development of our ability to concentrate. For example, I ask you to close your eyes and envision that you hold in your hands an orange. You can scratch it and smell it. You can see it from the outside and from within in every detail. It is possible to concentrate on this orange more fully than you have ever concentrated on a physical orange. It is even possible to cut it, eat it and be nourished by it. If you are a powerful master, the orange you constructed can serve as a womb for the materialization of a real natural orange that anyone can eat. With fantasy such a feat would be impossible. It is not with fantasy that we achieve healing phenomena, but with concentration and creative thought.'

Daskalos went on to elaborate further on the differences between fantasy and creative thought and claimed that many mediums fall into the traps of fantasy and 'see' things that do not exist. This is particularly problematic with 'psychometry.'

In an earlier conversation Daskalos elaborated that psychometry is the ability to concentrate on an object and re-experience every event associated with it. Psychometry is possible because every object is imbued with elementals that human beings created in relation to that object.

'The psychometrist,' Daskalos said, 'must be able to attune himself with the vibrations of an object and begin to see without coloring what he sees with elementals that he himself creates. For example, if he perceives a battle associated with the object, he must see it in every detail without any subjective interference with what he sees. In psychometry fantasy can easily interfere with our perceptions. Mediums often fall into the traps of fantasy and perceive the desirable rather than the real. They are sincere in their perceptions but they are unable to distinguish fantasy from reality.

'We can appreciate the difficulties in psychometry when we realize how easily our fantasy can distort our perceptions of ordinary phenomena. Several persons are watching a television program. If you ask them to describe what they have seen, I guarantee you most of them will color the plot with their own fantasies. Can you imagine how much more difficult it is to see clearly in the past? That is why concentration exercises are so crucial for the development of our psychonoetic powers.'

'Are there any dangers for the present personality in fantasy?' I asked.

'Most of the people who end up in asylums are victims of fantasies. A master, therefore, must be on guard over his students to make sure that their work, that is the construction of psychonoetic images, is the product of creative thinking and not of fantasy. In the case of ·the latter the master should interfere and stop his stude:.t from proceeding on such a dangerous path.'

After elaborating further on the difference between creative thought and fantasy we had a break of about half an hour. Daskalos was concerned about the whereabouts of his grandson who apparently was lost somewhere in the neighborhood. He went out into the street calling Marios several times. The little boy finally emerged from a neighbor's orange grove holding in his hand a quail given him as a present by one of Daskalos' students. He gently reprimanded Marios for taking the bird out of its cage. He then caressed the child's blondish hair and we resumed our conversation.

'How is fantasy associated with dreaming?' I asked when we settled down.

'Fantasy is an imperfection of the present personality. We are all victims of this malady to some extent and it requires great effort to overcome it. We imprint images in our subconscious either through fantasy or through concentration and creative thought. We are under the spell of fantasy when our interests and thoughts are incoherent, and under creative thought when we consciously decide what to register in our subconscious. Let me give you an example taken from ordinary life. Suppose we go on a trip. I consciously create within me the interest to enjoy the countryside. During the entire trip I focus my attention on the beautiful scenery and architecture. Someone else may pay no attention to all that. Instead he may indulge in whatever is ugly and unpleasant. We may have spent several hours driving. If you ask him to recollect what he saw during the trip, he may be unable to do so. Every human being can bring to the surface

surface of his consciousness what is already stored there.

'For a Researcher of Truth, dreams are logically coherent and in proper sequence. For a person plagued with fantasy, impressions and experiences come and go in a haphazard manner. His dreams are grotesque, incoherent and confusing. Someone told me the other day of a strange dream he had experienced. He saw himself in a very pleasant room with a handsome walnut-wood chest. The moment he opened the chest a river poured out of it. Then he saw green worms coming out of the river. What happened? Within his subconscious there was the experience of green worms, of rivers, and of walnut-wood chests. He may have seen only a river flowing within a psychic plane. He already had in his subconscious the experience of green worms and walnut-wood chests. Perhaps he did not see such things at that moment, but he associated them with the image of the river.'

'Is it possible,' I suggested, 'that what he saw was symbolic of something else?'

'No. What is symbolic is not grotesque. You will see the symbolic within the symbolic, not within a hodgepodge. Fantasy is a passive state of the present personality, causing it to experience uncontrolled and oppressive perceptions, to see nonsense, either one's own or that of others. Reality is not nonsensical. When one dreams one has seen everything in proper order. The problem lies in one's inability to transfer lucidly to the material brain what one experienced in the dream. It is as if a child gets a camera, takes a picture of a lovely landscape then, without turning the film, takes more pictures. When the negative is developed everything will appear mixed and confused. It does not mean that reality itself is confused. It is the way it has been imprinted within the brain. In nature, whether it be on the material, the psychic, the noetic planes, or beyond, everything is in its right place. It is when we transfer information from one plane to the next that we encounter difficulties.'

'How can we succeed in remembering our dreams without confusion?' Emily probed.

'By incessantly experimenting with meditation exercises so that our brains become disciplined to receive impressions properly.'

'How can we determine,' I added, 'whether the dreams we

see are not just fantasies but that we are in fact in contact, say, with beings living on the psychic plane?'

'Only experience will teach you how to differentiate fantasy from reality. Masters can tell the difference. Ordinary people usually recollect only what they already have stored within their subconscious. A master can spread himself over the reality he wants to examine and acquire whatever he needs to know. When you learn something that could not have been known in an ordinary state of mind, it may be a sign that you are in contact with something real. When you meet people in the psychic world and you are able to maintain their images within your experience, it is a sign that the contact is real rather than imaginary. Perhaps they are the ones who keep your attention and communicate with you. Quite often it is from their side that the desire to communicate originates. You will have to judge the reality of your experience yourself. "Could I possibly create such an experience from within myself or is it something I encountered within the psychic planes?" you may ask yourself. With concentration you will judge and discover whether your experience is genuine or the product of fantasy.'

'Will the present personality continue to see dreams once it becomes absorbed by the permanent personality?' I asked.

'Of course. I do not want to diminish the importance of dreaming. Whatever can be perceived is a form of dreaming.'

'Can we see dreams even when we become one with our self-conscious soul?'

'Definitely. We will not see dreams, however, in terms of past, present and future, but rather within the eternal present. Once you reach that stage you will no longer imprint experiences from only one point at a time. It is not necessary to sleep in order to dream. Dreaming means recording impressions on the subconscious from whatever dimension.'

'What is the purpose of dreaming?' Emily asked abruptly.

'If you explain to me the reason why you were born,' Daskalos replied with a smile, 'I will explain to you the reason why you dream. There is a purpose but it is difficult to explain with human reason.'

'Does the inner self intervene in our dreams?' Emily probed further.

'The inner self gives the freedom to the present personality to be as irrational as it wishes in order to acquire the necessary experiences. Nevertheless, the inner self is constantly supervising the present personality like a loving mother her child. The inner self interferes only to rescue the present personality from nightmares in order to modify the pain. For example, how often do you see yourself in a dream falling from a high spot? Have you ever hit the ground?'

'We wake up.'

'Who woke you up? Do you know that had you seen yourself hitting the ground you would have awakened with bruises on your body? It is your inner self that protects you from such unpleasant experiences by awakening you. Who do you think assists a Researcher of Truth to go through the various experiences associated with the initiations over the elements?'

'I assume it is the masters,' I noted.

'True. But always in cooperation with the inner self. It is the inner self that will help you go through the initiation of the elements. You find yourself, for example, inside a narrow hole. You pa..ic. How can you come out? Yet you are out. It is your inner self who helps you do that. It is the same with the initiation of water and the other elements. In short, the inner self always oversees the dream experiences of the present personality, but it is always from the side of the present personality that must come the initiative to approach the inner self.'

'If I understand you well, Daskale,' Emily said thoughtfully after a few moments' pause, 'you are saying that whatever is imprinted in our subconscious is experienced as real.'

'It is real,' Daskalos interrupted emphatically. 'It is real because it has existence and whatever has existence is real. Were it not so, there would be no possibility of adding to that great storehouse which is our subconscious. How can we prove this, you may ask. Let me give you an example. Suppose someone is an architect. He visits one city after another, inspects the various architectural styles and implants what he sees within his subconscious. Years later he sits down and recollects what he saw. He brings up from his subconscious what he studied and observed as an architect. On the basis of his experience he creates on paper something new and concrete. The substance of what he created came from within himself. It is something real. On the gross material plane buildings can be blown up or an earthquake can destroy them in a few minutes.

They are gone forever. Yet you call them real because you can touch them, they are tangible. What he has created on the material plane can be destroyed in no time. But who can destroy in the architect's mind the original conception which he expressed on paper? When the material building is destroyed he can create many more like it, given the appropriate conditions and available means, of course. You may say suppose the architect is killed, then what? The architect will cease to exist in a gross material body but he will exist as a full personality within the psychic worlds. You can come in touch with him. Whatever he has within himself is there. It will be possible for an architect living on the material level to contact telepathically the dead architect, exchange information with him, and see whatever the dead architect sees. In what kind of light will he be able to see? In the light of the subconscious of the departed, and the light of the subconscious of the living architect, the one who receives. One architect serves as a broadcasting station and the other as the receiving apparatus. When the dead architect is reincarnated he will bring along with him the substance of all his experiences as an architect. Whatever is imprinted within our subconscious is never lost.'

'Can we assume that the word "subconscious" is identical to the realm of ideas?' Emily asked.

'No, the realm of ideas is something else. As I have said many times before, the realm of ideas is what we call the higher noetic world where there are the archetypes, the laws, the causes upon which everything else is built. When I say subconscious, I mean the sum total of our knowledge and experience which remains in a dormant state but which can reach the surface at any moment.'

'As an idea or as a reality?' Emily persisted.

'What's the difference? What you call reality is just a temporary existence. It is not reality in the strict sense. An idea cannot be destroyed. That's what Christ had in mind when He admonished us that we should not rely on the treasures of this Earth, treasures that can be destroyed or stolen by thieves. "Your worth is in Heaven," He said, and by that He meant our subconscious and superconscious. There is where our treasures are stored and there is where reality is. Our life as an existent personality in this material world may cease at any moment. Yet we continue to exist. We are.'

223

'When we have a dream,' Daskalos went on after a coffee-break, 'in reality we perceive phenomena in the etheric and psychic worlds. Are these dreams real? Since they are experienced, they are real. Objects do not have to be tangible on the three dimensions to be real. In fact what we consider as tangible objects is a misconception. Our hands vibrate within the same frequency as the object we touch. That is why an object appears solid to us. With the etheric hands we create, we can go through solid matter. We can see the solid object as solid but the etheric hand can go through it like X-rays. Where, then, is the reality people call tangible and solid?

'Within the material world we see objects only after light is reflected on them. We can see only the surface of objects. In the etheric and psychonoetic worlds it is quite different. We receive vibrations not in the ordinary way of seeing but of being or existing within the object. We can observe something from all sides simultaneously.'

'That means,' I added, 'that if I look at a chair on the gross material level I have no way of knowing what is behind it since I can only observe it from a certain perspective. In the psychic world, on the other hand, I can be within the chair and experience it from all angles.'

'Precisely. Now, by which light do we receive the vibrations within the psychic worlds? In the realm of the four dimensions every atom and molecule of matter has its own light. It is not necessary to have a source of light that can strike on surfaces. You can, however, with your fantasy create a sun or anything else you like. In reality you do not need a sun in order to see in the psychic world. It is for this reason that the mystics of medieval times called the psychic realm the "astral plane."

'Bear in mind that everything which exists in the material plane has its etheric, psychic and noetic counterpart. Otherwise it cannot exist. There are things that exist in the psychic plane which do not exist in the material plane. There are things in the noetic plane which do not exist in the material plane or the psychic plane. But there is nothing material which does not have its etheric, psychic and noetic counterparts. When I find myself in the fourth dimension I can attune myself with the object and perceive it in its totality. I then experience certain feelings associated with the object such as pleasure, pain and the like. Can I also understand the object with my psychic body? To do that I must see it in its noetic nature and understand it with my noetic body, my mental power. So, to repeat myself, there are the material, the psychic and the noetic worlds. We call the last two the psychonoetic world because the psychic world cannot exist by itself. As I understand it, everything that exists within the psychic world must have within itself the noetic side because what we call psychic matter or substance cannot have shape or color unless it acquires it from the noetic plane. The psychic world is like a mirror which can have no shape unless it is joined to the analogous noetic plane which shapes it.'

'It seems as if the psychic plane is like a blank sheet of paper,' Emily observed.

'Yes, but upon which everything within the material world and the noetic plane is reflected. Strictly speaking, therefore, the psychic element must be shaped by other means.'

'It is an infinitely malleable substance,' I added.

'Exactly. All the hells, paradises and purgatories in which people find themselves are there. But they exist in the psychic world because the person who created them lived within matter and within the noetic world. Of the three worlds, the most real is the noetic world. It has primacy over the other two. Both the material and the psychic worlds are mirrors that reflect what is within the noetic world, what you earlier called the world of ideas.

'Within the psychonoetic worlds there are more vivid and refined colors than on the material plane. Colors, like everything else, are simply frequencies of vibrations. I am a painter myself and am always enchanted with the texture of colors I perceive within the psychonoetic worlds. Colors are alive there. You not only perceive them, you also experience them. Believe me, those worlds you call "dreams" are more real than this world of dirt and dust.'

'How can one know that unless one has the experience?' Emily asked.

'Some day you will have the experience, particularly once you train yourself. Suppose you experience the death of the material body. Do not assume that automatically you will know what has happened to you. I have met atheists there who still insist with tenacity that there is no God. They lead exactly the same lives as when they existed on the material level. One must have long training before one has clear understanding of what is happening to him. Lucid reasoning does not come automatically in the psychic world.'

'What does it mean, then, when one reasons within the dream state?' I asked, having in mind my own experiences.

'It means one lives consciously within that plane. But why call it "dream" and not say "being in contact with realities in another dimension"? It is gradually that you will be able to live fully and consciously within other realities. Masters live continuously and consciously in the material, psychic and noetic worlds. They know when they are in the material, in the psychic and in the noetic worlds and do not confuse them. They are aware of the differences between the worlds. When you one day also become conscious of the psychic worlds, you will be able to differentiate between those worlds and the psychic counterpart of the material world.'

'What is the difference?' Emily asked.

'Everything material, as I said before, has both its psychic and noetic counterpart. It cannot exist otherwise.'

'How can you tell, Daskale,' I interjected, 'whether you are observing something within a purely psychic plane or within the psychic counterpart of the material world?'

'Suppose I am in exomatosis and I come into this room. To find out whether I am in a purely psychic environment rather than the psychic counterpart of the material world, I try to move things around. If I notice that they are too heavy to move or lift, it is an indication that I am in the psychic counterpart of the material plane. The psychic part of that chair cannot be moved unless the chair is moved. If I can move it, it means that my hands are on the psychic environment and not on the psychic counterpart of the material world. What will I have to do then in order to move the chair? I will have to lower the vibrations of my psychic hand, materialize my hand and move the chair along with its psychic counterpart. Masters do that all the time. As invisible helpers they get out of their material bodies and travel to distant places where there are battles, earthquakes and similar disasters. When they are at the place where they want to be, they know whether they are on the psychic counterpart of the material plane. I know from experience that I can see human beings, objects, animals, trees, everything. If I want to help someone wounded I cannot do so unless I materialize my hands to take off his shirt and tie his wound. Believe me this is possible. But you will not know how to do that unless you know how to materialize yourself from the psychic plane down.'

'But if you are able to get out of your body and travel to distant places does it not imply that you have the ability and training to also materialize yourself there?' I pondered.

'Not necessarily. Sometimes people through their great love to be of service may find themselves out of their bodies in faraway places, but unless they have the training on materialization, they will not be able to accomplish anything. They will wake up thinking that they have experienced a vivid dream. It is what the ordinary psychics see.'

Just as Daskalos finished his sentence the telephone rang. I picked it up. It was a call from Athens. The Washington correspondent of a leading Greek newspaper wished to come to Cyprus, meet with Daskalos, and then fly back to the United States the same day.

'You mean you want to come all the way from Athens just to see me?' we heard Daskalos say on the phone. 'Fine. Call me as soon as you arrive at the airport.'

'Who knows?' Daskalos said and shook his head as he put the earphone down. 'Maybe in some mysterious way the time has come for these teachings to reach the general public.

'So, where were we?' Daskalos said as he sat down and folded his hands.

'Daskale,' I said, 'Emily has some questions to ask you about Freud, particularly in regard to his theory of the unconscious.' But before Emily said anything, Daskalos began commenting on what he thought of the father of psychoanalysis.

'Freud expressed what was possible to know, given the times he lived. His understanding of man was the sum total of the available knowledge on psychology which is still in its embryonic stage. Psychologists explore the surface of the ocean but not the depth of the ocean. Neither psychology nor parapsychology, for that matter, can tell us much about how personality is constructed.'

'However, Daskale,' Emily added, 'the twentieth century brought about impressive theoretical ideas on personality development.'

'Perhaps, but they are still far behind. Freud as well as most psychologists today arrive at their theoretical conclusions on the basis of studies about other subjects. They do not arrive at their theories on the basis of personal experience, through self-analysis.'

'Nevertheless,' Emily insisted, 'Freud speaks of the importance of subjectivity and how crucial it is to take into account personal experiences, something no other scientist to my knowledge had ever said before.'

'Fair enough, but he was still at the ABC's of knowledge. Perhaps he did not have the time to explore deeper into human nature. And let us not forget that Freud was not in the best of health emotionally and otherwise. His personal problems interfered with his understanding of reality. He was a first-rate scientist for the time and the place he lived. But his biggest mistake was that he was contemptuous of metaphysics and mysticism and consequently his understanding of personality suffered accordingly.

'When we speak of subconsciousness, unconsciousness and superconsciousness, we do so on the basis of our experiences. The subconscious for us is the fundamental essence of the present personality. It is the underground of what we call consciousness. In reality there is no difference between the two.'

'Freud,' Emily repeated, 'was the first who showed that there is such a thing as the unconscious.'

'Fine, he did so for modern science. Mystics have known this throughout the ages.'

'Perhaps Freud failed to define precisely what the unconscious is,' I remarked, somewhat amused with the debate between Daskalos and Emily.

'But can you define what the unconscious is?' Emily replied.

'Of course you can. We can.' Daskalos replied sharply in his typical confident tone. 'What did Freud do? He was on a boat and for the first time he looked down, put his hand in the water and discovered that the sea has depth. But he was not a diver. Had he been a diver he would have known what the depth of the ocean is all about. He spoke of the water under the surface theoretically. He had never dived himself to know, as a diver, what is down there. In the Research for Truth we aim at becoming good divers into our subconscious.'

Daskalos' metaphor on Freud brought to mind an anecdote

228

cited by Amaury de Riencourt (*The Eye of Shiva*) on the difference between Western and Eastern thought. At a crossroads there were two signs. One pointed right with the inscription, 'to heaven,' and the other pointed left to 'lectures on heaven.' Two travellers, a Westerner and an Easterner, walking side by side, approached the signs. The Westerner turned left to attend the 'lectures on heaven' while the Easterner followed the way straight to 'heaven.'

'When you say subconsciousness, Daskale,' I asked after awhile, 'do you also imply unconsciousness?'

'No. Subconsciousness, as I said, is the great force of your existence. It is the material from which the entire edifice of your existence is constructed. It is the sum total of the elementals which make up your present personality. Unconsciousness means bringing consciousness to a state of non-receiving impressions. Such a state can be attained by injecting morphine. Unconsciousness does not really concern us. For me subconsciousness becomes consciousness because I am imprinting images consciously there. So it is a way of giving names. What is conscious to me is subconscious to you. When you tell yourself you will bring something to the surface of your consciousness, it is what you do now subconsciously. In reality there is only one state, call it self-consciousness if you will. In this self-consciousness there are many many chambers within which you must work and attain mastery.'

'What would you consider the conscious part of our present personality?' I wondered.

'There is no conscious part. Whatever you perceive consciously is recorded within the subconscious. In reality there is no conscious part as such since it does not have a stable point.'

'Suppose,' I added, 'that our self is like a sphere which we must get to know. At this very moment we manage to know a small portion of the sphere. Can we name that part the conscious part?'

'But who is the one who is knowing? You have as your basis the present personality. Why not absorb the present personality with the inner self? By so doing you become one with it and then you know everything. Why do you give so much importance to "knowing" by identifying it with the "conscious" as if it is something superior to the subconscious? The subconscious is you.

'Do you know when you will be able to understand what I am talking about?' Daskalos said, leaning back in his chair: 'When you stop taking the present personality so seriously.'

'But it is the present personality that must know in the end.'

'Just because it must know, it should not be allowed to take over the scepter and lead the way. Why place the subconscious at a lower level from its reverie which people call the conscious part? By doing so we give primacy and weight to the present personality and we retard our spiritual growth. The present personality thinks of itself as the important part. It is not. The conscious part of the self is the spacial-temporal expression of the subconscious. Why should we place so much importance on the little we know now and consider the present moment as the most serious moment? At every single moment the subconscious becomes conscious and the conscious, subconscious. What you call conscious I call reverie. The subconscious, on the other hand, lasts beyond the dissolution of the material body.'

'Suppose,' Daskalos went on, 'there is a beautiful gallery of one hundred art pieces and I tell you this is your treasure, your subconscious. You then decide to go and take a look at your treasure. It is your choice from which corner of the gallery you begin your examination. You are not in a position to see the paintings unless you use a flashlight you hold in your hand. The flashlight is what you call the conscious part of yourself. I would rather call it the focus of your thought. Whereas now you can see only parts of the gallery, with the help of the flashlight, one day you shall become yourself, the light which will illuminate the entire gallery. This is what we call superconscious self-awareness, a condition that I know from experience but I cannot express with words.'

'I suppose, Daskale, once you become conscious of your own gallery, you can then enter into the gallery of the cosmos which is the same for all human beings,' I remarked, having in mind Jung's idea of the 'Collective Unconscious.'

'"The few coins that I placed in your hands," Jesus said, that is, the ability to think in a limited spacial-temporal degree, "you have made into something much greater." Who can tell you that one day your gallery, that is your subconscious, will not be the mastery over an entire planet? Christians have been hearing this parable for centuries. But how many do you suppose have actually penetrated deeply into its meaning?'

230

I met with Daskalos and Kostas several more times before my departure from the island. Iacovos had already left to continue his education abroad and Kostas, during a session of the inner circle, was anointed 'earthly master' responsible for the circles internationally and custodian, along with Daskalos, of Yohannan's teachings. I was not present during that special meeting. When I pressed Kostas on the issue, whether it was indeed Yohannan who made the appointment and not Daskalos, he smiled and shook his head. 'Kyriaco,' he said with a reassuring tone in his voice, 'I know when it is just Daskalos speaking and when it is Yohannan.' Then he went on to claim that the moment he recognized the presence of Yohannan he felt the hair on his body rising. Kostas said that what 'that super-intelligence' assigned him was a heavy cross to carry, a phrase he was fond of using to imply duty and responsibility.

Daskalos mentioned to me later that he had had no idea what was going to happen that day and that he himself was surprised when the words began pouring through his mouth appointing Kostas caretaker of the circles and custodian of the teachings. Then he went on to say that Kostas had earned that title. He had reached the state in his evolutionary path as a mystic whereby, like Daskalos, he was capable of serving as an authentic channel for Yohannan and therefore was in a position to absorb knowledge and wisdom directly, 'from the very source itself,' without the need for an intermediary.

I was told that when Daskalos made the announcement all the members of the inner circle in a state of high emotion embraced and kissed Kostas and vowed commitment and support in his difficult task ahead. Daskalos told me that he was very satisfied with the way things had developed. The circles can now continue after his passing through the capable hands of his younger apprentice. In fact Kostas' reputation was beginning to grow on the island, so much so, that he was taking on many of his aging master's tasks, forming new circles and accomplishing 'miraculous' healing feats.

I spent the day before departing from the island with Emily and the two children at Akamas, our favorite spot in Cyprus. It was a ritual for us to visit that remote region, swim, hike and absorb its majestic pristine beauty before the long flight back to Maine. Nature lovers and the ecologically minded started a movement, which we joined, to declare the area a national park and a nature preserve to protect it for good from developers, cement and petrodollars.

I sat cross-legged on the tiny pebbles at the beach and rested my back on a smooth rock. I had behind me the wilderness of Akamas and in front of me the expanse of the northern Cypriot sea. I gazed for several minutes at the setting sun which was ready to submerge itself into the tranquil sea. Daskalos claimed that the rays of the sun at dawn and sunset are particularly beneficial. For this reason shamans and mystics throughout the ages have been paying special homage to the sun during these periods of the day.

I was all alone. Emily walked with the children up the hill to 'The Baths of Aphrodite,' a eucalyptus-covered spring where the goddess, according to tradition, has been habitually taking her baths since time immemorial. I closed my eyes and prepared myself to start a special meditation exercise taught to me by Daskalos on how to leave my body. It was the first time I had dared experiment on this matter. I felt somewhat apprehensive not knowing where it would lead me. At first I began in a special rhythmic way to breathe deeply as Daskalos prescribed. He warned that the breathing could quickly tire me but instructed me to consciously fight any yawning tendency and concentrate on the exercise.

After about ten minutes of over-ventilating myself I proceeded with the meditation. Soon after I experienced a sensation unlike anything I had experienced in the past. I was fully conscious of where I was and what I was doing. I felt as if time had stopped and with every ripple breaking at the pebbles thirty meters ahead of me, a huge mass of energy, like a gigantic tidal wave, was pouring all over me filling me up with some mysterious vital energy. I had the strange sensation that a part of my consciousness was inside the water and that at some subtle level the sea was, somehow, communicating with me in a very soothing and loving way. I was exhilarated and a bit frightened. I could have remained in that state for much longer had Vasia, my seven-year-old daughter, not started calling *papaki* from high up the hill behind me.

I opened my eyes, stood up and stretched. I checked my watch. I must have remained in that position for more than half an hour. The sun had already set minutes earlier and its last rays were touching a lonely cloud in the distance. I walked up the hill where Emily and the children were sitting and made a note to myself that, before leaving Cyprus, I ought to discuss with Daskalos that most extraordinary sensation I experienced near 'The Baths of Aphrodite.'

Glossary

Chakras Psychonoetic centers on the etheric-double of the individual. It is through the chakras that the human personality absorbs etheric vitality for its maintenance. Through appropriate discipline and meditation exercises the mystic tries to open his chakras for the acquisition of psychonoetic powers. To a clairvoyant the chakras appear like revolving discs.

Elementals Thought forms. Any feeling or any thought that an individual projects is an elemental. They have shape and a life of their own independent of the one who projected them.

Etheric-double The energy field that keeps the three bodies (the gross material, psychic and noetic) alive and linked to one another. Each particle of the body has its corresponding etheric-double. It is etheric vitality that makes healing possible. The universe is filled with etheric energy. It can be transferred from one individual to another, and it is absorbed through the chakras.

Exomatosis The ability to willfully abandon one's body, live fully conscious within the psychonoetic dimensions and then return back to the body. It implies remembering whatever one experiences in the out-of-the-body state.

Gross material body One of the three bodies that make up the present self-conscious personality. The material body. That part of one's personality that lives within the gross material world, the three-dimensional world. The lowest expression of self. The center of the gross material body is the chakra of the solar plexus.

Higher noetic world The world of ideas, of the archetypes. The world of causes and laws that provide the foundations of all phenomenal reality.

Holy Monad The component parts of the Absolute. Each Holy Monad emanates myriads of rays that pass through different archetypes and acquire shape and phenomenal existence. When one such irradiation passes through the Idea of Man, a human personality is constructed. Humans who belong to the same Holy Monad have a particular affinity for one another.

Holy Spirit The impersonal superconsciousness which expresses the power of the Absolute, making the creation of the universe possible. The dynamic part of the Absolute.

Holyspiritual That which pertains only to the Holy Spirit. Animals live within a holyspiritual state. They lack the logoic expression of the Absolute, that is, they lack self-consciousness. Man is both logoic and holyspiritual.

Idea of Man An eternal archetype within the Absolute. Once an emanation of a Holy Monad passes through the Idea of Man, human existence begins.

Invisible helpers Masters who live on the psychic and noetic dimensions and are invisible to material eyes. Also masters who live within the gross material dimension but who carry out exomatosis and assist humans living within the gross as well as the other dimensions.

Karma The law of cause and effect. The sum total of a person's actions, thoughts and feelings that determine his successive states of existence. A person is fully responsible for the creation of his Karma, his destiny. The attainment of Theosis implies transcending one's Karma.

Law of cause and effect See Karma.

Logos The part of the Absolute that makes possible the existence of self-consciousness and free will. As eternal entities men are both logoic and holyspiritual. Animals are only holyspiritual. Jesus as the Christ Logos represents the most complete expression of the logoic nature of the Absolute. The more spiritually advanced a human entity is, the more the logoic part of him is dominant.

Mind The means by which the unmanifest Absolute expresses Itself. Mind is the supersubstance by which all the universes, all the dimensions of existence, are constructed. Everything is Mind.

Noetic body One of the three bodies that make up the present self-conscious personality. The body of thoughts. The noetic body exists within the noetic world, the fifth dimension. Its image is identical with the other two bodies. The center of the noetic body is the chakra of the head.

Noetic world The fifth dimension. Within the noetic world, space as well as time are transcended. A human entity living within the noetic world can travel instantly, not only over vast distances but also across time.

Permanent personality That part of ourselves upon which the incarnational experiences are recorded and are transferred from one life to the next. Our inner self.

Present personality What is commonly known as the personality of the individual. It is made up of the noetic, psychic and gross material bodies. The present personality is the lowest expression of ourselves which is constantly evolving and tends to become one with the permanent personality.

Psychic body One of the three bodies that constitute the present self-conscious personality. The body of feelings and sentiments having as its center the chakra of the heart. The psychic body lives within the psychic world, the fourth dimension. Its image is identical with the other two bodies, the gross material and the noetic.

Psychic world The fourth dimension. Within the psychic world space is transcended. An individual living within the psychic world can travel instantly over vast distances.

Sacred discs See Chakras.

Soul That part of ourselves which is pure and uncolored by earthly experience. The soul is beyond the Idea of Man, beyond all manifestation. It has never been born and it will never die. It is that part of ourselves which is qualitatively identical with the Absolute. The soul is our divine essence, unchangeable and eternal.

Theosis The final stage in the evolution of the self after it has undergone the experience of gross matter through successive incarnations. Re-unification with the Godhead.

World of ideas See Higher noetic world.

ARKANA – NEW-AGE BOOKS FOR MIND, BODY AND SPIRIT

With over 150 titles currently in print, Arkana is the leading name in quality new-age books for mind, body and spirit. Arkana encompasses the spirituality of both East and West, ancient and new, in fiction and non-fiction. A vast range of interests is covered, including Psychology and Transformation, Health, Science and Mysticism, Women's Spirituality and Astrology.

If you would like a catalogue of Arkana books, please write to:

Arkana Marketing Department
Penguin Books Ltd
27 Wright's Lane
London W8 5TZ

ARKANA – NEW-AGE BOOKS FOR MIND, BODY AND SPIRIT

A selection of titles already published or in preparation

On Having No Head: Zen and the Re-Discovery of the Obvious
D. E. Harding

'Reason and imagination and all mental chatter died down . . . I forgot my name, my humanness, my thingness, all that could be called me or mine. Past and future dropped away . . .'

Thus Douglas Harding describes his first experience of headlessness, or no self. This classic work truly conveys the experience that mystics of all ages have tried to put into words.

Self-Healing: My Life and Vision Meir Schneider

Born blind, pronounced incurable – yet at 17 Meir Schneider discovered self-healing techniques which within four years led him to gain a remarkable degree of vision. In the process he discovered an entirely new self-healing system, and an inspirational faith and enthusiasm that helped others heal themselves. While individual response to self-healing is unique, the healing power is inherent in all of us.

'This remarkable story is tonic for everyone who believes in the creative power of the human will' – Marilyn Ferguson.

The Way of the Craftsman: A Search for the Spiritual Essence of Craft Freemasonry W. Kirk MacNulty

This revolutionary book uncovers the Kabbalistic roots of Freemasonry, showing how Kabbalistic symbolism informs all of its central rituals. W. Kirk MacNulty, a Freemason for twenty-five years, reveals how the symbolic structure of the Craft is designed to lead the individual step by step to psychological self-knowledge, while at the same time recognising mankind's fundamental dependence on God.

Dictionary of Astrology Fred Gettings

Easily accessible yet sufficiently detailed to serve the needs of the practical astrologer, this fascinating reference book offers reliable definitions and clarifications of over 3000 astrological terms, from the post-medieval era to today's most recent developments.

ARKANA – NEW-AGE BOOKS FOR MIND, BODY AND SPIRIT

A selection of titles already published or in preparation

Being Intimate: A Guide to Successful Relationships
John and Kris Amodeo

This invaluable guide aims to enrich one of the most important – yet often problematic – aspects of our lives: intimate relationships and friendships.

'A clear and practical guide to the realization and communication of authentic feelings, and thus an excellent pathway towards lasting intimacy and love' – George Leonard

The Brain Book   Peter Russell

The essential handbook for brain users.

'A fascinating book – for everyone who is able to appreciate the human brain, which, as Russell says, is the most complex and most powerful information processor known to man. It is especially relevant for those who are called upon to read a great deal when time is limited, or who attend lectures or seminars and need to take notes' – *Nursing Times*

The Act of Creation   Arthur Koestler

This second book in Koestler's classic trio of works on the human mind (which opened with *The Sleepwalkers* and concludes with *The Ghost in the Machine*) advances the theory that all creative activities – the conscious and unconscious processes underlying artistic originality, scientific discovery and comic inspiration – share a basic pattern, which Koestler expounds and explores with all his usual clarity and brilliance.

A Psychology With a Soul: Psychosynthesis in Evolutionary Context   Jean Hardy

Psychosynthesis was developed between 1910 and the 1950s by Roberto Assagioli – an Italian psychiatrist who, like Jung, diverged from Freud in search of a more spiritually based understanding of human nature. Jean Hardy's account of this comprehensive approach to self-realization will be of great value to everyone concerned with personal integration and spiritual growth.

ARKANA – NEW-AGE BOOKS FOR MIND, BODY AND SPIRIT

A selection of titles already published or in preparation

Encyclopedia of the Unexplained
Edited by Richard Cavendish   Consultant: J. B. Rhine

'Will probably be the definitive work of its kind for a long time to come' – *Prediction*

The ultimate guide to the unknown, the esoteric and the unproven: richly illustrated, with almost 450 clear and lively entries from Alchemy, the Black Box and Crowley to faculty X, Yoga and the Zodiac.

Buddhist Civilization in Tibet   Tulku Thondup Rinpoche

Unique among works in English, *Buddhist Civilization in Tibet* provides an astonishing wealth of information on the various strands of Tibetan religion and literature in a single compact volume, focusing predominantly on the four major schools of Buddhism: Nyingma, Kagyud, Sakya and Gelug.

The Living Earth Manual of Feng-Shui   Stephen Skinner

The ancient Chinese art of Feng-Shui – tracking the hidden energy flow which runs through the earth in order to derive maximum benefit from being in the right place at the right time – can be applied equally to the siting and layout of cities, houses, tombs and even flats and bedsits; and can be practised as successfully in the West as in the East with the aid of this accessible manual.

In Search of the Miraculous: Fragments of an Unknown Teaching   P. D. Ouspensky

Ouspensky's renowned, vivid and characteristically honest account of his work with Gurdjieff from 1915–18.

'Undoubtedly a *tour de force*. To put entirely new and very complex cosmology and psychology into fewer than 400 pages, and to do this with a simplicity and vividness that makes the book accessible to any educated reader, is in itself something of an achievement' – *The Times Literary Supplement*

ARKANA – NEW-AGE BOOKS FOR MIND, BODY AND SPIRIT

A selection of titles already published or in preparation

The Ghost in the Machine Arthur Koestler

Koestler's classic work – which can be read alone or as the conclusion of his trilogy on the human mind – is concerned not with human creativity but with human pathology.

'He has seldom been as impressive, as scientifically far-ranging, as lively-minded or as alarming as on the present occasion' – John Raymond in the *Financial Times*.

T'ai Chi Ch'uan and Meditation Da Liu

Today T'ai Chi Ch'uan is known primarily as a martial art – but it was originally developed as a complement to meditation. Both disciplines involve alignment of the self with the Tao, the ultimate reality of the universe. Da Liu shows how to combine T'ai Chi Ch'uan and meditation, balancing the physical and spiritual aspects to attain good health and harmony with the universe.

Return of the Goddess Edward C. Whitmont

Amidst social upheaval and the questioning of traditional gender roles, a new myth is arising: the myth of the ancient Goddess who once ruled earth and heaven before the advent of patriarchy and patriachal religion. Here one of the world's leading Jungian analysts argues that our society, long dominated by male concepts of power and aggression, is today experiencing a resurgence of the feminine.

The Strange Life of Ivan Osokin P. D. Ouspensky

If you had the chance to live your life again, what would you do with it? Ouspensky's novel, set in Moscow, on a country estate and in Paris, tells what happens to Ivan Ososkin when he is sent back twelve years to his stormy schooldays, early manhood and early loves. First published in 1947, the *Manchester Guardian* praised it as 'a brilliant fantasy . . . written to illustrate the theme that we do not live life but that life lives us'.

ARKANA – NEW-AGE BOOKS FOR MIND, BODY AND SPIRIT

A selection of titles already published or in preparation

The Networking Book: People Connecting with People
Jessica Lipnack and Jeffrey Stamps

Networking – forming human connections to link ideas and resources – is the natural form of organization for an era based on information technology. Principally concerned with those networks whose goal is a peaceful yet dynamic future for the world, *The Networking Book* – written by two world-famous experts – profiles hundreds of such organizations worldwide, operating at every level from global tele-communications to word of mouth.

Chinese Massage Therapy: A Handbook of Therapeutic Massage Compiled at the Anhui Medical School Hospital, China
Translated by Hor Ming Lee and Gregory Whincup

There is a growing movement among medical practitioners in China today to mine the treasures of traditional Chinese medicine – acupuncture, herbal medicine and massage therapy. Directly translated from a manual in use in Chinese hospitals, *Chinese Massage Therapy* offers a fresh understanding of this time-tested medical alternative.

Dialogues with Scientists and Sages: The Search for Unity
Renée Weber

In their own words, contemporary scientists and mystics – from the Dalai Lama to Stephen Hawking – share with us their richly diverse views on space, time, matter, energy, life, consciousness, creation and our place in the scheme of things. Through the immediacy of verbatim dialogue, we encounter scientists who endorse mysticism, and those who oppose it; mystics who dismiss science, and those who embrace it.

Zen and the Art of Calligraphy
Omōri Sōgen and Terayama Katsujo

Exploring every element of the relationship between Zen thought and the artistic expression of calligraphy, two long-time practitioners of Zen, calligraphy and swordsmanship show how Zen training provides a proper balance of body and mind, enabling the calligrapher to write more profoundly, freed from distraction or hesitation.

ARKANA – NEW-AGE BOOKS FOR MIND, BODY AND SPIRIT

A selection of titles already published or in preparation

Head Off Stress: Beyond the Bottom Line D. E. Harding

Learning to head off stress takes no time at all and is impossible to forget – all it requires is that we dare take a fresh look at ourselves. This infallible and revolutionary guide from the author of *On Having No Head* – whose work C. S. Lewis described as 'highest genius' – shows how.

Shiatzu: Japanese Finger Pressure for Energy, Sexual Vitality and Relief from Tension and Pain
Yukiko Irwin with James Wagenvoord

The product of 4000 years of Oriental medicine and philosophy, Shiatzu is a Japanese variant of the Chinese practice of acupuncture. Fingers, thumbs and palms are applied to the 657 pressure points that the Chinese penetrate with gold and silver needles, aiming to maintain health, increase vitality and promote well-being.

The Magus of Strovolos: The Extraordinary World of a Spiritual Healer Kyriacos C. Markides

This vivid account introduces us to the rich and intricate world of Daskalos, the Magus of Strovolos – a true healer who draws upon a seemingly limitless mixture of esoteric teachings, psychology, reincarnation, demonology, cosmology and mysticism, from both East and West.

'This is a really marvellous book . . . one of the most extraordinary accounts of a "magical" personality since Ouspensky's account of Gurdjieff' – Colin Wilson

Meetings With Remarkable Men G. I. Gurdjieff

All that we know of the early life of Gurdjieff – one of the great spiritual masters of this century – is contained within these colourful and profound tales of adventure. The men who influenced his formative years had no claim to fame in the conventional sense; what made them remarkable was the consuming desire they all shared to understand the deepest mysteries of life.